Governors State University
Library Hours:
Monday thru Thursday 8:00 to 10:30
Friday 8:00 to 5:00
Saturday 8:30 to 5:00
Sunday 1:00 to 5:00 (Fall
and Winter Trimester Only)

A Guide to

Literacy
Coaching

A Guide to
Literacy
Coaching

Helping Teachers Increase Student Achievement

Annemarie B.
JAY

Mary W.
STRONG

CORWIN PRESS
A SAGE Company
Thousand Oaks, CA 91320

For information:

Corwin Press
A SAGE Company
2455 Teller Road
Thousand Oaks, California 91320
www.corwinpress.com

SAGE Ltd.
1 Oliver's Yard
55 City Road
London EC1Y 1SP
United Kingdom

SAGE India Pvt. Ltd.
B 1/I 1 Mohan Cooperative
   Industrial Area
Mathura Road, New Delhi 110 044
India

SAGE Asia-Pacific Pte. Ltd.
33 Pekin Street #02-01
Far East Square
Singapore 048763

Printed in the United States of America

Library of Congress Cataloging-in-Publication Data

Jay, Annemarie B.
A guide to literacy coaching: helping teachers increase student achievement/Annemarie B. Jay, Mary W. Strong.
     p. cm.
Includes bibliographical references and index.
ISBN 978-1-4129-5154-8 (cloth)
ISBN 978-1-4129-5155-5 (pbk.)
   1. Reading teachers—Training of. I. Strong, Mary W. II. Title.

LB2844.1.R4J39 2008
428.4′071—dc22   2008004898

This book is printed on acid-free paper.

08   09   10   11   12   10   9   8   7   6   5   4   3   2   1

Acquisitions Editor:	Hudson Perigo
Editorial Assistant:	Lesley Blake
Production Editor:	Veronica Stapleton
Copy Editor:	Paula L. Fleming
Typesetter:	C&M Digitals (P) Ltd.
Proofreader:	Caryne Brown
Indexer:	Sheila Bodell
Cover Designer:	Lisa Miller

Contents

List of Figures

List of Resources

Foreword

The ongoing emphasis on improving literacy achievement in American schools and the recognition that high-quality teaching is an essential ingredient in generating improvement has led to literacy coaching as an approach for changing teacher practices and increasing student achievement. In *A Guide to Literacy Coaching,* Jay and Strong build on the present knowledge base about coaching to write a book that is thoughtful, practical, and comprehensive; it identifies specific ideas for coaches, who often struggle with questions such as "How do I begin?" "How do I handle conflict?" and "What are my tasks in terms of working with other support personnel in the school?"

In Chapter 1, Jay and Strong provide an overview of coaching, drawing on the various documents of professional organizations that address qualifications and activities of coaches. They also discuss differences between the positions of literacy coach and reading specialist, emphasizing the fact that although both positions require leadership skills in the schools, the literacy coach's primary responsibility is that of working with teachers, whereas most specialists focus on working with students. In Chapter 2, Jay and Strong identify and discuss four major roles of the literacy coach: facilitator, observer, colleague, and learner. They provide specific examples of how coaches fulfill these roles.

Chapter 3 is an essential chapter for all coaches but especially those who are new to the position. Jay and Strong provide specific examples of how the new coach can develop solid relationships with teachers. They take the readers through the first year of the coach, discussing how the coach can continue to build relationships and increase responsibilities. In Chapter 4, Jay and Strong provide an excellent overview of schools at the primary, elementary, middle, and high school levels; they describe the structure of these schools and identify curricular trends and issues. There is also a section on the special education classroom setting, and coaches are provided with ideas about how to work with special educators.

Chapter 5 provides information about how coaches can work with parents and various institutions, including universities. Jay and Strong highlight the importance of understanding governmental policies and dictates. In Chapter 6, Jay and Strong emphasize the importance of coaches working with leadership in the school. What is impressive is that they describe not only ways that the literacy coach can work with the principal but also the importance of working with central office administrators.

In Chapter 7, there is a discussion about working with teachers, especially those who might be experiencing some difficulties in teaching or managing the classroom. This chapter also provides specific information about how to deal with the teacher resistant to coaching. Chapter 8 provides an excellent description of how coaches can work with other professionals in the school, including the librarian and the reading specialist. Information about how literacy coaches can support paraprofessionals is also a key part of this chapter.

Chapter 9 focuses on assessment, and literacy coaches are provided with specific information about how to collect, analyze, and use various forms of data. Finally in Chapter 10, Jay and Strong provide a review of national documents and research reports with which literacy coaches should be familiar.

Several dimensions of this text on literacy coaching are especially impressive—aspects that will be helpful to all literacy coaches, both novices and those with experience. First, Jay and Strong include summaries of interviews that they held with various reading experts. Readers get an opportunity to read the reflections of experts such as Richard Allington, Cathy Roller, Rich and Joanne Vacca, Roger Farr, and others. These experts include researchers and those who are experiencing the job every day—literacy coaches themselves!

Second, in addition to the practical suggestions throughout the text, readers will find many checklists that can be used by coaches—forms for observation and demonstration lessons and questionnaires that can be given to teachers to solicit input about coaching, among others.

Third, at the conclusion of each chapter are topic extensions that provide ideas for follow-up work and activities. These ideas would be especially helpful when the text is being used in the university or college classroom. Finally, there are many resources and Web sites that will be useful to practicing literacy coaches who want to be able to continue their learning while on the job.

This is a book for many audiences: university faculty who want a text for students in their coaching classrooms, novice literacy coaches who need a daily guide, and experienced literacy coaches who want a resource that they can consult when they have questions or concerns. These authors used their knowledge of the research and literature along with their understanding of the field to write a book that is current, insightful, and practical.

Rita Bean
University of Pittsburgh

Preface

A *Guide to Literacy Coaching* is intended to help both novice and experienced professionals who serve as literacy coaches in our nation's schools. Professional development is an expectation and requirement for every teacher. Growing as professionals and learning our craft form a dynamic process that hinges on the pedagogical skills we possess, the culture of our schools, and the interactions in our classrooms. Using a guide to aid professional development is certainly an important aspect of coaching. We sincerely hope that this book will be considered worthy of frequent reference and cause for reflection by those who use it for individual or collective professional development. Professional development opportunities and funding are as varied as schools from east to west. Credible resources, such as this book, are tools for aiding collaboration between literacy coaches and the teachers, specialists, and administrators with whom they work.

The role of the coach is both challenging and rewarding. We feel that the availability of a competent literacy coach is the right of every school. However, we recognize that some American schools have no coaches while others have several. This book is not meant to take the place of a coach but to help guide the coaching process. It will be useful for those who study the coaching process in graduate classes and for those who are already coaching practitioners.

The structure of this book was designed to help with the practical nature of daily coaching and feedback to teachers. The ten chapters are arranged to connect the practical and theoretical issues that most coaches will encounter. The sequence of topics proceeds from the nature of the role and the multiplicity of tasks to the various groups of people with whom coaches must be able to collaborate. The final chapter contains information on recent documents that have an impact on instructional practices in our schools and of which coaches should be aware.

The charts and forms included in the resources and figures throughout the book provide practical items that may be used and reused by coaches in a variety of situations. Readers will find that each chapter is formulated according to a uniform structure. A scenario sets the stage for the content of material presented and the process of coaching that may be imminent for coaches. Each chapter closes with three specific features: (1) opinions of experts who were interviewed about relevant topics within the chapter, (2) a summary of pertinent content, and (3) extension topics for discussion in graduate courses or in professional development settings.

Chapter 1 is an introduction to the role of the coach and makes a case for the importance of literacy coaches within both the elementary and secondary schools. Position statements about the coach and qualifications necessary for coaching are discussed. Some historical information is provided about the evolution of the role of coaching.

The multiple roles of the coach, facilitator, observer, colleague, and learner are thoroughly reviewed in Chapter 2. We feel the discussion of multiple roles is a natural link between the nature of coaching and the chapters that follow, in particular the advice that is offered in Chapter 3.

Chapter 3 provides in-depth information for those just beginning to serve as literacy coaches. A time line and other practical forms and charts help to make clear, succinct statements about planning and implementing coaching techniques either as a novice coach or as a coach who is continuing in the role.

Chapters 4 and 5 address the specific situations and groups that the literacy coach will encounter in typical work experiences. Chapter 4 offers suggestions for working in primary/elementary, middle, and high schools and in special education classrooms. Since one rarely knows where a professional path may lead, it is important that the coach have a good overview of both elementary and secondary levels as well as what is involved in working in classrooms of special needs learners. The section on interventions offers current information on strategies that all classroom teachers should be aware of when assessing what their students need and how they will provide instruction to meet those needs. Chapter 5 discusses the coach's possible collaboration with parents and educational agencies. It also provides information about professional organizations that serve as resources for the coach.

Chapter 6, "Literacy Leadership," addresses one of the main roles of coaching. As an informal leader who is a colleague to teachers, the literacy coach needs to have a collaborative working relationship with school administrators and other leaders. This chapter addresses these relationships.

The topic of collaboration is thoroughly explored in Chapters 7 and 8. Since difficulties may arise when teachers struggle with either the content or process of teaching, Chapter 7 focuses on how the coach may assist these teachers. Chapter 8 deals with collaboration with other professionals and school personnel both within and outside the school. This chapter also emphasizes the important role of the coach in facilitating professional development.

Chapter 9 describes the various types of student data with which the literacy coach should be familiar: schoolwide assessments, classroom assessments, and individual student observations and assessments. As discussed in this chapter, the coach should be able to make sound decisions, share assessment information cogently, and write reports based on the data.

Chapter 10 shares information about national documents related to today's educational practices. Although the full documents are not included, we recommend that coaches read the primary sources themselves and have a full understanding of them. The information we have shared provides concise accounts of the documents, as well as some cautions and recommendations.

Whatever your professional role in the schools across America—whether teacher, specialist, or administrator—we hope you find *A Guide to Literacy Coaching* to be a valuable addition to your professional resource library and to your personal professional development.

ABJ and MWS
January 2008

Acknowledgments

A Guide to Literacy Coaching was a collaborative effort between the authors, who share a passion for teaching as well as for valuable professional development. We are fortunate to be good friends and colleagues who work together well and continue to learn from each other.

Writing a book is much like taking a journey: it takes much effort to prepare for it and a great deal of energy to persist. We were fortunate that our path took us on a joyful excursion of learning. The love and support of our families sent us on our way and provided the encouragement to keep us moving forward. We couldn't have made the journey without them. Two special friends, Georgie Girl and Greta, were also influential—and inspirational—as we embarked on the road to writing this book.

Our editors at Corwin Press/SAGE were consistently helpful and reliable. They enabled us to avoid roadblocks and appreciate the view. Hudson Perigo, executive editor, and Lesley Blake, editorial assistant, were always just a phone call or e-mail away. Their reassurance was the impetus needed to help us maintain a clear vision as the book developed. Production editor Veronica Stapleton and copy editor Paula Fleming were efficient and effective in their feedback. Our thanks to Caryne Brown, Sheila Bodell, Lisa Miller, and the other assistants at Corwin Press.

We consider ourselves extremely fortunate to have had the cooperation of many experts in the field, who allowed us to interview them for the book and use their words of wisdom as contributing features in each chapter. Their rich comments support the recognition that coaches deserve and give credence to the valuable work they do.

The contributions of each of the experts that we interviewed are very much appreciated and warmly acknowledged. These experts include Dr. Cathy Roller, director of research and policy for the International Reading Association; Dr. Roger Farr, nationally recognized expert on assessment from Indiana University, where he is the director of the Center for Innovation and Assessment; Dr. Richard Allington, University of Tennessee, one of the most highly recognized experts in the field of reading today and past president of the International Reading Association and the National Reading Conference; and Dr. Linda Katz, executive director of the

Children's' Literacy Initiative, a nonprofit organization that trains coaches and provides coaches and materials for schools throughout the country.

Dr. Jesse Moore, East Stroudsburg University, is the government relations chair for both the International Reading Association and the Keystone State Reading Association; Drs. Richard and Joanne Vacca, professors emeriti at Kent State University, are known for their work in content area literacy at the secondary level. They offered excellent advice for coaching in the secondary schools. Dr. Jack Cassidy, associate dean and professor at Texas A&M University and past president of the College Reading Association and the International Reading Association, shared his thoughts on why literacy coaching is a hot topic throughout the nation. Dr. Shelly Wepner, dean of education at Manhattanville College, friend, colleague, and prolific writer about literacy teaching and learning and the infusion of technology into the classroom, provided much valuable advice about what coaches need to consider and know about technology in the curriculum.

Both Theresa Manfre, a Nila Banton Smith Award–winning reading specialist from New York, and Laura Richlin, a well-respected literacy coach from Pennsylvania, willingly shared with us their insights and perspectives from their specific roles. These experts have daily hands-on experience with classrooms, and we are grateful for their poignant contributions to *A Guide to Literacy Coaching.* In addition, Dr. Ken Koczur, a superintendent from New Jersey, shared comments that he and his administrative team felt clarified the esteem they hold for coaches in their schools. These comments endorse the role of the literacy coach from a districtwide view.

We were honored that Dr. Rita Bean, professor of education at the University of Pittsburgh and an internationally recognized expert on the role of the reading specialist as well as the role of the coach, wrote the foreword for our book. She is a respected colleague and cherished friend. Currently, she is a member of the Advisory Board of the Literacy Coaching Clearinghouse. Having Dr. Bean's words introduce our book was a highlight of our journey. We are most appreciative of her thoughts, her time, and her talent. We learn something from her with each interaction.

Throughout *A Guide to Literacy Coaching,* we have stressed the importance of the literacy coach as collaborator, colleague, facilitator, and learner. As we proceeded with our writing journey, we encountered each of these four roles when we interacted with those whom we acknowledge here, and we encountered the roles as we interacted with each other and wrote together. Our heartfelt thanks is offered to our cherished families, Corwin's valuable editors, and the esteemed experts who shared their thoughts with us and our readers.

ABJ and MWS
January 2008

Corwin Press gratefully acknowledges the contributions of the following individuals:

Emme Barnes
Literacy Facilitator
Hawk Ridge Elementary
Charlotte, NC

Amy Q. Blocher
Reading Coach
Polk County School Board
Bartow, FL

Carrie Dillmore
Reading Coach
Port Charlotte, FL

Dolores M. Hennessy
Reading Specialist
Sarah Noble School
New Milford, CT

Natalie S. McAvoy
Reading Specialist
Elkhorn Area Schools
Elkhorn, WI

Connie Molony
Reading-Language Arts Specialist
Fargo Public Schools
Fargo, ND

Jennifer L. Palmer
Reading Specialist
Forest Lakes Elementary
Harford County Public Schools
Bel Air, MD

Victoria Seeger
Literacy Coach
Seaman USD 345
Topeka, KS

About The Authors

 **Annemarie B. Jay,** PhD, is an assistant professor of education at Widener University in Chester, Pennsylvania. Retiring after more than 30 years in public education, she joined the faculty of Widener, where she teaches graduate and undergraduate courses in reading.

She spent most of her career as a K–12 language arts curriculum coordinator for a large school district. She also served in the capacity of elementary principal and supervisor of elementary education and federal programs during her public school experiences. A hands-on administrator, Annemarie Jay spent a significant amount of her time coaching teachers about literacy practices. After earning her PhD from the University of Pennsylvania, Annemarie served as an adjunct professor at the University of Pennsylvania and Saint Joseph's University in Philadelphia for many years.

Currently, Annemarie Jay is the president-elect of the Keystone State Reading Association (KSRA) and also serves on its Long-Range Planning Committee. She has been a member of KSRA's board for many years and has served on the Government Relations Committee and chaired the Financial Assistance Committee in the past. She is also the president of the Delaware County Reading Council, her local council in Pennsylvania, for which she writes a bimonthly online newsletter.

A reviewer for publications of the International Reading Association and the Keystone State Reading Association, she is also a frequent presenter at the local, state, and national levels about literacy teaching and learning. In addition, she serves on a countywide advisory board for an organization that fosters volunteerism of senior citizens in special education classrooms.

Her research interests include early literacy, comprehension, and literacy leadership. She is a graduate of the Governor's Institute on Early Childhood Education. She facilitated a study group on literacy coaching over two years and has recently written two articles on the role of the elementary principal as a literacy leader.

In addition to her professional endeavors, Annemarie enjoys reading, traveling, and spending time at the beach with her family and friends.

 **Mary W. Strong,** EdD, is an associate professor in the Center for Education at Widener University, where she currently teaches undergraduate and graduate courses in literacy and literacy leadership. Prior to coming to Widener University, she taught literacy classes in the Department of Curriculum and Instruction at Iowa State University.

Before entering higher education, she was a classroom teacher and reading specialist at the primary and middle school levels in Pennsylvania, Ohio, and West Virginia. She also served as school principal at the elementary level for 20 years in West Virginia; one of the schools that she led won a National Rural and Small Schools Consortium Award and the National Council of Teachers Award for Programs for Schools at Risk.

She has given presentations on the topic of literacy education at the International Reading Association, National Reading Conference, College Reading Association, American Education Research Association, National Association of Elementary School Principals, and Association of Childhood Education International. She has had articles published in the *Reading Professor, Reading Horizons, Journal of Reading Education, Delta Kappa Gamma Bulletin,* and *Day Care and Early Childhood.* Additionally, she is on the editorial review board of *Journal of Literacy Research* and the *Journal of Adolescent and Adult Literacy.*

In other leadership roles, she is a member of the International Reading Association's Bylaws and Resolutions Committee and the former chair of the Teacher Awards and Grants Committee. She is the secretary/treasurer of the Language Experience Special Interest Group of the International Reading Association and has served as a board member to that group.

As an active member of the Keystone State Reading Association (KSRA), she is on the editorial review board of *Pennsylvania Reads: A Journal of the Keystone State Reading Association* and is the chair of KSRA's Community Involvement State Committee. She has also served as president of the Pennsylvania Reading Teacher Educators, a special interest group of KSRA. Presently, she is vice president of the Delaware Valley Reading Council.

To those who teach me the lessons and joys of life:
Jeff, Jim, and Christine
and
To Pip, my father, whom I miss dearly—a patient teacher
who always delightfully modeled lifelong learning

ABJ

To the memory of my parents, Harry and Adele Strong,
who always supported all of my educational endeavors
and
To my children, Mary Kaye, Beth, and John

MWS

To all of the educators and friends who have inspired us to
improve and reflect upon what we do

ABJ and MWS

The Nature of Literacy Coaching in America's Schools

1

INTRODUCTION

Since the enactment of the legislation for No Child Left Behind (2001), federal monies and other funding sources have been directed toward improvement of literacy instruction at the individual classroom level. An increasingly popular method of providing instructional improvement has been a coaching model in which an expert teacher coaches another teacher in the how and why of improving instructional practices. Although the model is widely used, the variability of qualifications and credentials of those providing literacy coaching has come under scrutiny. Allington (2006) identified this disparity when he stated, "in many, if not most, schools today you would find substantial numbers of reading specialists, reading teachers, and reading coaches who have never earned a reading specialist credential, even though most states have established such credentials" (p. 16). Despite the variability, coaches should be experts who are recognized as highly qualified by many stakeholders, including state departments of education, school districts, professional organizations, parents, and children. Every child deserves a quality education from a quality teacher. In every elementary and secondary school and classroom, quality instruction should occur because experts in the field have clearly delineated what good instruction should be. Literacy coaches can help ensure that quality instruction is a staple of every American classroom.

Whether states and/or schools call these experts reading coaches or literacy coaches is a matter of semantics. For the purposes of this book,

the term *literacy coach* will be consistently used, as we recognize and advocate the role of the coach in the instructional improvement in all of the
language arts' areas: reading, writing, listening, speaking, and viewing.
We identify a major aspect of literacy coaching as the teacher-to-teacher
observation and feedback of literacy practice with a core focus of instructional improvement. This component of literacy coaching is talked and
written about in many veins of the educational world today. The importance of literacy coaching is undisputed, but in many ways, educators are
embarking on a new frontier in finding the most effective techniques for
implementation.

This chapter contains a great deal of technical information that is
intended to help the literacy coach develop both a theoretical perspective
and a practical stance. It serves as a foundation to the practical applications presented in later chapters.

WHY LITERACY COACHING IS IMPORTANT

Literacy coaching is important because it has the potential to effect positive change in the learning culture of an entire school. Current literature
documents studies and initiatives for which literacy coaching has been
a positive change agent in the professional development of teachers
(Guiney, 2001; Moxley & Taylor, 2006; Poglinco & Bach, 2004; Toll,
2005; Walpole & McKenna, 2004). Coaching is not a new concept. What
is new about this concept as it relates to reading is the documentation of
coaching practices and the credentialing of coaches to work at particular
grade levels or within particular subject areas. Currently, national and
state standards are being published by professional organizations such as
International Reading Association (IRA), National Council of Teachers of
Science (NCTS), National Council of Teachers of Mathematics (NCTM),
and the National Council of Teachers of Social Studies (NCTSS). Federal
grants, such as Reading First (1999), have incorporated coaching as a
required component of implementing the grant directives. Initiatives
involving coaching, standards implementation, and grant requirements
have been instrumental in bringing coaching to the forefront. Coaching is
a key professional development endeavor to ensure best practices and raise
student achievement.

Many states are now issuing or considering issuing credentials to certify qualifying teachers as literacy coaches. Masterful teachers who are
organized and efficient, interact well with adults and children, keep confidences, and consistently exhibit professionalism in all realms of their
duties are likely to be successful coaches.

WHAT IS A LITERACY COACH?

The complex nature of literacy coaching is both difficult to define and difficult to recognize as a paradigm. The situational context and dynamics of each coaching experience is likely to dictate the form and function of a variety of coaching paradigms. This is because no two coaching experiences are alike. To produce a level playing field, however, we must define our perspective of what a literacy coach is and what the job entails. For the purposes of this text, *literacy coach* is defined as a reading specialist recognized as an expert teacher by peers and superiors whose main function is to provide professional development to teachers in both one-to-one and group venues with the goal of improving literacy instruction. Coaching as a professional development model is most often structured for one-on-one observation, feedback, and mentoring of teachers. However, coaching can be structured for small-group observation, feedback, and mentoring of teachers.

One way to think of the nature of literacy coaching is as multilayered, reflective practice. Not only is the primary practitioner, the classroom teacher, reflective of his or her own practice, but the coach is reflective of that teacher's individual practice as well. The coach's reflectivity focuses on what she might do to help the teacher improve in some way. In addition, coaching involves other types of reflection, including reflection on student learning, curriculum requirements, mandated testing, and the collective practices of the teachers for whom the coach is responsible. Just as reflective practice is multilayered with literacy coaching, so is the level of change. Improved instructional change occurs in individual classrooms as well as at different levels within the school system. When implemented effectively, literacy coaching can be a powerful tool to change positively the learning culture of an entire school.

In many ways, the position of literacy coach is analogous to that of a sport coach. In any sport, a coach is thought to be an expert and a person who will lead the team to victory. The coach needs to have experience and knowledge of the particular sport that is being played. The coach teaches the players what strategies will be used to win the game. The players confer with the coach with matters such as the game plan and environmental and weather issues. Tips for executing the game plan as well as difficulties that may arise will also be discussed by the coach with the manager and other personnel who assist with the daily activities of the team. The bottom line in American sports is that if the team has a losing streak, the fans are disgruntled, meaning that the coach and team must work harder to overcome deficiencies.

The concept of *coach* is inextricably connected to the concept of *team*. The coach needs to know the team well, both as individual members and as a cohesive unit; likewise, the team needs to be mindful of the coach's expectations. If we think of a team in a sports scenario, such as a football game, each player of the team has a specific talent and role that helps him to meet the general goal: winning the game. Individual preparation and work becomes orchestrated with team preparation and collaborative work. The coach observes, provides feedback, and fine-tunes these skills until the desired synergy is evident.

Generally, the basic principles that pervade the world of coaching sports teams can be applied to coaching teachers in the public or private school arena. In a school scenario, the team is the faculty. The literacy coach, like a sport coach, needs to be cognizant of each individual's strengths and contributions as well as specific area(s) that need improvement. For example, Ms. Hargy, a fifth-grade teacher, may be creative in having her students respond to what they read in texts or view on film or software. Her activity-centered classroom seems to motivate her students, as they consistently report that they are having fun doing skits and drawing posters. Although the fifth graders seem busy during their language arts class, they are not necessarily reflective or thoughtful about their literature responses. Her students do not engage in either sustained independent reading or re-reading of the texts to which they are required to respond. The teacher neither confers with the students about the quality of their responses, nor does she make standards-based decisions. Activity for activity's sake is never instructionally sound.

After observing several times in Ms. Hargy's classroom, the literacy coach recognizes that this teacher and her students have a nice rapport; the students seem happy and busy. The coach also recognizes that Ms. Hargy is not meeting the standards-based curriculum of the school district. The literacy coach must remind Ms. Hargy of the required reading curriculum that needs to be provided to all students. The overriding educational goal, providing a quality, standards-based instructional program, drives the work of the coach and the team. The coach needs to be acutely aware of this goal and communicate the goal to this teacher so that her level of awareness is raised to meet the "team's" expectations.

Often, the coach's awareness of the quality instructional program is dependent upon her observation and assessment of instructional delivery. In the example above, the coach was keenly aware that instructional delivery was a weakness for Ms. Hargy. Instructional delivery may be made through use of textbooks, such as basal anthologies or content area texts, or through thematic units written by teachers themselves. Whatever resources are used, instructional delivery should ensure that learners acquire knowledge of content and apply appropriate strategies to guide their understanding of what is being learned. The literacy coach's job is to ensure that quality teaching occurs so that quality learning is possible.

To function as a literacy coach, one must have high foundational knowledge of literacy curriculum and pedagogy as well as knowledge of educational standards. In addition, the coach must maintain rapport and have a good working relationship with the faculty. An effective coach has the ability to remind, encourage, and inspire individual teachers to hone their skills. He is also able to communicate to administrators, teachers, and the community how the school as a whole is maintaining reading standards. In general, the coach should be able to retain high sustainability for the responsibilities and demands of this challenging role.

As apparent in the sports analogy presented above, coaching is not a new concept. What is new is the documentation of coaching practices and the credentialing of coaches to work at particular grade levels or within particular subject areas. At this time, educators are also grappling with how to promote coaching so that its nature, the essence of the craft of coaching, is understood at a high level of recognized standards. According to the International Reading Association (IRA; 2004), quality control guidelines need to be considered and established to ensure standard training and background requirements. This seems to be especially important with the plethora of federal, state, and local curriculum standards mandated today. As a result of this need, standards and principles are being published by professional organizations, and some U.S. states are creating certification requirements and even certification programs for coaches. However, other states have not formally begun to consider these issues.

Additionally, educators are seeking to establish a specific set of parameters for coaching teachers. Shaw, Smith, Chesler, and Romeo (2005) define the literacy coach as a collaborator with classroom teachers and paraprofessionals who undertakes the following activities:

- Conducting demonstration lessons
- Supplying assistance to teachers in the selection of best practices
- Helping to design programs that motivate all students
- Providing training for classroom teachers in the administration and interpretation of assessments
- Presenting professional workshops
- Facilitating study groups
- Providing assistance to classroom teachers in preparing curriculum materials
- Assisting with student assessment
- Working with the teacher to plan appropriate instruction for students

Shaw et al. (2005) further state that some universities, just beginning to initiate the coaching model in their graduate reading programs, are incorporating hands-on coaching experiences in their courses based on the nine tenets listed above.

Although this type of professional development is complex due to the time-consuming tasks of preparation, observation, and feedback, the literacy coach must have a solid foundational knowledge of literacy curriculum and pedagogy. The coach must also have a clear knowledge of educational standards to ensure a quality standards-based instructional program.

WHAT ARE THE DIFFERENCES BETWEEN A LITERACY COACH AND A READING SPECIALIST?

After the Reading First legislation was enacted in 2000, the role of the literacy coach emerged. Reading specialists, on the other hand, have been working with teachers and students since the mid-1960s, when the Elementary and Secondary Education Act was passed during the Johnson administration. As a result of this legislation, pullout and in-class models have been used historically. At first, the predominant method was pullout instruction. Eventually, a blend of both models was accepted and often implemented in the same school.

As the role of the literacy coach became more prevalent, the literacy coach and the reading specialist began to work side by side in the same school. In some states and school districts, the literacy coach works only with students in the classroom, but in other states and school districts, the literacy coach works only with teachers. In still other situations, the literacy coach works with both students and teachers. Whatever the structure of providing reading services and coaching services, there are distinct differences in the primary function of each role.

In several states, there is a distinction between the literacy coach and the reading specialist. The reading specialist may work with both teachers and students. In fact, the Position Statement developed by the International Reading Association calls for the reading specialist to fulfill three roles: instruction, assessment, and leadership. However, the literacy coach generally works only with teachers. Regardless of how the state or school implements these services, the role is to improve the teaching and learning that occur as part of the educational program.

Figure 1.1 (Jay, 2005) conveys the contrasts that *may* exist between the two roles. However, in most areas of the chart, you will notice a duality of goals. The categories provide similar areas of focus, but the clientele is different. For the literacy coach, the direct recipient of services is the teacher; for the reading specialist, the direct recipient of services is the student.

The essential function of both the coach and the reading specialist is to improve instruction. While the reading specialist models and guides the work of children, the literacy coach models and guides the work of teachers. The reading specialist meets with the same groups of children routinely throughout the year for the purpose of providing instruction (Bean, 2005). The literacy coach may or may not work with the same teacher(s) throughout the course of the year. If the coach determines that a teacher has met an improvement goal, that teacher may be coached for only a part of the year, and the coach would then focus on working with other teachers in the school.

The professional roles of both the literacy coach and the reading specialist require high skill in observation, note making, and foundational knowledge of literacy teaching and learning. Although both roles demand knowledge of the curriculum, the literacy coach generally needs a more global understanding, as the coach is usually responsible for schoolwide or districtwide curricular efforts. The reading specialist, in contrast, often may be focused on particular grade-level or adjacent grade-level curricula (Wepner, Strickland, & Feeley, 2002). Additionally, the role of the literacy coach requires skills in working with adult learners.

The literacy coach needs to plan to work with teachers, not only in the classroom but also in professional development groups and feedback sessions (see Figure 1.1). The reading specialist's planning is situated in two distinct settings: with students in the regular classroom as a part of a coteaching model and in a second setting of self-contained small-group sessions. Regardless of their roles, the coach and the reading specialist should have strong organizational skills. They should be able to organize their time and resources so they can efficiently and effectively meet the demands of their positions. The planning role of the coach requires collaboration with principals and other administrators, whereas the planning role of the reading specialist requires collaboration with teachers and parents. The reading specialist often works as part of a child-study team in which she shares testing results and observational reports, and she may offer suggestions for reading strategies to be implemented both at home and at school.

Professionals in both roles are required to provide both formal and informal reports to stakeholders. Standard, efficient use of both oral and written communication is necessary. It is critical for coaches to communicate effectively with teachers and administrators. The reading specialist should communicate effectively with children, classroom teachers, staff who serve as part of child-study teams, and parents (Wepner et al., 2002).

Figure 1.1 Essential Differences Between the Literacy Coach and the Reading Specialist

Essential Differences	Literacy Coach	Reading Specialist
Function	• Improving instruction through focused work with regular classroom teachers • Planning, modeling, observing, and feedback; resources are targeted toward teachers' learning.	• Improving instruction through focused work with children • Teaching designated group(s) of children daily/regularly • In class: Coplanning occurs between teacher and reading specialist. • Pullout instruction: Planning, modeling, observing; feedback and resources are targeted toward children's learning.
Skills	• High foundational knowledge of documented curriculum • High knowledge of taught curriculum and reasons that it differs from documented curriculum • High foundational knowledge of reading and writing • Observational skills of teacher's strategy use, verbal and visual cues, questioning techniques, use of resources, etc. • Note making	• High foundational knowledge of reading and writing • Observation skills of children's strategy use and other reading behaviors • Note making
Planning	• Instructional formats for modeling in classrooms • Professional development (group meetings) • Feedback sessions • Participation in meetings with principal(s) and/or other administrators	• Instructional formats for working with students • Parent-teacher conferences • Child-study team meetings
Reporting	• Usable feedback to classroom teachers • Formative feedback to principals (and/or other administrators/stakeholders) • Written reports and communication for school or districtwide distribution	• Feedback regarding strategy use to children • Feedback regarding strategy use/misuse by children to teacher • Report cards to parents; conferences • Team meetings: Grade-level teams, support teams, child-study teams

Assessments	• Ongoing assessments of teachers' progress • Self-assessment regarding preparation, implementation, and feedback of coaching sessions • Match between coaching-instruction progress and school's long-term improvement plan • Match between coaching-instruction progress and standardized test improvement	• Ongoing reading assessments of children's progress • Self-assessment regarding pedagogy, resources, etc. • Match between instructional progress and standardized test improvement of both individual children and groups of children

Source: Jay, A. (2005, May). *Leading a winning literacy team: The complex roles of coaching, training and management.* Paper presented at meeting of the International Reading Association, San Antonio, TX.

Another aspect of duality is the critical nature of reflective practice for both the coach and the reading specialist. Self-assessment is essential to the ongoing rigor of the school-improvement process. Both professionals must have a thorough understanding of standardized tests, as well as informal checklists or other data-collecting instruments used by the teachers in their schools.

No matter what the role, foundational knowledge is essential. But the players are different due to their developmental nature. Adult learners have different needs than children. The dynamics of sharp skills, efficient planning, effective reporting, and quality assessment are critical for the literacy coach. These qualities will breed rapport, respect, motivation, and collaboration, and, more important, these interactions should promote a "we are in this together" mentality.

COACHING LABELS

In the educational arena, the concept of coaching has been given different labels such as *peer, technical, team, collegial, cognitive,* and *challenge* coaching (Garmston, 1987; Wong & Nicotera, 2003), and these also apply to literacy coaching. While the term *coaching* can be given different labels, all of these labels give a picture of the various functions of a literacy coach. In common among the terms is the notion of the coach as skilled mentor and the teacher of literacy to a less skilled yet able colleague. The labels vary in that some of the terms connote individual coaching exclusively, while others may refer to both individual and group coaching. Figure 1.2

provides an overview of the coaching labels presented, and the next sections in the text will discuss the terms in more detail.

Peer Coaching

The *peer coaching* label first appeared in American public education in the 1980s to designate peer or master teachers who were very skilled at teaching. They were assigned to assist other, less-skilled teachers with curriculum implementation and the development of teaching strategies (Joyce & Showers, 1996). However, Bean (2005) indicates that sometimes the teacher only watched while the peer coach demonstrated lessons in the classroom. In this situation, no rich discussion of the demonstration lesson occurred between the teacher and the coach. Shared reflection was missing because there was no dialogue at the end of the lesson.

To shed further light on Bean's comments, we might consider a situation in which two third-grade teachers have been assigned to peer-coach each other as part of a schoolwide peer-coaching endeavor. These teachers

Figure 1.2   Coaching Labels, Descriptions, and Implementation

Label	Coach's Description	Teacher's Description	How Implemented
Peer Coach	Master teacher	Less-skilled teacher	Individually
Technical Coach	Expert in new technique or new curriculum	Less skilled or unfamiliar with new technique or new curriculum	Individually, team
Team Coach	Assists, plans, and coteaches with teacher	Plans and coteaches with coach	Individually
Collegial Coach	An expert who leads a group or department	A group or department that interacts with the coach for professional development	Team
Cognitive Coach	A goal setter who assists teacher in skill reinforcement or expansion after observing and conferring with the teacher	A practitioner who is observed by the coach and then confers with coach and sets goals for future instructional implementation.	Individually
Challenge Coach	A problem solver with a focus on a specific classroom or a specific curriculum implementation issue.	Practitioner(s) who work toward a solution of a problem with the guidance of the literacy coach.	Individually, team

have been working together for several years but are now given the opportunity to observe in each other's classrooms. After taking turns observing, the teachers may offer general comments about positive impressions of each other's teaching. They may remark about each other's positive interaction with the students. However, they do not exchange concrete suggestions about missing elements in the lesson: pacing, pedagogical techniques, or resources used. Discussion of these elements would have made the peer coaching more thorough.

In schools today, the peer literacy coach does model and demonstrate the teaching of lessons. Although the coach may well express positive impressions of the class observed, in the peer-coaching model, he will also share feedback and possibly set goals with the teacher for practices that need improvement. In the example above, the third-grade peer coaches omitted goal setting.

The literacy coach, who is always considered a peer coach, does discuss the lesson with the classroom teacher. She thoroughly covers all elements of the lesson. Thus, good communication skills are an important asset for the literacy coach in promoting professional development and growth in the classroom teacher.

Technical Coaching

The *technical coaching* label implies that the literacy coach has instructional expertise. In this role, the literacy coach assists the classroom teacher in implementing new curricula and new instructional techniques into current procedures (Wong & Nicotera, 2003). The classroom teacher focuses on incorporating the new strategies and techniques based on guidance from the coach. The coach must have skills in working with adults in this situation.

If a literacy coach has expertise in writing instruction, the classroom teacher may call upon the coach for assistance with conducting writing conferences in a middle school classroom. Possible areas of discussion might include scheduling and organizing writing conferences, actually conducting conferences, minilessons, and the physical rearrangement of the classroom. For example, the coach might show the teacher some examples of note taking during an actual student writing conference. As the coach models, the middle school teacher watches the coach conduct the conference. After the conference, the coach and teacher meet to discuss what was done and why. The next step would be for the teacher to conduct conferences with the coach participating as an observer. A feedback session would follow. In technical coaching, it is important that the steps of the process as demonstrated by the coach remain intact. At the same time, however, the teacher should be able to maintain his own style and creativity while interacting with the student.

Team Coaching

When *team coaching* occurs, the literacy coach plans with the teacher, pools experiences with the teacher, and shares aspects of pedagogy with the teacher as a member of a team. This type of coaching creates an environment that is conducive to teamwork. The coach can provide additional materials and supplies that the classroom teacher may need.

In this setting, the coach assumes an equal share of the planning and teaching responsibility. In addition to planning, this coaching concept includes selection of resources and rehearsal of what should happen when the teacher implements the lesson.

An example of team coaching is conveyed in the following elementary scenario. If a primary grade teacher is struggling with developing fluency, the literacy coach may introduce the concept of readers' theater to the teacher. Together, the coach and the teacher would demonstrate to the children how to read the different parts in the play. They would then guide the children through their own reading; both adults would rehearse with the children, reading the parts of the script for the entire instructional period. This joint effort is a true team effort and most closely resembles what reading specialists do when they coteach with classroom teachers.

Collegial Coaching

According to the position statement *The Role and Qualifications of the Reading Coach in the United States* issued by the International Reading Association (IRA; 2004), literacy coaches collaborate with classroom teachers to achieve particular professional objectives. This definition describes *collegial coaching.* The coach engages classroom teachers in professional dialogue about their teaching, and the coach provides feedback as a mentor. However, the literacy coach does not assume the position of supervisor or evaluator of the classroom teacher.

The following vignette is offered as an example of collegial coaching. In a high school English department, some of the teachers would like their students to begin using electronic response journals. The coach might be asked to provide assistance if the teachers need to develop electronic response journals to literature. In this particular English department, a few teachers are uncomfortable with using this format. At first, the coach could meet with the entire department for several sessions to reaffirm the department's goal and help everyone feel included. These sessions could be used to offer tips on how to incorporate this tool into routine practices. Then, the coach could facilitate other sessions for those who were hesitant to use the electronic response journals. In this way, technology integration into the English curriculum would be promoted. The coach has functioned in a collegial manner by creating a cohesive team and by providing additional support to those who needed it.

Cognitive Coaching

In *cognitive coaching*, the emphasis is on improving the classroom teachers' practices by assisting them with refining and expanding their skills (Bean, 2005).

For example, after videotaping a lesson, the teacher and the coach could sit down and discuss what went well and what might be improved. The teacher is encouraged to reflect on the specific strengths and weaknesses of the lesson during the conference with the coach. This is the essence of cognitive coaching. The conference becomes a springboard for goal setting for future work with the coach. The literacy coach reflects on the observed lesson and on the teacher's reflections and considers the next steps in the process of coaching this teacher.

Challenge Coaching

When a specific problem arises and is identified by the literacy coach, this situation is considered *challenge coaching*. The problem may not be confined to a specific classroom but may occur in a larger setting, such as a particular grade level or even at the school level (Ackland, 1991; Becker, 1996). Here, the coach puts on a mystery sleuthing hat, which may include problem solving and lead to action research (research conducted by teachers in their own classrooms).

Consider the following scenario. The year after the district adopted a new reading text, three of the four fifth-grade teachers retired. The remaining teacher had a negative attitude about the newly adopted text. The principal and the coach were both concerned that newly hired teachers and the remaining veteran teacher might not plan and work together well to provide high-quality instruction. In that case, all four teachers would need coaching. The question for the coach is whether the fifth-grade teachers should be worked with individually or as a grade-level group. The answer to the question will depend on the coach's consideration of these variables: individual personalities of the teachers, reading philosophies of the teachers, and the group dynamics of the teachers.

POSITION STATEMENTS ON THE LITERACY COACH

National teacher organizations, such as the International Reading Association and the National Council of Teachers of English, as well as prominent committees, such as the National Reading Panel, have either directly or indirectly had an impact on the role of the literacy coach. Each U.S. state looks to these organizations for guidance in forming certification programs and guidelines. As stated previously in this chapter, establishing a certification as a literacy coach is being considered by many states and has already been established by some. The IRA has been instrumental in emphasizing standards in an effort to promote quality for coaching regardless of where it occurs or who does it. These position statements may be accessed from the Web sites of these organizations:

- International Reading Association (www.reading.org)
- National Council of Teachers of English (www.ncte.org)

ROLE AND QUALIFICATIONS OF THE LITERACY COACH

The International Reading Association's position statement on the *Role and Qualifications of the Reading Coach* (2004) delineates five criteria that should demarcate the role of the coach. The document states that a literacy coach should have the following characteristics.

1. Be an excellent classroom teacher.

2. Have an in-depth knowledge or reading processes, acquisition, assessment, and instruction.

3. Have experience working with teachers to improve their practices; be a reflective practitioner herself.

4. Have excellent presentation skills; have knowledge and experience in presenting at local, state, and national conferences.

5. Have experience or preparation that enables him to observe and model in classrooms and to provide feedback to teachers. This final criterion includes the skills necessary to be sensitive to the needs of the teacher and to engender trust in the relationship with the teacher.

STANDARDS FOR MIDDLE AND HIGH SCHOOL LITERACY COACHES

Recently, the IRA collaborated with the National Council of Teachers of English, the National Council of Teachers of Mathematics, the National

Science Teachers Association, and the National Council for the Social Studies to issue the *Standards for Middle and High School Literacy Coaches* (2006). This document structures the standards into two distinct parts: leadership standards and content literacy standards.

The leadership standards are written for the middle and high school literacy coaches without reference to the particular content area in which they are giving assistance. The content area literacy standards are written to ease the challenge that coaches face when assisting teachers in a particular curricular area, such as English language arts, math, science, or social studies.

The four key components of middle and/or high school literacy coaching as stated in the document (IRA, 2006) involve the need for the coach to be skillful as a *collaborator, instructional coach, evaluator of literacy needs,* and *instructional strategist.*

Collaborator

As a skillful collaborator, the literacy coach will assist the principal in developing a school literacy team. The coach will work with the school's literacy team to determine the school's instructional strengths. Collaborating with the literacy team, the coach can then develop a needs assessment plan for the whole school. In this role, the literacy coach promotes and facilitates productive relationships with and among the staff.

As a collaborator, the literacy coach in the middle or high school might need to focus on a teacher's weakness in guiding sufficient practice of a new skill taught to children. For example, the principal has concerns about a sixth-grade teacher based on both his informal observations and some communication with parents. The parents are distressed that their children are not grasping concepts because the teacher has not allotted much learning time before the students are tested on the material. The principal approaches the literacy coach about helping the teacher guide student practice. The literacy coach and the principal need to communicate in an honest, confidential manner so that the coach can work with the teacher to help him recognize areas in which he could improve his instructional practice. Effective coaching can certainly help to improve the literacy team at this grade level or the entire department if the struggling teacher becomes able to perform at a similar level as his peers.

Another example of the literacy coach as collaborator might involve work in a middle or high school that lacks print materials for students' use. The coach might be responsible for leading or coleading a committee to examine and carefully select materials. Then the committee can adopt those materials that are the best fit for the curriculum and the students.

When the committee's work is finished, the coach's work would continue as she helps the teachers learn to use the materials effectively in a variety of ways.

Instructional Coach

As a skilled instructional coach, the literacy coach works with teachers in the core content areas (math, science, and social studies), providing practical suggestions on a full range of reading, writing, and communications strategies. This work may be done with individual teachers, in collaborative teams consisting of teachers from several departments, or with individual content area departments. In this role, the literacy coach observes and provides feedback to teachers on instruction related to both literacy development and content area knowledge.

The coach's ability to recognize the absence or misuse of instructional strategies is dependent upon the regularity with which the coach observes a teacher at length (at least a full class period as opposed to a few minutes). Close teacher observation and careful note making should enable the coach to provide useful feedback to the teacher. For example, if a teacher is consistently giving directions but neglecting the demonstration or explanation of how to do a required task, the coach needs to be mindful of the oversight and tactful in making the teacher aware of the need to incorporate strategy use into his instructional routines.

Evaluator of Literacy Needs

As a skillful evaluator of literacy needs, the literacy coach interprets and uses assessment data to inform instruction within various subject areas. The literacy coach assists faculty in the selection and use of a range of assessment tools to make sound decisions about student literacy needs. Analysis of the assessments will provide the coach with data to implement a literacy improvement plan—one of the end goals of the collaboration effort. The literacy coach also conducts regular meetings with content area teachers to examine student work and progress. The examination of and reflection upon student work provides information for action planning for the present year and for the next year. For example, after working for a few years in the middle school and at the high school, the literacy coach notices that the expectation for ninth-grade report writing is very different for the English department and the science department. The literacy coach could provide professional development venues in which the two departments come together to examine and reflect on actual writing samples of students. Criteria could be discussed and established; the dialogue would certainly help one department understand the other's rationale for expectations in writing. Rubrics and standards might be introduced to help provide common ground for the two departments to continue examining students' work and to achieve coherence in their expectations and goals for students' writing.

Instructional Strategist

As an instructional strategist at the secondary level, the literacy coach is an accomplished middle and high school teacher who is skilled in developing and implementing instructional strategies for improving academic literacy in the core content areas (English language arts, math, science, and social studies). After careful observation, the literacy coach may realize that most of the middle and high school teachers are using graphic organizers with their students. Some use them as individual worksheets, while others use them as preteaching frameworks to structure class discussion. The graphic organizers range from basic to complex, and few organizers are used more than once or twice. To help teachers use graphic organizers more effectively so that the middle and high school students become familiar with their purpose, the coach might select and share some key graphic organizers that could be used across content areas. These graphic organizers could be used as before-reading/writing activities and after-reading/writing activities. The goal would be to reduce the number of graphic organizers used and increase the productivity of student responses based on the organizers.

Additional definitions of literacy coach can be found in the *Standards for Middle and High School Literacy Coaches* (IRA, 2006), which provides a chart of six key sources and details the roles, qualifications, and responsibilities of coaches cited by each source.

LITERACY COACHING CLEARINGHOUSE

Two of the nation's most respected teachers' organizations have collaborated to form a clearinghouse for literacy coaches. This collaboration is a model of the cooperation inherent in the ideal role of literacy coaches within their schools. The goal of the Literacy Coaching Clearinghouse, sponsored by IRA and the National Council of the Teachers of English (NCTE), is to provide information on how literacy coaches are being prepared and supported and how literacy coaches are being utilized in schools. The clearinghouse provides information about what research concludes about their effectiveness and what is needed to extend their contributions to student learning. Models for assessing literacy coaching programs will also be provided by the clearinghouse. For more information on the clearinghouse, contact Ken Williamson, executive director at NCTE, at kwilliamson@ncte.org or Nancy Shanklin, director of the Literacy Coaching Clearinghouse at the University of Colorado at Denver, at nancy.shanklin@cudenver.edu. The Web site for the Literacy Coaching Clearinghouse is www.literacycoachingonline.org.

LITERACY COACHING CERTIFICATION THROUGHOUT THE UNITED STATES

As we have mentioned previously in this chapter, literacy coaches have been given different titles depending on the state and the school district in which they teach.

Reading specialists and reading teacher positions are also given different labels according to state certification standards. In Resource A, you will find a survey that was conducted by the authors of this text regarding the certification status of reading specialists, literacy coaches, and reading supervisors across the United States. You will notice that only a few states have certification for literacy coaches either listed or pending on their Web sites.

If you would like more information about the reading teacher/specialist, supervisor, or literacy coach certificate for a particular state, a contact list including street addresses, telephone numbers, fax numbers, e-mail addresses, and/or Web sites is located in Resource B.

AN EXPERT'S THOUGHTS: DR. CATHY ROLLER

Reading Today featured a prominent front-page article titled "IRA, Others Develop Middle, High School Literacy Coaching Standards" ("IRA, Others," 2005) in which Dr. Cathy Roller, director of research and policy for IRA, emphasized the critical need to improve adolescents' literacy skills in American schools. The article stressed the collaborative work of IRA with NCTE, NCTM, the National Science Teachers Association (NSTA), and the National Council for the Social Studies (NCSS) in producing the document *Standards for Middle and High School Literacy Coaches* (2006).

Dr. Roller's expertise as a prominent researcher and her many experiences with these acclaimed national and international organizations led us to seek her comments concerning current issues involving the role of the literacy coach. The authors' interview with Dr. Roller follows:

Q: What does the present research say to you about literacy coaching?

A: There are not very many specific research studies about literacy coaches. Some evaluation research has been conducted by Pogonroff in New York and by a consortium in Southern California. There is a document by Elizabeth Sturdevant published by the Alliance for Excellence in Education.

Right now we are in a second stage of research evidence. We know that the type of research model with a coach and long-term site-based professional development has good sound research support. But there are not a great number of research studies related to specifics of reading coaching.

Q: Will the International Reading Association (IRA) be conducting research on literacy coaching?

A: IRA will probably not do specific research on coaching. Although some of IRA's research grant awards have been given to coaching studies, most of the research information about coaching is coming from the Reading First evaluations. The research studies are analyzing how coaches spend time. One of the preliminary findings is that coaches spend a lot of their time in support activities like organizing materials and doing scheduling. Unfortunately, reading coaches are spending less time than is desirable in working with teachers in classrooms.

Q: What do you know about certification of literacy coaches in different states?

A: Ohio has developed a certification program that involved all of the universities. There is a brief report about the program on the IRA Web site (www.reading.org). The name of the article is "Ohio Creates New Career Path in Literacy" by Beth Cady. It appeared in *Reading Today* under the "Best Practice" section (Cady, 2005).

Q: What do you see as the strength of promoting literacy coaching at this time?

A: The real strength at this time is the recognition that site-based professional development can improve reading scores. I think that it is really important that we use a site-based, long-term research approach to improving reading achievement through improving teachers. That approach is its strength.

Q: What about the political underpinnings of literacy coaching?

A: I am not as concerned about the politics as I am about the lack of consistency across the national, state, and district requirements that the person in the reading coach position be a reading specialist and have an extensive knowledge of reading. The nature of education in the United States is that it is locally controlled, and that is why there are inconsistencies across the states.

Q: Districts are hiring coaches from nonprofit organizations because they do not want to take teachers out of the classroom. Many of the reading coaches from nonprofit organizations are not reading specialists. Do you think that this is a problem?

A: I think that is a big concern. This is the same situation that often occurs with educational innovations. You have a good idea, and everybody latches onto it. However, the implementation isn't consistent, so the results aren't consistent. Then people draw the conclusion that the innovation doesn't work. Nothing that is badly implemented works.

Q: What do you think universities and professional development experts should be doing to ensure that quality literacy coaching occurs?

A: The first and most important thing is that universities should have good connections with state departments of education. That is an agenda that faculty members and administration in the universities in the past understood. They paid attention to the state departments. As the emphasis in universities shifted to achieving more publications and more publications, those relationships were viewed as less important. There are many states where there is no relationship between the university and the state department and in some states, there is a very adversarial relationship between the state department of education and the university.

It is very important that universities understand that it is *the state department* of education that certifies teachers. When university faculty start complaining about academic freedom, they must remember that they may have academic freedom in teaching their courses, but the state may choose not to certify. Once you ask the state department to certify the graduates of the universities, you have to pay attention to what the state department is asking. They best way to make sure that your program is accepted is to be aligned with the state department and make sure that your expertise has an impact on state requirements for certification. If you influence certification requirements, you can be sure that state requirements are consistent with good teacher preparation. That is one of the really important things that universities need to do.

We are just completing a review of the literature of teacher preparation at the undergraduate level, and essentially research in teacher preparation and reading coaches would fall into that group. We have noticed that it is a cottage industry. There are single studies, conducted at single sites, done by a single professor trying to improve their own practices. So another thing that has to happen is that we have to have big money for research. We are very pleased that the Education Research Center at the Institute for Educational Sciences has now included teacher preparation as a part of the agenda for education research. Thus, there have been some very big teacher quality grants, and teacher education programs have become a target for research funding. Some grants have been awarded, and some more grants have been submitted. So we are beginning to see some large-scale research in teacher preparation. We have been working for that, and we are beginning to see it happen.

Another thing that universities need to do is to strengthen their programs. What we are finding with the NCATE approval process is that most university programs do not have a coaching aspect. So we are granting conditional approval and 18 months to revise coursework so that programs *do* address coaching issues and responsibilities.

Q: Do you think that more courses from the educational leadership program should be incorporated into the literacy coach programs?

A: Actually, what I think would be useful is a practicum in how you help teachers improve their practice. You could do that easily in summer institutes. You could have teachers working with kids, and then reading coaches could work with groups of teachers and provide input and feedback on instruction. That is another thing that universities need to do to strengthen their programs. Then you would have a really top-notch reading coach in every school.

Q: How do you think some of the national mandates, such as Reading First and Reading Next, will play out in the future?

A: A lot depends on how effectively the money is used. If the Reading First research shows some strong positive effects, the coaching model with the reading emphasis will really catch on. The secondary model in Striving Readers, which began with a small program that included strong evaluation research, may have a long-term effect because you don't have a lot of money flooding the market at one time. In some places with both state and federal initiatives moving in, you have what I call "slap dash hire a warm body" kind of coach situations. That is bound to lead to poor implementation. To start small and do more research as you go is a more rational approach to implementing coaching.

Q: Is IRA working on quality control issues, and are they looking at the standards and qualifications of literacy coaching?

A: IRA already has standards. In the "Standards for the Professionals" document, information about the reading specialist/literacy coach is very prominent. In *Standards for Middle School and High School Literacy Coaches,* there is more of a focus on the subject matter issues. Thus there are two sets of standards that IRA has related to reading and literacy coaches, and there is a position statement.

We find that the standards do have an impact, particularly through the NCATE process, but most schools of education do not feel compelled to get their reading specialist program approved by IRA. One of the things that NCATE requires is a six-hour practicum. There are many universities across the nation where there is no practicum required.

Q: Why do graduate reading students not participate in the practicum?

A: Universities need to be a little more sensitive to the practicing teachers in their programs. They should consider permitting practicing teachers to do the practicum in their own classrooms and schools. A really good practicum program could be structured with teachers teaching in their own settings. It would make it harder for the university to supervise under this plan because each teacher might be doing something different in each individual classroom. However, it would make it more possible for the teacher to complete a practicum.

Universities should also have strong summer course offerings. Many university faculty do not want to teach in the summer. Universities need to be more customer-sensitive. This is one of the reasons that the neighboring school districts or regional educational consortiums and everyone else enter into the teacher-training act. These outside entities are willing to look at the needs of the customer. Universities seem to take the position that looking at customer needs is not good. But customer sensitivity does not have anything to do with quality. I think that you can have strong quality and still meet the needs of your customer.

Q: What final comment would you like to share about literacy coaching?

A: My big hope is that we will get a strong implementation of literacy coaching, but my fear is that we won't due to all of the issues that I have previously mentioned.

Source: Dr. Cathy Roller, Director of Research and Policy for the International Reading Association.

SUMMARY

Chapter 1 provided information about why literacy coaching is important as a focused professional development venue. The daunting task of improving teaching and learning in America's schools should be a constant effort of all in the educational field. The role of the literacy coach as an expert with strong foundational knowledge in teaching, assessing, curriculum, and standards has become critical in national efforts to maintain and incorporate quality instruction in classrooms today. This chapter emphasized the experience and the knowledge of the coach and addressed descriptions of the various labels of a coach as peer, technical, team, collegial, cognitive, and challenge.

A clear distinction was made between the role of the literacy coach and the role of the reading specialist. The IRA position statements on these roles were used as the basis for comparison. The *Standards for Middle and High School Literacy Coaches* (IRA, 2006) state that literacy coaching has been defined in the literature according the various roles that literacy coaches perform. The IRA standards detail the qualifications that coaches need and explain the responsibilities that coaches have. Both of these documents reflect different aspects of literacy coaching and their definitions.

Information regarding certification requirements throughout the 50 states was rendered in a comprehensive chart. In addition, an interview with Dr. Cathy Roller, director of research and policy for IRA, was included in the chapter.

TOPIC EXTENSIONS FOR CLASS SESSIONS OR STUDY GROUPS

1. Compare the IRA literacy coach qualifications in Appendix A to the requirements of the reading coach in your state. If your state does not have standards for the literacy coach, develop ideal criteria based on the IRA position statement. (See IRA, 2004.)

2. Refer to the scenario given in the section on "Challenge Coaching." Design a written action plan for working with those fifth-grade teachers on a weekly basis over six months. Be prepared to give an oral bimonthly report to the principal on the progress and issues you observe for each two-month period.

3. With four other colleagues, role-play a literacy coach working with the eighth-grade social studies and science departments. The departments are concerned because their standardized test scores have

been weak. Have each member of the group assume one of the following roles as delineated in *Standards for Middle and High School Literacy Coaches* (IRA, 2006):

Collaborator

Instructional coach

Evaluator of literary needs

Instructional strategist

Create and report on a plan for the professional development needs of each of the represented department teachers.

RESOURCE A: CERTIFICATION BY STATE

State	Read Spec	Lit Coach	Read Supv	2nd Endorse/ Cert	Other Terms or Labels to Check
Alabama (AL)	Yes	No	No	x	
Alaska (AK)	No	No	No	x	
Arizona (AZ)	Yes	No	No	x	
Arkansas (AR)	Yes	No	No	x	
California (CA)	Yes	No	Yes	x*	
Colorado (CO)	Yes	No	No		English/Language Arts + Reading Teach
Connecticut (CT)	No	No	No		
Delaware (DE)	Yes	No	No		
District of Columbia (DC)	No	No	No	x	K–12 Reading Licensure
Florida (FL)	Yes	No	No	x	
Georgia (GA)	Yes	No	No	x*	Instructional Supervision
Hawaii (HI)	No*	No	No		
Idaho (ID)	Yes*	No	No		
Illinois (IL)	Yes	No	No		General Reading
Indiana (IN)	Yes	No	No		General Reading; Indiana Standardss
Iowa (IA)			No		General Reading; Reading K–6; Reading 6–12
Kansas (KS)	Yes*	No	No	x	
Kentucky (KY)	Yes*	No	No	x	Reading and Writing
Louisiana (LA)	No	No	No	x	Language Arts
Maine (ME)	Yes*	No	No		Literacy Specialist
Maryland (MD)	Yes	No	No		Specialist
Massachusetts (MA)	Yes	No	No		Specialist
Michigan (MI)	Yes	No	No	x	
Minnesota (MN)	No	No	No		K–12 Reading Licensure
Missississippi (MS)	No	No	No		K–12 Remedial Reading
Missouri (MO)	No	No	No		
Montana (MT)	No	No	No		Reading

(Continued)

Resource A (Continued)

State	Read Spec	Lit Coach	Read Supv	2nd Endorse/ Cert	Other Terms or Labels to Check
Nebraska (NE)	Yes	No	No		Curriculum Supervisor
Nevada (NV)	Yes	No	No		Reading Teacher
New Hampshire (NH)	Yes	No	No		
New Jersey (NJ)	Yes	No	No	x	
New Mexico (NM)	No	No	No		Reading
New York (NY)	No	No	No		Reading Teacher
North Carolina (NC)	Yes	No	No		K–12 Reading Education
North Dakota (ND)	No	No	No		Reading Licensure
Ohio (OH)	No	Yes*	No		"Literacy Specialist" & Reading
Oklahoma (OK)	Yes	No	No		
Oregon (OR)	Yes*	No	No		
Pennsylvania (PA)	Yes	Pend	Yes	x	
Rhode Island (RI)	Yes*	No	Yes*		*Generic Supervisor
South Carolina (SC)	Yes	No	Yes*		Reading Teacher; Clinician; Consultant; Coordinator; Director
South Dakota (SD)	Yes*	No	No		
Tennessee (TN)	Yes	No	No	x	
Texas (TX)	Yes	No	No		
Utah (UT)	Yes*	No	Yes*		Reading Specialist; Supervisor
Vermont (VT)	Yes*	No	Yes*		Coordinator & Specialist
Virginia (VA)	Yes*	No	Yes*		
Washington (WA)	No	No	No		General Reading
West Virginia (WV)	Yes	No	Yes		
Wisconsin (WI)	Yes	No	Yes*		General Reading
Wyoming (WY)	Yes	No	No		

* = National Board Certified Teacher (NBCT) certification

RESOURCE B: HOW TO CONTACT STATE DEPARTMENTS OF EDUCATION FOR CERTIFICATION REQUIREMENTS

State	Address	Phone/Fax/E-mail
Alabama	Alabama Department of Education Teacher Education and Certification Office 5201 Gordon Persons Building PO Box 302101 Montgomery, AL 36130-2101	T: 334-242-9977 F: 334-242-0498
Alaska	Alaska Department of Education 801 W. 10th St., Suite 200 Juneau, AK 99801-1878	T: 907-465-2831 F: 907-465-2441 E-mail: tcwebmail@ eed.state.ak.us
Arizona	Arizona Department of Education Certification Unit PO Box 6490 Phoenix, AZ 85005-6490	T: 602-542-4367 E-mail: certification@ade.az.gov
Arkansas	Arkansas Department of Education Office of Professional Licensure 4 State Capitol Mall, Room 106B/107B Little Rock, AR 72201	T: 501-682-4342 F: 501-682-4898
California	California Department of Education (CDE) 1430 N St. Sacramento, CA 95814	T: 916-319-0800
Colorado	Colorado Department of Education State Office Building, Room 105 Educator Licensing 201 E. Colfax Ave. Denver, CO 80203	T: 303-866-6628 F: 303-866-6866 E-mail: educator.licensing @cde.state.co.us
Connecticut	Bureau of Certification & Professional Development Connecticut State Department of Education PO Box 150471, Room 243 Hartford, CT 06115-0471	T: 860-713-6969 F: 860-713-7017 E-mail: teacher.cert@po.state.ctus
Delaware	Delaware Department of Education Licensure/Certification Office 401 Federal St., Suite 2 Dover, DE 19901	T: 302-739-4686

(Continued)

Resource B (Continued)

State	Address	Phone/Fax/E-mail
District of Columbia	Office of Workforce and Professional Development Logan Annex 215 G St. NE Washington, DC 20002	T: 202-698-3995
Florida	Florida Department of Education Bureau of Educator Certification Suite 201, Turlington Building 325 W. Gaines St. Tallahassee, FL 32399-0400	T: 800-445-6739 E-form: www.fldoe.org/edcert/ contact.asp
Georgia	Georgia Department of Education Teacher Quality 1852 Twin Towers East 205 Jesse Hill Jr. Dr. SE Atlanta, GA 30334-9048	T: 404-463-1411 E-mail: wehughes@doe.k12.ga.us
Hawaii	Hawaii Department of Education Hawaii Teacher Standards Board 650 Iwilei Rd. #201 Honolulu, HI 96817-5318	T: 808-586-3230/3232 E-mail: mars@notes.k12.hi.us
Idaho	Idaho Department of Education Bureau of Certification & Professional Standards 650 W. State St. PO Box 83720 Boise, ID 83720-0027	T: 800-432-4601
Illinois	Illinois State Board of Education` 100 N. 1st St. Springfield, IL 62777-0002 or 100 W. Randolph, Suite 14-300 Chicago, IL 60601-3283	T: 866-262-6663 (Springfield); 312-814-2220 (Chicago) E-mail: certification@isbe.net
Indiana	Indiana Department of Education Division of Professional Standards 101 W. Ohio St., Suite 300 Indianapolis, IN 46204-4206	T: 317-232-9010; 886-542-3672 F: 317-232-9023 E-mail: bbridges@psb.in.gov
Iowa	Iowa Department of Education Board of Educational Examiners Grimes State Office Building Des Moines, IA 50319-0146	T: 515-281-3245 F: 515-281-7669 www.state.ia.us/boee/

State	Address	Phone/Fax/E-mail
Kansas	Kansas State Department of Education 120 SE 10th Ave. Topeka, KS 66612-1182	T: 785-296-3201/1978 F: 785-296-7933 E-mail: ddebacker@ksde.org
Kentucky	Kentucky Education Professional Standards Board 100 Airport Road, 3rd Floor Frankfort, KY 40601-6161	T: 502-564-4606 F: 502-564-7092 T: 888-598-7667 E-mail: dcert@ky.gov
Louisiana	Louisiana Department of Education Certificate of Preparation PO Box 94064 Baton Rouge, LA 70804-9064	T: 225-342-3566; 877-453-2721 F: 225-342-3499 E-mail: stan.beaubouef@la.gov
Maine	State of Maine Department of Education Certificate Office 23 State House Station Augusta, ME 04333-0023	T: 207-624-6603 F: 207-624-6604
Maryland	Maryland State Department of Education Attn: Certification Branch 200 W. Baltimore St. Baltimore, MD 21201	T: 410-767-0412
Massachusetts	Massachusetts Department of Education The Office of Educator Licensure 350 Main St. Malden, MA 02148-5096	T: 781-338-3000 Web site: www.doe.mass.edu/educators/
Michigan	Michigan Department of Education 608 W. Allegan St. PO Bo30008 Lansing, MI 48909-7508	T: 517-373-3324
Minnesota	Minnesota Department of Education Educator Licensing 1500 Highway 36 W. Roseville, MN 55113	T: 651-582-8200 E-mail: mde.educator-licensing@state.mn.us
Mississippi	Mississippi Department of Education Educator Licensure Central High School 359 N. West St. PO Box 771 Jackson, MS 39205-0771	T: 601-359-3483 E-mail: ccoon@mde.k12.ms.us; cchester@mde.k12.ms.us

(Continued)

Resource B (Continued)

State	Address	Phone/Fax/E-mail
Missouri	Missouri Department of Elementary and Secondary Education Educator Certification PO Box 480 Jefferson City, MO 65102-0480	T: 573-751-0051/3847 F: 573-522-8314 E-mail: webreplyteachcert@dese .mo.gov
Montana	Montana Office of Public Education Educator Licensure PO Box 20251 Helena, MT 59620-2501	T: 406-444-3150 E-mail: cert@mt.gov
Nebraska	Nebraska Department of Education 301 Centennial Mall S. PO Box 94987 Lincoln, NE 68509	T: 402-471-2496 E-mail: tcertweb@nde.state.ne.us
Nevada	Nevada Department of Education Teacher Licensing Office 1820 E. Sahara Ave., Suite 205 Las Vegas, NV 89104	T: 702-486-6458 F: 702-486-6450 E-mail: license@doe.nv.gov
New Hampshire	New Hampshire Department of Education Bureau of Credentialing 100 Pleasant St. Concord, NH 03301-3860	T: 603-271-3491 F: 603-271-1953
New Jersey	New Jersey Department of Education 100 Riverview Plaza PO Box 500 Trenton, NJ 08625-0500	T: 609-777-2140 F: 609-633-0291
New Mexico	New Mexico Public Education Department Professional Licensure Bureau 300 Don Gaspar Santa Fe, NM 87501-2786	T: 505-827-5800 E-mail: license@ped.state.nm.us; mgonzales@sde.state .nm.us
New York	Certification Unit New York State Education Department 5N Education Building 89 Washington Ave. Albany, NY 12234	T: 518-474-3901 E-mail: tcert@mail.nysed.gov

State	Address	Phone/Fax/E-mail
North Carolina	North Carolina Department of Public Instruction Employment and Licensure 301 N. Wilmington St. Raleigh, NC 27601	T: 919-807-3300
North Dakota	North Dakota Education Standards and Practices Board 2718 Gateway Ave., Suite 303 Bismarck, ND 58503-0585	T: 701-328-9641 F: 701-328-9647 E-mail: espbinfo@state.nd.us
Ohio	Ohio Department of Education Office of Certification/Licensure 25 S. Front St, Mail Stop 105 Columbus, OH 43215-4183	T: 614-466-3593 Web site: www.ode.state.oh.us/ teaching-profession/ teacher/certification_ licensure
Oklahoma	Oklahoma State Department of Education Professional Standards 2500 N. Lincoln Blvd. Oklahoma City, OK 73105-4599	T: 405-521-3301 F: 405-521-6205 E-mail: karen_nickell@sde.state .ok.us
Oregon	Oregon Department of Education 255 Capitol St. NE Salem, OR 97310-0203 or Teacher Standards and Practices Commission 465 Commercial St. NE Salem, OR 97301-3414	T: 503-378-3569/3586 F: 503-378-5156 E-mail: ode.frontdesk@ode.state .or.us
Pennsylvania	Pennsylvania Department of Education 333 Market St. Harrisburg, PA 17126-0333	T: 717-783-6788
Rhode Island	Rhode Island Department of Education 255 Westminster St. Providence, RI 02903	T: 401-222-4600; 401-254-3019 E-mail: rmccormack@rwu.edu
South Carolina	Office of Teacher Certification 3700 Forest Dr., Suite 500 Columbia, SC 29204	T: 877-885-5280 F: 803-734-8264 E-mail: certification@scteachers.org

(Continued)

Resource B (Continued)

State	Address	Phone/Fax/E-mail
South Dakota	South Dakota Department of Education 700 Governors Dr. Pierre, SD 57501	T: 605-773-3134 F: 605-773-6139
Tennessee	Tennessee Department of Education Andrew Johnson Tower, 6th Floor Nashville, TN 37243-0375	T: 615-532-4880 F: 615-532-1448
Texas	Texas Education Agency Educator Certification and Standards 1701 N. Congress Ave., WBT 5-100 Austin, TX 78701-1494	T: 512-463-9734; 888-863-5880
Utah	Utah State Office of Education 250 E. 500 S. PO Box 144200 Salt Lake City, UT 84114-4200	T: 801-538-7740
Vermont	Vermont Department of Education 120 State St. Montpelier, VT 05620-2501	T: 802-828-2445 E-mail: edinfo@ education.statete.vt.us
Virginia	Virginia Department of Education PO Box 2120 Richmond, VA 23218	T: 800-292-3820 E-mail: ppitts@ mail.vak12ed.edu
Washington	Dr. Terry Bergeson Washington Department of Education Old Capitol Building PO Box 47200 Olympia, WA 98504-7200	T: 360-725-6000
West Virginia	West Virginia Department of Education Office of Professional Preparation (Certification) Building 6, Room 252 1900 Kanawha Blvd. E. Charleston, WV 25305-0330	T: 304-558-2703; 800-982-2378 F: 304-558-7843 E-mail: mfmiller@ access.k12.wv.us
Wisconsin	Wisconsin Department of Public Instruction 125 S. Webster St. PO Box 7841 Madison, WI 53707-7841	T: 800-441-4563
Wyoming	Teaching Certification Professional Teaching Standards Board 1920 Thomes Ave., Suite 400 Cheyenne, WY 82002-3546	T: 307-777-7291; 800-675-6893 E-mail: bmarti@state.wy.us

The Multiple Roles of the Literacy Coach $\quad$ **2**

*Facilitator, Observer,
Colleague, and Learner*

INTRODUCTION

Chapter 2 explores the multiple roles of literacy coaches. Literacy coaches teach, and they learn. The roles and responsibilities of the literacy coach are defined and refined as the position evolves. The information in this chapter concerning various types of facilitation and observation will help both the new and the seasoned literacy coach refine the craft of coaching. Practical suggestions are provided for the literacy coach as colleague and learner.

SCENARIO

Harry, a literacy coach, needs to schedule six hours of professional development for the teachers in his middle school to meet state mandates. These meetings will take place over several sessions. All of the 153 teachers on the staff will be involved. Harry can't decide the best times to meet or how to divide the time into meaningful segments that will be convenient for all of the teachers. He also needs to decide where to hold the meetings; how to coordinate the facility, technology, books, and handouts; and what type of food to have available.

Harry tried to meet with the middle school's principal three times this week, but each time, the principal was involved in a school emergency or in a meeting out of the building. Harry decided to create two possible plans and have them ready for when he would be able to meet with the principal. Both plans will meet the required six hours of professional development.

Review the two plans that Harry prepared in Figure 2.1. Which of the two do you think is more effective? Why? Would you modify anything?

COACH AS FACILITATOR

Facilitating committees, projects, and meetings is a common responsibility of a literacy coach. To facilitate means to provide a level of ease and comfort to a process for all of those who participate in it. When the coach acts as a facilitator, he may be performing the roles of the team coach (assisting, planning, and coteaching with the teacher) or the collegial coach (leading the group or department as an expert) as described in Chapter 1. Whatever the situation, the literacy coach will need strong foundational knowledge of language arts' processes, adult learners' traits, and the purpose/mission of the facilitated event. According to the International Reading Association (2004), the following criteria related to facilitation are viewed as "minimum qualifications" for the literacy coach:

- Have in-depth knowledge of reading processes, acquisition, assessment, and instruction.
- Be an excellent presenter and group leader.

The literacy coach should be recognized as a good resource for providing these services and acting as facilitator before, during, and after the facilitated event.

Facilitating Before the Event

Before facilitating a committee, project, or meeting, the literacy coach needs to plan carefully. As Harry did, the literacy coach must consider who the participants will be, when the meeting will take place, where the event will be held, and how the event will be conducted. The literacy coach may face three distinct planning situations: planning specifics for the group meeting as they relate to general guidelines set forth by administrators, planning entirely on one's own for the content and context of the meeting, or planning in collaboration with some or all of the teachers who will be involved in the group meeting.

Figure 2.1   Plans A and B for Harry

PLAN A* From Scenario

	MEETING 1 (October 19)	MEETING 2 (October 26)
9:30 AM	Welcome and Overview. • Coffee, tea, and pastries (Principal Goldman).	Review of task from Meeting 1.
9:45 AM	Setting the Task: Aligning state standards and assessment reports (Harry McKinney).	Teachers continue to work in departments to create draft of assessment reports.
10:00 AM	Review of Literacy and Content Area Standards. • PowerPoint presentation (Harry McKinney)	Teachers continue to work in departments to create draft of assessment reports.
10:30 AM	Teachers work in departmental groups to create draft of assessment report categories.	Teachers continue to work in departments to create draft of assessment reports.
	Boxed Lunch: During lunch, departments will share their drafts with the whole group.	Boxed Lunch: Departments share final reports.
	Closure: Reminder about next week's meeting to continue this work (Principal Goldman).	Closure: Remind the teachers that copies of completed forms will be distributed by mid-November to all staff. Teacher evaluation of the meetings.

*Considerations for Plan A

> Number of meetings: 2
> Place: School auditorium
> Logistics: Microphone, screen, computer, table to display materials (books, handouts, pencils)
> Food: School food service will provide coffee, tea, and pastries and boxed lunches

(Continued)

Figure 2.1 (Continued)

Plan B From Scenario**

MEETING 1 October 22	MEETING 2 October 30	MEETING 3 November 7	MEETING 4 November 13
3:30–5:00 PM	3:30–5:00 PM	1:00–2:30 PM (Half-day inservice)	3:30–5:00 PM
Overview of task and review of standards.	Teachers will meet in departments to begin creating draft of assessment reports.	Teachers will meet in departments to continue drafting assessment reports. Departments share work on drafts with the whole group.	General discussion about the quality and cohesion of draft documents; consensus about final, uniform report forms. Teacher evaluation of the meetings.

**Considerations for Plan B

    Number of meetings: 4

    Place: Connie's Restaurant (across the street from Middle School)

    Logistics: Microphone, screen, table to display materials

    Food: Light snacks (provided by Connie's restaurant and paid for by district professional development budget)

Specific Planning With Administrators

State mandates are communicated to administrators, who delegate responsibility for implementing the mandates to those in leadership positions, such as literacy coaches. The administrator then meets with the literacy coach to apprise her of what is expected, what funding is available, and when time lines need to be met. This information assists the collaborative process of the administrator and the coach as they anticipate how many group meetings will be needed to meet the requirements of the new mandate. A preliminary agenda can be drawn up as the administrator and literacy coach initiate plans. A final agenda may be designed by the literacy coach and approved by the administrator.

Planning on One's Own

The second situation, planning on one's own, may occur after a literacy coach has had numerous opportunities to observe in classrooms, review assessment data, and survey instructional resources. The coach may create a committee or set forth a project as a professional development endeavor to help improve instruction related to his experiences in observing and reviewing over an extended period of time. In other words, the literacy coach has collected some data that supports the purpose for the committee or project. This type of planning may occur at both the individual school building level as well as at the district level.

Collaboration With Teachers

The third scenario for planning involves collaboration with teachers. Whether an upcoming professional development session is assigned to the literacy coach or whether she determines that it is necessary, the coach should solicit the help of teachers in planning what needs to be done. This goal can be accomplished in several ways. A representative group of teachers could be asked to assist with planning, if the committee or project will eventually include all of the school's or district's teachers. Another method for soliciting the help of all teachers in the district is through an electronic survey or conducting individual surveys. The survey or interview should focus on the data that the coach collected. Yet another approach is to provide a questionnaire to the teachers to ask what time and place would be desirable for the meeting to be held.

Each of the three situations outlined above are likely to be ongoing professional development meetings rather than "one and done" meetings. Fullan (2001) reminds us that sustained improvement occurs when a clear purpose for the event is delineated, there is understanding of the change that takes place, a knowledge base is created and shared, and coherence is achieved through collaboration. After all, the goals of facilitated group meetings are sustained professional development and long-term instructional improvement. Episodic reform, a frequent product of "one and done" meetings, does not yield the desired goals. Preparing for what one desires to happen (and what might actually happen) takes brainstorming and flexibility.

It is imperative for the literacy coach to keep the purpose of the event in mind and to share that purpose with the participating teachers. The following guidelines are recommended *before* facilitating a committee, meeting, or project:

- *Be prepared.* Know your data well and be able to explain them. Relate them to district concerns so that they are relevant to the participants.
- *Plan ahead of time.* Anticipate what you can accomplish within the time frame of the meeting. Have your ideas and your resources organized.

- *Have a written agenda.* Distribute a general agenda to the participants at the beginning of the meeting. However, the coach should have a detailed agenda and checklist. (See Figure 2.2.)

Figure 2.2   Checklist for Facilitating a Meeting

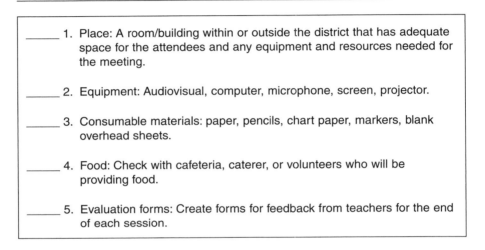

_____ 1. Place: A room/building within or outside the district that has adequate space for the attendees and any equipment and resources needed for the meeting.

_____ 2. Equipment: Audiovisual, computer, microphone, screen, projector.

_____ 3. Consumable materials: paper, pencils, chart paper, markers, blank overhead sheets.

_____ 4. Food: Check with cafeteria, caterer, or volunteers who will be providing food.

_____ 5. Evaluation forms: Create forms for feedback from teachers for the end of each session.

If possible, the coach may want to survey the teachers who will be attending the meeting to find out what time would be most convenient for them to meet and where the best place to meet might be.

Facilitating During the Event

One guideline that was suggested in the section on "Facilitating Before the Event" was to distribute the agenda. The next step is to provide an overview of the agenda. Tell the group what needs to be accomplished while they are together so that expectations and a time frame can be adhered to. Being prepared for what one desires or expects to happen (and what actually happens) takes brainstorming and flexibility on the part of the coach. It is imperative for the literacy coach to keep the purpose of the event in mind and to share that purpose with the participating teachers.

Pacing

Pacing is just as important in a teachers' meeting as it is during a classroom lesson. Just as teachers make multiple decisions and determinations during instruction, the literacy coach also makes multiple decisions and determinations during the facilitation of a group professional meeting with a focused agenda. For the new coach, this skill must be learned through experience. One tip is to gauge your time depending on the importance of the task. For example, as you preview the agenda, if item A is of less importance than item B, you might devote only 20 minutes to item A but 45 minutes to item B.

The Schedule

Keeping to a schedule is key. Remain on task and help the members of the group to avoid traveling down a rabbit trail. However, be able to read the group. If it becomes obvious that discussion about an agenda issue is warranted, time may be granted for teachers to discuss the particular issue in depth. In this case, the agenda should be adjusted. The facilitator/coach who recognizes the importance of the discussion as an enhancement of teachers' understanding and who is flexible enough to allow for time adjustment demonstrates good professional judgment. When teacher input is valued, facilitation takes place in the true meaning of the word. Collaboration is evident among the teachers and also between the facilitator and the participating teachers. The positive power of committed collaboration is essential in a learning community (Aseltine, Faryniarz, & Rigazio-DiGilio, 2006). On the other hand, if the participants are presenting only negative comments that are detrimental to the group's work, then the facilitator/coach must bring them back to the agenda's focus quickly. Thus the commitment to the goals and purposes of the meeting, professional and curriculum development, is honored.

Facilitating After the Event

When a meeting comes to a close, it is a good idea to recap what concepts were covered. It is also helpful to state what work was completed and what is incomplete. If possible, the facilitator/coach should also inform the group what he can do to transition incomplete work between the current meeting and the next meeting. Sometimes the facilitator/coach can solicit volunteers from the participants to help with minor incomplete tasks that can be ready for the next meeting. For example, if the group brainstormed ideas and they were jotted on a chart, someone from the group may volunteer to type the information as an outline or a table. The typed information can be submitted to the facilitator/coach before the next meeting so that it can be photocopied and distributed when it is needed.

Of course, much of what the coach will reflect on about the meeting will depend on the feedback she receives from the meeting's participants. The feedback may be oral, but generally it is given in writing. If a written response form is used, it should be easy for teachers to complete and relevant to the work they did in the meeting. Some examples of brief and user-friendly feedback forms for meetings are included offered here:

- *WILT (**W**hat **I** **L**earned **T**oday).* On a half-sheet of paper, type WILT. Give the teachers a few minutes to write their thoughts about the meeting. They may write a few sentences or use just a list of phrases. The coach should decide if the form should be submitted anonymously or not.
- *I Learned/Feedback to Presenter.* Provide each participant with an index card. Ask the teachers to use one side to write what they learned as a result of the meeting. Ask them to provide feedback to the presenter on the other side.
- *Colored Sticky Notes.* This technique works well when the facilitator/coach would like to have two, three, or more specific types of feedback. For example, participants may be asked to jot on a yellow sticky, "What topics I feel comfortable with." On a blue sticky, they may be asked to jot, "I question . . ." The facilitator/coach may want the teachers to post their responses by color on a bulletin board or wall as they exit the meeting. This makes it easy for the facilitator and the participants to do a quick review of the responses by category. The facilitator can save them and type the responses by category for distribution at another meeting if desired. They also serve as part of the record of documentation of the meeting.

When a meeting comes to an end, whether it is the first meeting, fourth meeting, or final meeting, the literacy coach's reflection on the meeting will help her to plan for subsequent meetings. At this time, the coach can also assess progress made toward the goal(s) of the committee, meeting(s), or project. If the literacy coach is accustomed to facilitating meetings and/or doing presentations, she may have a first reaction to assessment of the completed meeting. The reaction will be based on her knowledge of the content that was shared, the staff that participated, and what was accomplished or needs to be accomplished.

She may feel total satisfaction because the participants were actively involved and in agreement with each other's ideas. She may sense that the meeting was productive and the group is ready to move forward in its work, because everyone seems to be looking forward to continuing the meetings and to understand the level of professional responsibility they are undertaking as part of the group. The literacy coach has then determined that the meeting progressed as well as expected and then some!

Perhaps after facilitating a meeting, however, the literacy coach may feel mixed emotions of satisfaction and impending need. She feels satisfaction because progress was made, but she has a sense of impending need because more time and resources may not materialize for the remainder of the year's schedule. She may have to prioritize details for future meetings and move forward in an intrepid manner. In her reflection, the literacy coach has assessed the meeting as adequate but does not feel completely satisfied.

One possible reflection, which we would hope would not occur, is that the literacy coach would feel utter dissatisfaction with the meeting. A disjointed agenda, awkward pacing, and disgruntled participants could combine to create such dissatisfaction about the day's meeting. In this situation, the coach has assessed the meeting as flawed and realized that she must "dust herself off and start all over again."

Although each of these reflective considerations is hypothetical, the point is that literacy coaches who facilitate committee work, ongoing meetings, or project work must reflect on each meeting as both a separate entity and a connective link to the data collected. At the first meeting, she must be able to initiate the group's work. The reflection about that particular meeting is a separate entity. It also must be thought about in a manner that will help the facilitator/coach plan for the meeting that follows. In subsequent meetings, the coach must be able to facilitate the ongoing efforts of the professionals involved in the work. Each subsequent meeting should be reflected on as a separate entity, for how it links to past meetings, and how it connects to those yet to occur.

Whether a novice or veteran facilitator of professional development in group settings, the literacy coach will find it helpful to pose questions (such as those listed in Figure 2.3) to aid in reflecting on a meeting after it has been conducted.

Figure 2.3   Literacy Coach as Facilitator: Questions for Reflection After
Meetings

- What went well at today's meeting?
- What strategies did I (or others) use that helped things go well?
- What did not go well at today's meeting?
- What did I (or others) do that hindered this meeting from going well?
- How did the planned written agenda compare to the dynamic agenda (what actually happened at the meeting)?
- What perceptions or concerns of the group became evident at this meeting? Were they ongoing perceptions or concerns, or were they new because they were specific to something that happened at this particular meeting? (For example, if a discussion of phonics instruction emerged, should it be explicit or implicit?)
- Could anything have been done differently to facilitate fluency of the professional development process? If so, should a specified change be incorporated into the next planned meeting? (For example, two speakers were on the agenda for 45 minutes each, but Speaker #1 spoke for 75 minutes.)
- Were tasks set for participants during the meeting "just right," or were they overwhelming for most of the group? (For example, the coach might evaluate jigsaw reading of articles, evaluating materials, viewing a number of video clips for comparisons, listening to a consultant's presentation, and so forth.)
- How did the physical setting promote or hinder the group's work at the meeting?
- How was the pacing: on target, too slow, too quick?
- Based on feedback (evaluation form), do I (and the group) feel comfortable moving forward as a result of today's meeting?
- What do I feel needs to be revisited or revised as a result of today's meeting? How will the group feel about this?

In addition to the questions for reflection, three general guidelines for important consideration *after* facilitating a group meeting are recommended:

1. *Use other venues for feedback.* Design a structure that works for providing feedback (e.g., a teacher-friendly form at the close of the meeting such as those mentioned above, informal individual interviews with teachers within a day or two of the meeting, a quick survey of participants via e-mail, a brief meeting with a representative group of participants).

2. *Maintain meeting documents.* Maintain a file of agendas. Include any articles, handouts, materials from publishers, etc. that are related to the content of the meeting. In addition, file menus, supply lists, or any other type of information that is pertinent.

3. *Communicate.* Be prepared to communicate progress of meetings through written reports, e-mail, newsletters, and memoranda. Thank teachers for their participation and notify them of future meetings. Prepare written and/or oral reports to stakeholders such as school directors and the community at large.

COACH AS OBSERVER

One of the major purposes for which most coaches are often hired is to provide individual professional assistance to teachers in the classroom. Walpole and McKenna (2004) and Lambert (2003) state that literacy coaches must move from providing professional development outside the classroom to providing professional development inside the classroom. One of the responsibilities of the coach is to assist teachers with the process of reflection. To accomplish this goal, the coach must understand the daily activities in the teacher's classroom. In this instance, the coach is posing questions about classroom instruction rather than telling the teacher what must be done. Meaningful dialogue about the workings of the classroom can occur only when both parties understand the set of circumstances. Lambert (2003) states that true understanding happens when we listen to each other, build on shared ideas, and construct knowledge and understanding. The coach can observe the teacher, the teacher can observe the coach, and the coach can observe other coaches. Professional development is not restricted to the classroom teacher; the coach can also participate in the process as a learner.

Coach Observing Teachers

The one-to-one observation that takes place in an individual classroom of a teacher by a coach is the heart of literacy coaching. The information gained from directly observing in individual classrooms as well as collective classrooms should provide significant data to the coach about the instructional strengths and shortcomings within the school. According to Walpole and McKenna (2004), "literacy coaches who do not observe find themselves making incorrect assumptions about instruction" (p. 204). Formative observations should guide the individual teacher to examine and improve instructional practice. Walpole and McKenna (2004) suggest that observation must be carefully defined and described to teachers. Clarifying what will happen can take place in a collegial manner in a preobservation meeting between the teacher and coach. The preobservation meeting is a great place to begin building rapport if the teacher and coach are unknown to each other. The coach should assure the teacher that the nonevaluative observation will be done in a helpful manner.

The first step of the observation process would be to ask the teacher to describe several of his teaching strengths. Then, ask the teacher to identify one area that he would like to strengthen. Discuss the possibility of using the area of perceived need as a focus of the observation. For example, a teacher may describe his strengths as pacing, organization, and question posing. He may cite the use of context clues as an area to be strengthened. The coach can let the teacher know that during the observation, she will focus upon the teaching and guiding of context clues and share her observations with the teacher at a feedback session.

A second step of the observation process may be for the coach to share several sources for the teacher to read about the topic. (Articles, DVDs, Web sites, etc. can be given to the teacher later.) As a third step, the literacy coach may also make a note of this area and plan to use it in a demonstration lesson for this teacher at a later time. Aseltine et al. (2006) state that

> focusing on a "slice" of teaching and learning supports the teacher's developing pedagogical capacity for analyzing student performance data in general; for designing professional development connected to student learning needs; and for developing instructional interventions that align essential curriculum, related instructional methodology, and the monitoring of student progress. (p. 22)

Whole Group Versus Small Group

Depending on the outcome of the preobservation conference, the coach and teacher may agree that the coach will be observing either whole-class instruction or the instruction of a small, guided group. In either case, the coach is focusing upon the quality of instruction. If small groups are being observed, the coach needs to be acutely aware of the teacher's purpose for working with that group. If guided reading is being conducted, for example, is it for comprehension focus, fluency focus, or another skill focus? Is the lesson an introduction or a review for this particular group of students? If guided writing is being done, is it a skill-building lesson, a process lesson, or a craft lesson?

Whether the coach plans to use an observation checklist or take running notes, the checklist or plan should be shared with the teacher at the preobservation meeting. When this information is shared before the coach observes in the classroom, the teacher and the coach are both cognizant of the goals of the observation. The coach should also ask the teacher where he should sit during the observation: at a table with a group of children, at the teacher's desk, or on a chair in an unobtrusive place in the classroom. Whichever mutually agreed upon seating placement is chosen, the site should be one where the coach can carefully see the interactions between the teacher and the students. He should also be able to view any visual aids that are used or referred to during the lesson.

It is important for the coach to arrive on time for the observation lesson. He should introduce himself to the students so they are not distracted by his presence. Any materials (notebook, clipboard, laptop computer, pens) should be organized and ready to be placed on a desk to use in a manner that is not distracting. During the lesson, the coach should use the observational checklist and focus on the instructional process and procedures. Figure 2.4 provides a blank form for the coach's use. Figure 2.5 provides a model of a completed form for the coach's review. Share the completed checklist with the classroom teacher before the observation so that she can see the types of notes that will be part of the observed lesson.

The coach could create her own checklist or refer to one that is already created. Bean's (2004) checklist of domains for reading specialists could be adapted, or Walpole and McKenna's (2004) recording form for time increments might be used. As an additional resource, the coach may want to refer to Lyons's (2002) six components of analytical coaching. The components (preparing to coach, observing the lesson, reflecting after the observation, coaching for shifts in teaching, reflecting after coaching, coaching for self-analysis and reflection) may help the coach to create her own checklist.

Although the literacy coach will be making notes, the focus should be upon the agreed focus/agenda from the preobservation conference. Copies of the literacy coach's notes and/or a completed observation checklist should be left with the teacher immediately after the observation. If using a laptop, print out the notes and leave them in the teacher's mailbox the same day as the observation.

Make certain that positive information is provided in the observation feedback. The report to the teacher should provide suggestions for improving teaching and learning based on what is observed during the lesson. A follow-up conference should then be scheduled with the teacher. The teacher and the coach should determine whether another observation by the coach would be helpful. Subsequent observations may take place within a few days of the original observation or after a period of time has elapsed. The scheduling of a follow-up observation would be based on the level of need for instructional improvement. The teacher should also have the opportunity to see the literacy coach demonstrate techniques related to the instruction that was observed.

Figure 2.4   Literacy Coach's Note-Making Form for Observing Classroom
Lessons (Blank)

Teacher: _____   Date: _____

Time: (from _____ to _____)   Grade: _____

Instructional Focus: _____

Generalized Observation: _____ Focused Observation: _____

Notes	Comments	Suggested Actions

Key: T = Teacher   S = Student   Ss = Students

? = Abbreviated form of question being asked

Figure 2.5   Literacy Coach's Sample Note-Making Form for Observing
Classroom Lessons (Completed Sample)

Sample #1

Teacher: _____Greta Sterling_____   Date: __May 28__

Time: (From 9:15_____ to 10:15_____)   Grade: __5__

Instructional Focus: Reading (second day using this text)_____

Generalized Observation: _____x_____ Focused Observation: _Use of context clues_

Notes	Comments	Suggested Actions
9:15 Teacher opens lesson by asking Ss questions related to yesterday's reading ? remember about yesterday's reading S-1 gives some info ? else S-2 adds on ? Do you recall what we talked about after reading that section? (No S response) T: summarizes for Ss	Nice T-S rapport All oral responses	 Record summary phrases or key words from prior day's reading to display for Ss' review.
9:27 T: Read next chapter to find out what else happens. Ss read silently T—seated at desk	Good—silent reading!	
9:31 S goes to T's desk with book—asks question (inaudible)		
9:40 T asks if Ss need more time—allows more time		
9:45 T asks Ss ? What happened in Chapter 4 S-1 answers T: OK S-2 gives another answer T: restates S-2 response S-3 tells another event that happened S-4 attempts to add information but is confused on some of the terms used T restates S-4 response and clarifies the terms.	 T is doing restatement & clarification rather than Ss.	Have teacher consider having Ss work in small groups for discussion after reading the chapter; encourage them to help one another with problems with key terms or concepts. Have all students refer to text; have S-4 use context to determine and clarify confusion; allow other Ss to help him if necessary.
10:15 Further reading assignment given; observation ends.		

Key: T = Teacher   S = Student   Ss = Students

? = Abbreviated form of question being asked

(Continued)

Figure 2.5 (Continued)

Sample #2

Teacher: _____Ronald Barron_____   Date: ___January 10___

Time: (From 9:15_____ to 10:15_____)   Grade: ___6___

Instructional Focus: _____

Notes:	Comments:	Suggested Actions
9:15 Teacher opens lesson by asking Ss questions related to yesterday's reading ? What do you remember about the man S-1 responds ? else S-2 adds on ? Do you recall what we talked about after reading that section? (no student response; teacher summarizes that section for the class)	all oral responses	Record summary phrases or key words from prior day's reading to display for Ss' review.
9:27 T: Read next chapter to find out what else happens. Ss read silently. T—seated at his desk	Sets purpose. Good—silent reading	
9:41 S to T's desk w/book— asks question of teacher (inaudible); S returns to his seat.		
9:50 T asks if Ss need more time; allows more time.		
9:53 T asks ?: What happened in chapter 4? S-1 gives some information. T: OK S-2 gives some information. T: Restates S-2's response. S-3 adds a bit more information. T: Restates S-3's response. S-4 gives some information. T: Restates S-4's response and summarizes entire chapter for the class.		1. Change restatements to questions: Can you add on? Can you say it differently? Do you agree/disagree w/S? 2. Have Ss discuss in small groups.
10:08 T: Assigns homework: Write a summary statement for Ch. 4 and a prediction for what you expect to happen in Ch. 5. Tells Ss to write this assignment in notebook. Ss jot; pack up; chat informally until bell rings.		
10:15 Bell. Observation ends		

Key: T = Teacher   S = Student   Ss = Students

? = Abbreviated form of question being asked

Collective Observations

Collective observations can be used to determine patterns of strength or areas of instructional need within the school. The information that the coach has gathered from the collective observations is a source of planning for future professional development sessions. Once the coach has determined these plans, the plans should be shared with the principal. A schedule of professional development activities can be arranged. If areas of instructional need are mentioned to the principal, they should be discussed in generalities to maintain confidentiality between the coach and the teachers. For example, the literacy coach has noticed that several ninth-grade teachers need to provide more writing activities in their classrooms. The coach should tell the principal that writing is a general area of needed improvement rather than specifically mentioning teacher X, W, Y, or Z. This is important to maintain both confidentiality and the nonevaluative role of the literacy coach.

Teacher Observing the Coach

The opportunity for one teacher to observe another actually instructing a lesson is a rare occurrence in our field. Teachers often have opportunities to talk about instruction but not to view it. When a coach is demonstrating a lesson for a teacher, the teacher is able to observe another professional working with her students. This presents an opportunity for the teacher to view her students from a different perspective. She is the observer of the lesson in her own classroom, not the implementer.

The teacher's observation of the coach will be multifaceted, and she should be prepared to focus the observation on several items. The teacher should be encouraged to make notes during the observation session. The notes could then serve as a basis of discussion after the demonstration lesson, but they also could be used later as a guide for the teacher when she decides to implement a similar lesson herself. The checklist in Figure 2.6 could serve as a guide for the teacher to use during the demonstration lesson.

Whether statements or questions are posed, they should have positive connotations. For example, for each of the categories in the checklist in Figure 2.6, the observing teacher could respond to the following open statements:

- The students seem to . . .
- I noticed that the technique that you used to . . .
- The materials used in the demonstration helped to . . .

Figure 2.6 Checklist for Teacher Observation of the Coach's Demonstration Lesson

Focus	Focus Question	Yes or No	Teacher's Notes
Students	• Are the students active participants? • Does the observing teacher note that the students make typical responses or reactions? • Are student responses and reactions surprising to the teacher? • Are weaker readers/writers able to do the tasks within the lesson? • Is there enough time for student engagement in the tasks?		
Techniques	• Is the introduction to the lesson typical of what the teacher does? • Is there a nuance or change in the technique that the coach uses to introduce the lesson? • Is the purpose of the lesson clearly set? • Is time allotment the same as what the teacher provides to introduce the lesson? • Is the class taught as a whole for the entire lesson? • Does the demonstrating teacher address the individual needs of students? • Is the closing of the lesson appropriate? • Does it link to the introduction and the work that the students did throughout the lesson?		
Teaching materials/aids	• Were any ancillary materials used as part of the demonstration lesson? • Was technology integrated into the lesson? • Were visual aids (word walls, flowcharts) included?		
Other: _____			

The statements could also be used for further discussion during the conference, because they will help the coach describe the pedagogical rationale that was used during the lesson.

Planning Demonstration Lessons

Throughout this book, we mention the fact that demonstration lessons are a necessary tool in the literacy coach's kit. Thoughtful planning is the key to conducting a successful demonstration lesson. Erickson (1995) makes some suggestions on how to make the demonstration lesson a worthwhile activity:

- Demonstration lessons should focus on relatively narrow topics of concern. If the topic is too broad, there is danger of missing what is important.
- One demonstration lesson should cover only one or two points. If you need to cover more concerns, plan a series of lessons.
- First practice the demonstration with a skillful teacher and receive her feedback to refine and clarify the main points.
- Prepare the teacher observers prior to the lesson by supplying them with a packet of materials or a detailed lesson plan. Tell them what to focus on in the lesson.
- Be aware of your timing and move into the lesson quickly. Introductions should be short, and you should tell the teacher observers that there will be time for discussion and questions after the lesson.

The lesson should include a follow-up activity so that the teacher observers can discuss their reactions to the lesson, review the purposes of the demonstration lesson, and relate their perceptions of what they have witnessed.

When the demonstration lesson is completed, the coach and the teacher should schedule time to review it. The teacher can bring the observation checklist and notes to the conference for discussion. The teacher may also bring the packet or detailed lesson plan provided by the coach at the onset of the demonstration. Resource C offers a blank form that can be used as a template to help coaches provide a detailed written lesson plan to the teacher before the demonstration. In most cases, it is also helpful to submit a copy of the plan for the demonstration lesson to the principal or other supervisor. The lesson is part of the documentation of the work of the literacy coach.

Resource D is a sample of a completed plan for a demonstration lesson. In our experiences with demonstration lessons, we have found it helpful to present the written plan to the observing teacher before the demonstration begins. The observing teacher can write questions or comments directly on the plan as the literacy coach provides the demonstration lesson. After the lesson, the teacher and the coach can use the plan, as well as the observing teacher's written notes, to confer about the demonstration. Of course, everything cannot be written in plan, but the observing teacher can pose questions about what is written in the lesson plan as well as what happened. Areas that the teacher might probe with questions could include (1) the time given to allow a student to respond to a question, (2) the posting and reference to the skill chart, and (3) the use of grouping techniques for various activities throughout the lesson.

Once the coach is established in the school and the staff feel comfortable concerning the coach's helpful role, the coach should provide a demonstration lesson for more than one teacher at a time. For example, if literacy coach George Brindle has been in Greta Black's classroom several times and they have formed a good working relationship, George could ask Greta if he may invite other teachers to observe a demonstration lesson. If Greta is agreeable and the principal is able to provide substitute teachers, George can invite Greta's grade-level partners to the demonstration lesson in Greta's classroom. Afterwards, a small-group grade-level meeting with rich discussion is held. The teachers' shared experience has opened doors for more dialogue among the teachers themselves and for including George in further consultation.

Coaches Observing Coaches

Since the literacy coach's contributions are becoming widely recognized as a valuable part of professional development in the schools, coaches need to be prepared to share their knowledge base and wide experiences. They also need to learn from each other as an integral part of their own professional development. This could happen via a videotaped session, in an actual live situation, or behind an observation glass. The videotaped and live observation sessions could be scheduled for either demonstration teaching or conducting professional development sessions. The behind-the-glass situations could be for either demonstration teaching or pre/post-observations of teachers. When others are observing a teacher-coach conference behind the glass, both the teacher and the coach should have previously agreed to being viewed by a group of outsiders.

Coaches observing coaches should not be a rare occurrence but a frequent means of refining skills. Reading professional books and articles can certainly be beneficial to coaches, but firsthand observations are especially valuable because they allow the coach to ask questions, clarify points, and determine whether he will be able to implement or adapt what he has seen. Once a network is established, it gives coaches a forum for ongoing communication and discussion.

COACH AS COLLEAGUE

The topic of "coach as colleague" was first addressed in Chapter 1, where it was defined as collaboration with classroom teachers to achieve particular professional objectives (IRA, 2004). As mentioned many times throughout this text, the primary purpose of the coach-teacher collaboration is instructional improvement. All relationships are built on respect. It is important for the literacy coach to have the disposition to establish respect and trust within the school (Moxley & Taylor, 2006). When there is mutual respect between the coach and the teachers with whom she works, the coach will be accepted as a colleague. Whether the coach is a known colleague (someone who has been at the school for several years), a new colleague (someone who has not worked in the school before), or an itinerant colleague (someone working part of the week in one school and part of the week in another), she must collaborate with teachers to promote the work of good teaching and learning.

According to Radencich (1995), when a team of teachers gathers to learn new skills and polish old ones, coaches can lend support. Perhaps a literacy coach will have the opportunity (and the funding) to take several teachers to a regional conference. As the group travels to and from the event, attends sessions, and shares meals, the literacy coach is engaging in the role of "coach as colleague." Being together in a professional forum outside of the school allows for both informal and professional opportunities to "talk shop." In this situation, the literacy coach is among his peers and can observe and interact with the others as an equal participant.

A coach who is a colleague can provide professional companionship, give regular technical feedback, help determine appropriate use of a new skill, help to gauge student response to a new technique, and provide emotional support as teachers try new skills in front of students. (Alvermann, Moore, & Conley, 1987; Joyce & Showers, 1982). The general dimensions of leadership involve intellectual, emotional, social, and moral areas (Wepner & Quatroche, 2002). Each of these areas is pertinent to the leadership skills involved in being a literacy coach.

Dimensions of Leadership

The intellectual dimension of coaching involves not only the high foundational knowledge of literacy but also knowledge of various facets of the literacy coach's position. It requires one to be able to juggle responsibility within one's own work context. The emotional dimension requires the literacy coach to provide emotional support to teachers as they encounter change and as they need coaching in their practices. In addition, the literacy coach must look after her own emotional well-being as she works with various teachers throughout each day and over the school year. Having the ability to acknowledge inner conflict and express feelings convincingly is crucial (Wepner & Quatroche, 2002, p. 23).

The social dimension may be described as transacting with others in social and organizational relationships. The literacy coach is certain to find himself in both types of transactions. For the literacy coach to be an effective colleague, it is important that he deal with conflict rather than flee from it and be tolerant and respectful of others. Being a good listener is essential, since the literacy coach must acknowledge the ideas and issues shared by teachers and administrators. It is an especially important skill as the literacy coach supports teachers in trying new techniques and programs. With constant support, the literacy coach will observe strategies that work with particular teachers who struggle with instructional change or who have struggling readers who are experiencing difficulty (Moxley & Taylor, 2006).

The moral dimension involves a sense of conscience and accountability. It helps the literacy coach promote a desire to negotiate energetically for mutually satisfactory solutions to problems. One of the most significant aspects of the moral dimension of leadership for the literacy coach is maintaining confidentiality. When each of the four dimensions of leadership is in alignment, the coach is able to perform her role as a colleague well.

Collaboration With Other Groups

Although coaching in the classroom, conferencing with teachers, and doing presentations for the faculty are part of the routine responsibilities of the coach, the literacy coach may find himself working with his own professional staff and others from outside of the school. Some examples of this type of collaboration would be inviting speakers and experts, serving on district teachers' committees, and leading a Teachers As Readers group (TAR).

Inviting Outside Experts/Speakers

Part of the high foundational knowledge that the literacy coach possesses is knowing experts in the field of reading and writing. The coach may know these experts from reading the research and attending professional conferences at the state and national level. The coach may become aware that an expert is in the area through her professional organization and may wish to invite this person to her school or district. Invitations should be extended to those teachers that would benefit from hearing the professional address a need or practice that is lacking within their schools. Although the literacy coach working in a particular building may be responsible for contacting and securing the speaker, the coach may want to invite teachers from throughout the school district or from within the immediate region to attend the presentation.

The coach should be in contact with the expert or invited speaker by e-mail, telephone, or letter. If a publisher sponsors the speaker, the direct contact may have to be made with the publisher. When the speaker has agreed to do a presentation at the coach's school, both the logistical and pedagogical aspects of the visit should be discussed. The logistical topics should include the following:

- Arrival and departure times
- Transportation and directions
- Facilities (place, room arrangement)
- Number of teachers in attendance
- Classroom visits (Will these be part of the day's agenda?)
- Technology or any other audiovisual needs
- Length of the presentation (all day, half day, split sessions, etc.)
- Videotaping of presentation (Is it allowed? Who will do it?)
- Fees and expenses

The pedagogical topics should include the following:

- Specific topic to be presented
- Background information on the school's (or district's) endeavors related to the speaker's topic
- Resource materials (Is the expert familiar with materials used in the schools? Would the expert like the coach to send her materials or vice versa?)
- Handouts (Can handouts be faxed or e-mailed to the coach ahead of time for copying?)
- Administrative policies related to the topic (inform the speaker concerning administrative support or issues)

The goal of inviting a speaker to a school is to motivate teachers as well as provide salient information that will support the schoolwide collaborative work the coach and the teachers do together. The support may be geared toward work already begun or work that is about to begin.

Serving on Committees

The literacy coach may be asked to serve on committees as well as lead committees. For example, the school's librarian might convene a schoolwide committee to create a summer reading program. Not only is the coach's expertise in literacy and knowledge of books needed, but also his knowledge of the school and the community should make him a significant contributor to the committee. However, his role is one of a peer and colleague to be valued equally with the other committee members.

The summer reading program committee also includes reading teachers, classroom teachers, parents, and school board members. The librarian asked these people to serve on the committee because of her respect for their knowledge, work ethic, and ability to collaborate. In this instance, the literacy coach will not serve as a committee leader. However, his service as a responsible member and contributor to the committee will earn this coach recognition as a valued colleague in a role other than that of being a direct coach of teachers.

The superintendent or the chief academic officer often forms districtwide committees. Districtwide committees are formed because the work of the committee is relevant across the district but is too extensive for one school to undertake. Some examples of this type of meeting are those that involve curriculum renewal, textbook adoption and selection, technology integration, or report card revision. The literacy coach's expertise would be valuable in any or all of these committees, and her service would be a contribution. She is not leading the committee, but she is a colleague in equal standing with the other members of the committee. If the coach is the only representative from her school on a districtwide committee, she should be able (and is often required) to provide summaries or updates of the work of the committee to the principal and teachers of her school.

Teachers as Readers

The literacy coach may be able to organize a book club for teachers in their building. Book clubs for teachers are phenomenon that is steadily increasing in popularity (Daniels, 2003). School districts are supplying the funding for the books, meeting places, and even professional development credit for the sessions, because they realize that book clubs are invaluable tool for enhancing school faculty camaraderie as well as a way of promoting personal growth (Strong & Lander, 2005). According to Goldberg and Pesko (2000), one reason for this growth is that when teachers meet to discuss nonprofessional literature, they renew their own love of reading while enhancing their understanding of students' needs.

Starting a TAR Group. For a teachers' book club to be successful, teachers must be free to choose books that appeal to them. Smith (1994) recommends some TAR program ingredients that will make your program more manageable, such as holding at least six meetings per year with a structure, studying common themes, and including a variety of interests at all grade levels. Research about the author/illustrator under discussion should be presented when reviewing a particular book at the meeting. Smith also suggests that an administrator should be invited to be part of the group.

According to Carmichael (2001) and Goldberg and Pesko (2000), the steps that should be included in the process of starting a group are as follows:

- Choose a group leader.
- Mail a flier to local teachers.
- Ask the school district to provide the meeting place and the books (from professional development funding, grants, etc.).
- At the first meeting, the teachers should complete a survey about their personal reading and what types of books they may want to use in the classroom.
- Based on the survey, the teachers should reach a consensus about the genres that they are going to read in the TAR groups and the particular books that they will read for the first few meetings.
- The teachers should try to choose the top six choices (one for each meeting).
- Teachers should have the flexibility to change genres after the initial meetings.

At the first TAR group meeting, people may read historical and contemporary fiction. But as Goldberg and Pesko (2000) explain, the groups usually expand to reading other genres, including nonfiction.

A further point to consider when ordering books for your TAR group is whether or not paperbacks are the best to use. Paperbacks are convenient and inexpensive (Carmichael, 2001). However, if you want to write for grant money to purchase books, you may need to place the books in the school library after they have been read. In this case, you should purchase hardback books or library-bound books. Daly (1994) suggests that if you have small groups, you can meet in people's homes. Danielson and Rogers (2000) also recommend meeting in libraries or even local bookstores.

COACH AS LEARNER

Literacy coaching is not an easy task. The coach is responsible for helping teachers learn to refine their instructional skills with the expected outcome of instructional improvement in each classroom throughout the school. However, in addition to helping teachers learn, the coach is a learner herself. She is learning about the role of coaching, and she is learning about the evolving literacy development of both students and teachers within the school. Learning involves growth and change and requires individuals to redefine both their roles and their identities (Vogt & Shearer, 2004, p. 265).

Modeling and observing are discussed throughout the first three chapters. Both are important techniques for learning to improve skills. Both techniques can be beneficial to the coach as a learner as well. When the coach has the opportunity to view good modeling as part of his formal or informal training as a literacy coach and to observe other coaches at their craft, he is adding to his own professional development. Two main areas in which the coach should continue to develop as a learner are self-learning and learning about the school. Self-learning requires self-discipline and motivation. Learning is an active process; it requires a desire to improve in one's area of expertise. Learning about the school is a job-related task that helps the literacy coach stay informed about the instructional progress of literacy as well as any needs. The coach may need to individualize plans for both areas of learning. It is important that both areas are priorities to the coach and that ongoing self-assessment and schoolwide literacy assessment occur as part of her role. She is a learner with much to learn about. The two priority areas of the coach as learner, self-learning and learning about the school, are discussed in the following sections.

Self-Learning

Moxley and Taylor (2006) state that few literacy coaches arrive at the position with all of the skills and knowledge that they need to be effective coaches. Learning to be a literacy coach evolves from the first day of the assignment and continues throughout the journey. Those who advocate literacy learning need to be readers and writers themselves.

Professional journals and personal journals provide valuable resources and insights into one's learning as a literacy coach. Reading professional literacy journals to keep current is a wonderful way to renew oneself. A variety of professional journals can give information about new children's books, materials and texts, and Web sites. Whether perusing bound journals or online journals, extensive professional reading can lead to the marriage of theory and practice. When reading professional journals, the literacy coach should ask, "How does the information presented in the articles relate to what I believe and what I teach?" and "Can the information help me to help my teachers improve their instructional practices?"

As a result of his professional reading, the literacy coach may find articles that can be shared with staff (or the principal) at meetings or in study groups. If an article is lengthy, the literacy coach could highlight or underline key paragraphs or sections for the teachers. Articles can be kept in a binder as a professional reference for teachers and placed in an area those teachers frequent. This is especially helpful when implementing a new technique schoolwide, such as guided reading, reciprocal teaching, or integrating technology with language arts. Making the articles readily available as a reference when a change is initiated can help support the literacy coach's efforts.

Another type of journal, a personal journal, assists the process of reflection for the self-learner. Entries are made in the journal after reading articles, observing in classrooms, attending professional conferences, and examining data. Journal entries may promote ideas for action research within the school. They may provide ideas so that the coach can assist the teacher in making visual aids (bookmarks, posters, study guides, rubrics, graphic organizers) to support learning.

Reading professional journals and writing in one's own journal are activities that are usually done in isolation. The literacy coach can also learn as a member of a group by joining professional organizations at the local, state, and national levels. These organizations typically provide quality presentations and conferences. They are also a wonderful venue for networking with other literacy coaches and reading professionals.

University courses and seminars are ways to renew one's skills and learn cutting-edge ideas. University courses provide theory-to-practice connections and are a strong basis for action research in schools. As more and more states initiate certification for literacy coaching, it will be imperative for coaches to take advantage of course offerings.

Finally, videotaping has been widely used as tool for self-observation by teachers. Coaches should also take advantage of this medium to reflect upon their own practices. Demonstration lessons, inservice presentations, teacher conferences, parent workshops, and any other types of meetings can be videotaped. While watching the video, the coach should make notes about strengths and weakness of her presentation skills.

Self-learning is focused on reflection of practice. Walker (1995) states that adult learners must be able to draw upon their experiences, knowledge, and values if learning is to have meaning for them and if they are to experience constructivist learning as a basis for constructivist leading (p. 171). As the time-honored adage says, "Those who dare to teach should never cease to learn."

Learning About the School

In addition to self-learning of the role, the literacy coach must be a continuous learner about the school in which he works. The chief means of learning about the school is the collection of data. Walpole & McKenna (2004) address the critical notion of data as part of a professional support system. They emphasize the idea that literacy coaches build knowledge when assisting teachers to understand the data that have been collected in the building from testing children.

> In our experience, literacy coaches are expert in collecting data, and expert at interpreting data for an individual child, but reticent about looking for larger trends within or across grade levels. However, this type of knowledge-building session has been particularly powerful in the work of many literacy coaches. (p. 196)

In addition to learning about the school from test data, the literacy coach can learn a great deal from two additional data sources: data from classroom observations and data from self-learning. The key word here is *data.* Collecting facts and evidence from these three sources will provide volumes of information for the literacy coach to know the school well enough to determine strengths and create action plans for improving areas of weakness. Each of these three data areas will be discussed in the following section.

Testing in American schools emanates from several sources: the classroom, the state, and the national government. Classroom assessments include both teacher-made tests and tests produced by companies that publish reading and writing programs. Most states require standardized assessments at selected grade levels in reading, writing, and content areas as well. Some schools volunteer to participate in national assessments such as the National Assessment of Educational Progress. The public outcry for accountability of schools aims spotlights at schools that are high-achieving and those that are low-achieving. Stronge (2002) states that pressure is placed on schools to prepare students to be successful on tests by aligning instruction with state standards. Graduation requirements are often linked to required state assessments.

Literacy coaches are often responsible for collecting and reviewing the school assessment data. Analyzing and interpreting schoolwide test data is a complex task. In addition to creating a clear picture of the overall strengths and weakness of the school's language arts program, the literacy coach must be able to report the findings of her analysis to a variety of constituents and design a course of action to improve any areas of significant weakness. Looking at test data through a schoolwide lens helps the literacy coach learn about the school. Specific areas may need to be addressed across the school. For example, if writing in response to a prompt is a generalized weakness, the literacy coach knows that this aspect of writing instruction needs to be refined, and her coaching responsibilities should include a renewed look at writing instruction.

Needs at certain grade levels may also become evident to the literacy coach when analyzing schoolwide test data. For example, if all kindergarten and first-grade children score in the bottom quartile on the phonemic segmentation portion of a state test, the literacy coach should work with teachers of those grades to improve that skill in young learners.

Analyzing test data on a schoolwide basis does not necessarily reveal just weaknesses. Literacy coaches may also determine areas of strengths across the school or grade levels. When this information is shared, teachers and students should be praised and complimented for their efforts and encouraged to sustain them.

Comparing test data from one year to the next can reveal some information about instructional programs in the school, but literacy coaches should be careful not to make faulty assumptions. Since teaching and learning are dynamic processes and student populations change, making generalizations about teaching strengths and shortcomings, core materials, and time allotments for language arts teaching may be erroneous. Cross-referencing the test data with other data sources should help the literacy coach clarify such assumptions.

As the literacy coach works in classrooms throughout the school, he should ask teachers who create their own tests to share copies with him. Since we know that all statewide tests are not created equal, the same holds true for teacher-made tests. Tests that require students to use high-level thinking may be shared at grade-level and/or schoolwide meetings. Samples of well-created tests can serve as models for the staff. In addition, tests created by publishers of reading and writing programs can serve two goals: professional development endeavors for the staff and means for the literacy coach to learn about the school. A professional development meeting in which teachers examine a unit or theme test from a publisher can help them determine the strengths and weaknesses of certain items or even entire tests with the guidance of the literacy coach. The literacy coach can learn about the school when examining publishers' tests over time to determine whether certain scores occur because of excellent teaching (or poor teaching) or strong construction of test items (or weak construction of test items). The accuracy of the literacy coach's analysis of such tests will help him know whether schoolwide improvement needs to occur or whether tests need to be replaced or discarded.

A second source of data that will help the literacy coach learn about the school is the data collected from her own observations in classrooms. The notes made and checklists used during observations are resources that can be used in compiling information. In addition, her observations of the literacy materials used (and not used) in classrooms, the quality of student work posted on bulletin boards, and the availability of visual references in classrooms for students' use provide insights about strengths and needs within the school. Comparing and contrasting the data garnered from observations with test data can assist the literacy coach in making informed decisions.

The third type of data that helps the literacy coach learn about the school is the data included in his self-learning: journal entries from his own reflections on observations and readings and notes from university classes, conferences, and meetings. These data can aid the literacy coach in assessing the school's strengths and needs based on knowledge of what actually happens instructionally in the school and expert pronouncements—the tried-and-true research-based documentation of best practices in literacy education. Careful review of this information before initiating any change, small or significant, is recommended.

The literacy coach learns about the school when she carefully considers the three data sources: tests, observations, and self-learning. None of the areas should be used in isolation to make sweeping changes within the school. Instead, the three areas should be triangulated so that the literacy coach can help her school move forward in a positive direction through her leadership role. Self-learning and reflective practice are crucial aspects of the "coach as learner." McAndrew (2006), generalizing about literacy leaders, accurately describes the "coach as learner" when he states that a literacy leader "constantly collects information, reflects and evaluates, and tries new ideas based on what he or she has learned" (p. 128).

AN EXPERT'S THOUGHTS: DR. JACK CASSIDY

Dr. Jack Cassidy, Texas A&M University, is known nationally and internationally for his expertise in literacy teaching and learning. He served on the International Reading Association's task force "Role of the Reading Specialists," chaired by Dr. Rita Bean. He is known for writing about hot topics in literacy education. Here are Dr. Cassidy's thoughts about the current status of literacy coaching in America:

> Each year, I interview 25 literacy leaders from around the world on hot topics. The results are published in *Reading Today's* December/January issue ("IRA/NCTE," 2005). For this year's article, 23 respondents from throughout the United States identified "literacy coaches/reading coaches" as a hot topic.

At this time in our country, literacy coaching is becoming the first concentrated effort to use the reading specialist for the professional development of classroom teachers. Literacy coaching has the potential to be one of the most positive developments in the reading field. However, it is unfortunate that some areas of the country are misusing the role of the literacy coach (e.g., hiring unqualified coaches, spreading the literacy coaches over more than one school, failing to document student achievement). Unless changes are made *soon,* literacy coaching may go the way of whole language, Reading Recovery, and many other excellent practices that once were very "hot."

Source: Dr. Jack Cassidy, Texas A & M University.

SUMMARY

This chapter began with a scenario about a middle school literacy coach facing a major responsibility for a schoolwide professional development endeavor. The scenario sets the stage for the multiple leadership aspects of the role of the literacy coach detailed in the chapter: facilitator, observer, colleague, and learner. Several checklists are provided throughout the chapter to aid the literacy coach in using or adapting forms to facilitate note making during observations. Three points of discussion are provided below for reflecting on the multiple roles of the literacy specialist.

TOPIC EXTENSIONS FOR CLASS SESSIONS OR STUDY GROUPS

1. Review the two plans that Harry prepared in the opening scenario for this chapter. What type of a plan would you create if you were facilitating a long-term professional development opportunity for a large group of teachers? Like Harry, create both a Plan A and Plan. Be prepared to share your plans.

2. Put yourself in the place of a literacy coach facilitating the first of a series of staff development meetings dedicated to a focus topic. Consider what you might do when participants begin a discussion that is truly a "commitment of collaboration" about the topic. In addition, consider what you might do when participants begin a discussion that is a campaign of negativity about the school and that circumvents the focus topic.

3. Develop a checklist to be used during and after a classroom observation. Think about the components you feel are important for inclusion.

RESOURCE C: FORM FOR THE LITERACY COACH'S DEMONSTRATION LESSON (BLANK)

Demonstration Lesson for _____ Grade: _____
                        (Classroom Teacher's Name)

Lesson Demonstrated by _____ Date: _____
                        (Literacy Coach's Name)

Purpose of Lesson:

Text:

Story:

Skill:

Strategy:

Lesson Introduction (Before Reading or Writing)

Active Student Engagement (During Reading or Writing)

Lesson Close and/or Assessment (After Reading or Writing)

RESOURCE D: SAMPLE FORM FOR THE LITERACY COACH'S DEMONSTRATION LESSON (COMPLETED)

Demonstration Lesson for <u>Ms. Elizabeth Williamson</u> Grade: <u>_5_</u>
    (Classroom Teacher's Name)

Lesson Demonstrated by: <u>Mrs. Carrie McDermott</u> Date: <u>April 10 & 11</u>
    (Literacy Coach's Name)

Purpose of Lesson: To demonstrate modeling and guiding of skill and strategy instruction

Text: *Coast to Coast* (5-1 text from "Signatures" series of Harcourt, 2004)

Story: *Yang the Youngest and His Terrible Ear*

Skill: Identifying character traits

Strategy: Drawing conclusions

Lesson Introduction (Before Reading or Writing)

1. Begin with a discussion about *talent.* Ask students to define or give examples of someone who has a particular talent. Then ask the following questions for discussion:

   What if we all had the exact same talents?

   What if no one in the world ever had musical talent?

   Tell about the concert in Philadelphia last month (cellist and pianist). Then ask the students to discuss what talents they think the performers had and what skills they needed to make the most of their talents. Guide this discussion by doing a T-chart on the chalkboard:

Talent	Skills
Playing the cello	(Possible responses): Concentration Practice a lot Motor skills (to move bow, hold cello) Patience
Playing the piano	(list Ss' responses)
(Generate some others, such as artist/painter)	(list Ss' responses)

Tell the students that they will read about a very talented family and how important it is for the family members to express themselves through this talent. Tell students that focusing on the characters in the story is very important (as in many stories); they need to be able to identify the characters' traits.

2. Post chart: Character traits describe how a character thinks, feels, and acts.

   Guide students as they recall something recently read and describe a character's traits. (Note: It is a good idea to keep an ongoing posted list of traits, as students can use these terms in their oral and written responses to literature.)

3. Introduce strategy: Drawing conclusions

   Define the strategy: *Drawing conclusions* means using evidence from a story and your knowledge of character traits to make a sensible statement about why or how something happened:
   a. Model: Tell briefly about seeing a moving van at a house on my street that has been empty for a while. Shortly after, a family arrives in a car. My conclusion is that a new family is moving into the empty house on my street.
   b. Guide: Divide students into pairs. Give each pair a scenario card and have them draw a conclusion (see attached).

4. Introduce vocabulary: In context on an overhead (see attached)

5. Set purpose for reading: Read pages 371–375 silently to find out about the main character's traits and to draw a conclusion about why/how something is happening in the story.

Active Student Engagement (During Reading or Writing)

1. Students will read silently to meet the purpose set. Facilitate a discussion after the first reading chunk to address a character's traits and possible conclusions.

2. Continue to chunk story (pages 376–379) to meet same purpose. Facilitate discussion after each chunk.

Lesson Close and/or Assessment (After Reading or Writing)

1. After the entire story has been read, complete discussion of the final portion of the story by facilitating a discussion about the main character's traits and the story's conclusions. Talk about how the main character's traits changed or remained the same throughout the story.

2. Have students form same pairs as in "before reading" take turns re-reading the entire story.

3. Have two pairs of students join together. Using the cards for the drawing conclusion activity in "before reading," have the students choose one of the two cards for which they can (1) conduct a brief skit and (2) have the other students determine which character's traits they are emphasizing in the skit. Keep a running list of the traits as each small group performs. Remind students that character traits will influence the interpretation of each work of fiction that they read.

4. Optional activity: After all of the skits have been performed and traits listed, have the class select one skit and write about it. Writing should take place independently. The goal of the writing task is to reveal a character's thoughts, feelings, or actions through clear writing. This activity could be used as an assessment.

Assistance and Resources for New and Experienced Literacy Coaches

3

INTRODUCTION

Chapter 3 explains some of the assistance and resources available to literacy coaches, including technology and human resources. An important feature of this chapter is the specific information given about first-year coaching possibilities. A suggested time line is offered for implementing key components of coaching during the first year in the position. The benefit of study groups for both new and seasoned coaches is also presented in this chapter.

Specific information about technological resources is offered, since the use of technology has brought about changes within literacy teaching and coaching. Whether the coach is experienced or a beginner, having information about where and how to access resources and assistance readily available is important.

SCENARIO

Marguerite Floyd tossed and turned throughout the night because she is both happy and nervous about a new teaching assignment at the start of the school year. Today she will begin working as a literacy coach at Winthrop School, a K–8 school. Marguerite previously worked in another school in the district. The district administration recently decided to place literacy coaches in each of their K–8 buildings and at the high school. After she successfully interviewed for a coaching position, Marguerite had anticipated staying at Carney School, the K–8 school in which she had taught for the past 11 years. Although she'll miss her friends and her students, she is looking forward to a change and the challenges of doing something completely new.

During the summer, Marguerite went to Winthrop to meet with the principal, introduce herself to the office staff, and organize her office. She had the opportunity to meet some of the teachers and felt comfortable with the greetings and good wishes she received from them. She wanted to receive some input from the principal on the strengths and concerns he perceived about instruction. The principal met briefly with Marguerite on only one occasion, although she had been to the school several times over several weeks and had asked to meet with him on each visit. The principal told her that summer was his time to catch up on paperwork and he would rather wait until school started to begin meeting with her. She felt awkward and nervous about interacting with the principal. Marguerite wondered why he was so distant with her. She also questioned why he couldn't spare an hour or two all summer for a professional discussion with the new literacy coach.

However, because the school district had both a core curriculum guide and core materials, Marguerite felt comfortable with the curriculum. She had taught second and sixth grades at Carney before serving as a K–8 reading specialist for her last four years there. She was familiar with the state and district standardized tests and knew the district's report card system.

During Marguerite's restless night before the first day of school, these were her questions: What would go well? What could she expect to accomplish in the first few months, in the first year? How would her relationships with others impact the quality of her work? Would she have the full support of the principal? Would the faculty be as cooperative and cohesive as the one she just left? Had she been foolish for wanting a career change while things were going so well? Would she feel as connected to the students and parents here as she did in the former school? Why was she so excited about this new position, yet so nervous?

Marguerite's range of emotions and ambivalence at the onset of her coaching career are common for many beginning literacy coaches across the nation. It is difficult to know what to expect, even in a field for which you are thoroughly trained and prepared, when multiple influences impinge on daily situations.

A GLIMPSE OF FIRST-YEAR COACHING

Entering any new position usually prompts both anticipation and trepidation. Those who take on positions as literacy coaches have similar emotional responses when assuming the tasks and responsibilities of being such an important informal leader. The literacy coach who is new to the role can expect that the demands of the role at the end of the school year will be quite different from those at the beginning of the year. Thus, the start-up techniques used by a new coach and the expectations of the role at the beginning of the second year are likely to be much different from those for the initial year.

The new coach should expect a variety of reactions from staff concerning the coaching position. Teachers may also experience anticipation and trepidation when a new colleague in a brand-new role enters the scene. Some teachers will embrace the coach while other teachers will attempt to avoid him or her. The dynamics of staff interaction are complex and vary from school to school. Inherent in the coaching role is building cohesive relationships between the coach and the individual teacher, between the coach and the entire staff, and among the entire staff. The coach is not expected to work miracles and bring social rivals together or engage in psychological analysis for the betterment of all. The coach's role in fostering a cohesive staff is to create what Kise (2006) calls "instructional collaboration." According to this model, the coach leads, participates, and observes the team of teachers who collaborate as resources, learning partners, and mentors for one another.

Well-prepared, confident coaches are able to meet many of the challenges that cross their paths as they begin coaching and as they continue their work through the years. Their coaching experiences help them hone essential skills. One of the biggest adjustments the new coach faces is working with adult learners, rather than children, full-time.

The following sections provide an overview of a typical year in the life of a first-year coach and the types of encounters the coach might have with school staff.

Change Over Time

The new coach needs to have strong foundational knowledge of literacy and strong skills for dealing with people. These strengths should have been obvious to those who interviewed the coach and offered her the position. However, the new coach usually has much to learn through on-the-job training. She will have to learn about the culture of the school, the principal's leadership style, the impact of parent involvement, and the dynamics of staff interactions. This can be done only through acquiring information as the synergism of the coaching role becomes evident through daily experience over time.

School Culture

School culture refers to the way teachers and other staff members work together (McBrien & Brandt, 1997). The new coach is wise to recognize what impacts the culture of the school; that is, what issues unify or fragment those who teach there. According to Vogt and Shearer (2004), organizational culture, such as school culture, "is constantly emerging." In time, those in leadership positions within the organization, including coaches, will be able to define the behaviors that support the culture of the organization.

The coach can observe the interactions of colleagues within the school during professional development meetings and collaborative work sessions. The new coach can gain information about the school culture by observing the interactions of the teachers during professional development meetings and collaborative work sessions. The professionalism exhibited by teachers as they interact with each other and as they respond to presenters reveals a significant cultural aspect of the school. As Robbins and Alvy (1995) point out, the culture of a school reflects what its members care about, talk about, and spend time doing.

When coaches perform as collaborators, facilitators, and colleagues, they can influence teachers to join together for focused discussions. They can help teachers find common ground for in-depth discussions about important instructional issues that affect the entire school. Taylor and Gunter (2006) assert that getting the faculty to agree on expectations for everyone's classroom is challenging. However, when a coach has a keen sense of school culture and an accurate picture of which literacy practices are effective and which aren't, he or she is capable of convening a group of teachers for a series of meetings to discuss literacy practices. According to Fullan (2001), educators "thirst for more" sharing when positive, collaborative structures are put in place. The challenge of agreeing on instructional expectations is easier when teachers share and learn as a collaborative group. Literacy coaching can and should become embedded in the culture of the school. It is the positive force that provides collaborative elements to define the culture of the school.

Principal's Leadership Style

Principals wear many hats as they both lead and manage their schools. In the daily realities of school life, management tasks require much of the principal's time and attention (Portin, 2004; Smith & Andrews, 1987). The National Association of Elementary School Principals (NAESP, 2001), published standards for what principals should know and do to place student and staff learning at the center of their leadership. Principals who are leaders move their schools forward as a cohesive team of educators with a shared vision and shared goals. To achieve "coherence making" (Fullan, 2001), principals need to focus on student learning and external ideas that may further the thinking and vision of the school. It is essential, then, for all principals to be aware of the literacy goals for their particular schools.

Jay and McGovern (2006) state that

> principals are expected to be knowledgeable and evaluative of all instructional trends and practices in general as well as what is specifically happening in each classroom in the building. The principal's ability to distinguish between strong and weak practices is critical; quality instruction must be recognized and promoted in order to promote literacy learning. (p. 22)

Like literacy coaches, principals should have their eye on the target: improved teaching and learning of literacy skills.

According to Booth and Roswell (2002), it is important for the principal to encourage individuals in leadership positions within the school. The literacy coach, an informal leader in a school, has an explicit role in improving instruction at the school level. Ideally, the building's principal has a keen awareness of the demands of the work of the literacy coach and a strong appreciation of the craft necessary to help bring about change in classroom instruction. The leadership of these two professionals is two sides of the same coin: a unified plan that promotes sound literacy instruction in each and every classroom within the school. Principals can positively affect the culture of the school if they and the literacy coaches (1) engage in frequent, focused discussion about the goals and needs of the language arts program and (2) develop a viable plan for implementing change over time.

But what if the principal is not aware of the importance of the role of the literacy coach? If a disparity exists in the manner in which the principal and coach view the coaching process, and if the principal is unsupportive of the ongoing professional development necessary to implement positive change, little or no change is likely to result. The principal's support is crucial to the success of a coaching model within a school. Teachers who understand that the principal and coach are united in leading the school through systemic change will realize that coherence making is a long-term goal rather than this year's trend. The collaborative, the resistant, and the weak will be unable to form separate factions. The "we" mentality starts with the principal and includes all staff.

Parent Involvement

Literacy learning begins in the home. When parents remain active in the literacy learning of their children throughout their school years, children tend to view literacy as an essential part of life and not merely a school-related task (Pressley, 2002). Literacy is a lifelong endeavor. Today's American families are busy with activities that often result in hectic schedules. Having the time to participate in school meetings or volunteer in classrooms is just one more thing that parents juggle to fit into crowded schedules, *if* they consider their involvement in the school a priority.

Historically, reading specialists have done a wonderful job getting parents to attend school events about their children's reading programs. Literacy coaches can collaborate with reading specialists in fostering parent involvement through workshops, visitations, and demonstrations. Being comfortable interacting with professional staff helps parents feel welcome in the school environment. When parents have a clear understanding of what is being taught in their children's schools and the roles various professionals play in literacy instruction, they are likely to participate actively in programs provided by the teaching staff and to volunteer for committees related to curriculum matters.

Literacy coaches can be a tremendous source of parent information by regularly contributing to newsletters, posting information on the school's Web site, and speaking with parents informally and at scheduled presentations. Keeping parents informed of instructional practices, assessment results, and the rationale for or against programmatic change promotes parents' trust and confidence in the teaching staff. When parents are assured that both their awareness of instructional programming and their participation in the events mentioned here are valued, they are more likely to be involved in their children's schools. Parents should always be considered important partners in the literacy process.

Staff Interactions

Human dynamics are a fascinating phenomenon. The interactions observed among a school staff are similar to those of any workplace where people have a need to interact and collaborate. It seems likely that regardless of the working context, people have their own opinions about how things should be done. Some workers will band together when their ideas are similar, and others will remain isolated when their thoughts are different from the norm.

In addition to being an attentive, analytical observer of teaching practices, the literacy coach needs to be acutely aware of staff interactions that impact the assumptions and realities of literacy instruction in the school. As stated earlier in this text, these interactions may be observed in informal situations as well as during professional development venues facilitated by the coach.

Positive interactions thrive in a respectful environment. People do not have to be in total agreement about everything. But the school environment should be one in which respectful discussion of different opinions, and listening to them, can take place. The coach should interact professionally and respectfully with staff members, individually and collectively, at all times. Teachers will form a trusting, collaborative relationship with the literacy coach who treats them as valued colleagues.

Lambert (1998) found that teachers who comprise a "professional community" do so because of the habits and conditions that promote joint responsibility for instructional outcomes. Literacy coaches serve as model participants of a professional community as they lead the teaching staff in assuming joint responsibility. The energy to move forward with continuous schoolwide improvement is easily channeled when positive interactions among staff are the norm.

On the other hand, negative interactions among staff proliferate in a disharmonic environment. Past events may have fractionalized the staff in some way. An undercurrent of negative interactions among the school's staff makes it difficult to work as a coherent group. The negativity may be directed from teacher to teacher, teacher to principal, or teacher to new staff member, such as a coach. Negative interactions can greatly inhibit productivity.

The coach may be aware of negative interactions but may have no power to stifle subliminal or blatant negativity displayed by teachers. According to Lambert (1998), maximizing interactions that allow for relationship building can be accomplished through shared work and shared responsibilities. Glickman (2002) found that the culture of most schools reflects an "unspoken expectation that teachers will be instructionally private and isolated from each other" (p. 35). If this is normative school culture, bringing together comfortable isolates to interact about their teaching can evoke negativity. Glickman advocates infusing staff interactions with deep, wise, and practical talk about teaching and learning.

The coach needs to get to know each staff member as an individual. Those individuals who begin to build a working relationship with the coach can also build collaborative relationships with their colleagues in time. The skillful facilitation of the literacy coach in structuring group work and group membership is essential to dispelling any negativity that exists among the staff. When coaches are able to influence teachers to work with them individually and eventually begin working with each other, a professional community of learners evolves. The school culture can be transformed from disharmony to collaboration.

Sample First-Year Time Line

Walking into a school in a new role is an onerous experience, whether one is a classroom teacher, special area teacher, or principal. Questions usually arise as one begins a new position. Some of the questions that educators pose as they begin new roles include the following:

- How will other faculty perceive my work?
- How will the faculty perceive my interpersonal skills?
- What expectations will administrators have for me in this role?
- What might evolve from this position that isn't evident right at the moment?
- How will I relate to the student population?
- What contact will I have with parents?
- How will the parents react to me in this role?
- What changes will others expect of me?
- What will I expect of myself in this new role?
- How will I learn about the school's current curriculum and assessments?

The literacy coach is bound to pose the above questions to herself, or others may pose them to her. Responding to the questions above will help prepare the coach for the shift of circumstances that accompanies the new role. To plan for a new year in a new role, the coach will find it helpful to think broadly about the expectations and responsibilities that may evolve.

The time line in Figure 3.1 is offered to assist the coach in previewing the breadth of the first year's duties. The depth of situations will surely be specific to each coach's experiences and each school's needs. The time line is meant to enable the new literacy coach to be a visible, viable, and valued member of the school's professional staff.

Figure 3.1   Time Line for First-Year Literacy Coach

1st Three Months: Acquaintances	2nd Three Months: Adaptations	3rd Three Months: Adaptations and Assessments	4th Three Months: Assessments and Priorities
• Face-to-face introductions with each member of the staff. • Publication of first newsletter. • Organize work space and material resources. • Participate in initial meeting with principal about curriculum materials. • Establish a schedule with the principal for meeting regularly. • Meet with other administrators. • Arrange to meet with other administrators regularly. • Begin observations in assigned classrooms during language arts instruction. • Observe and confer with reading specialists in the building. • Begin to establish routine meetings regarding literacy instruction. • Make brief presentations at regularly scheduled faculty meetings. • Plan and implement professional development sessions. • Establish time for self-reflection and note making. • Attend schoolwide parent meetings.	• Continue regular publication of newsletter. • Meet with school principal regularly. • Continue to meet with other administrators and literacy coaches. • Increase the frequency of observations and conferences. • Continue to conduct meetings that assist groups of teachers. • Change faculty meeting presentations to focus on professional development. • Continue to plan and implement professional development sessions for which you are responsible. • Continue to participate in regular self-reflection and note making. • Initiate a survey of staff. • Continue to attend parent meetings.	• Continue working in each area mentioned in the "2nd Three Months." • Review and reflect on survey information. • Ensure a consistent strand of focus in professional development. • Administer and monitor schoolwide assessments.	• Continue working in each area mentioned in "2nd Three Months" and "3rd Three Months." • Analyze current assessment data. • Set literacy-oriented priorities based on assessments and year's literacy issues.

First Three Months: Acquaintances

In the first three months of the year, the coach becomes acquainted with personnel and establishes routines. At the beginning, coaches should schedule appointments to meet at length with each of the constituents. They should pace meetings or observations so that neither coach nor others involved feel rushed or unimportant. Because the beginning of the school year is when teachers and students become familiar with one another and with the curriculum, the coach may have the luxury of controlling the pacing of appointments now more than at any other time.

The teachers will become familiar with their students' responses to curriculum and instruction. Therefore, coaches should recognize that the daily and weekly events of their lives will not be as evenly paced during the remainder of the school year. The initial routines created will remain, but others will be added. The majority of the school year is a time of adapting to school situations and routines for the literacy coach.

Coaches who are new to the school as well as being new to the position should introduce themselves to each member of the school's staff from the principal to the janitor. Personal introductions are important so names and faces can be connected. The introductions should also give the message that the coach is happy to be in the new setting and is looking forward to knowing and working with each person there.

Keeping the lines of communication open is important in all relationships. One suggestion for making sure all staff are aware of literacy initiatives, meetings, and other events is to publish a friendly, professional newsletter. During the first few months of the school year, the coaches should provide newsletters (either hard-copy or electronic) that inform everyone of their willingness to be of assistance. The newsletters can also provide resources such as book reviews or helpful Web sites. Announcements regarding newly formed committees and meetings can also be included. As subsequent newsletters are issued, they become a record of communication and literacy events.

The start of the school year is also the time for the new coach to organize working space and materials. Some coaches may be fortunate enough to have a private office that is an entire room. Other coaches may have to share a room with others or situate themselves in a space that has been converted from a storage space into a room for them. Whatever the physical space may be, the coach should strive to organize it at the start and keep it organized throughout the year. The coach's office should be a professional setting. Once the coaches' schedules become more demanding, they will appreciate having organized space and easily accessible materials.

Every new coach should schedule an initial meeting with the principal to determine her expectations of the coach's role. This meeting should include a thorough review of standardized test data from the previous year(s). These two pieces of information—the principal's expectations and test data—should give the coach a strong historical perspective of the school's instructional program as well as which current issues should be addressed. Before the initial meeting with the principal, the new coach should familiarize himself with curriculum documents and published curriculum materials that are used throughout the building.

The principal is the chief literacy leader in the school. After the initial meeting with the principal, the literacy coach should establish a schedule for meeting regularly with the principal (perhaps weekly or biweekly at the beginning) to discuss issues related to schoolwide literacy instruction. Ideally, a shared vision for the school's literacy program will evolve as a result of these collaborative meetings.

The coach should also plan to meet with other administrators with whom she may have a direct line of communication (curriculum supervisor, assistant superintendent). Depending on the structure of the district and wishes of the administration, an initial meeting with central administrators may be either a one-time event or on ongoing event. If the new coach is able, she should arrange to meet with other coaches (literacy and math) from the building or throughout the district for networking and sharing of ideas.

One of the most essential duties of the coach during the first three months of the year is to begin observations in assigned classrooms during language arts instruction. The observations will be an ongoing part of the coach's role. The observations will also expand the role of the coach to include conferences, planning sessions, preparing professional development for groups of teachers, and ensuring that assessments are aligned to instruction.

Reading specialists are an important part of the literacy instruction that takes place in schools. The new literacy coach is advised to observe and confer with reading specialists in the building about their work with children and the areas they perceive needing improvement

During the first segment of the year, the new literacy coach should begin to establish routine meetings or other opportunities to be of assistance to teachers. These may include monthly grade-level meetings regarding literacy instruction or assessments, study groups, mentoring relationships, etc.

It is important for the new literacy coach to establish her role as an informal leader within the school. During the first three months, the coach should make brief presentations at regularly scheduled faculty meetings (overviews, reports, announcements, etc.) as part of the communications to the staff. This forum provides a schoolwide audience for the literacy coach's interactions with teachers. It is as important as, but different from, the one-on-one observations taking place in classrooms at this time.

It is also important that the literacy coach plan and implement the professional development sessions for which he is responsible. The coach may be the sole presenter at schoolwide sessions or the facilitator of sessions at which a consultant will present to the staff. The coach may also be asked to co-present with other coaches or reading specialists for interschool or districtwide professional development.

The beginning of the year is a busy time; the remainder of the year is bound to be busier. Therefore, the coach should establish time for self-reflection and note making on a regular basis. Time for reflection is important for the coach to determine the strengths as well as the needs of the school in terms of literacy education. Setting aside time for routine reflection and note making early in the coaching role can help to make reflective practice a habit.

It is usual for the first schoolwide parent meetings (PTA, Home and School, Back-to-School Night, etc.) to be held during the first three months of the school year. As a new faculty member in a new role, it is important for the literacy coach to attend parent meetings. Parents have the right to be informed of school practices that affect literacy instruction in the school. Often, parents are unsure of the purpose of teaching roles that are different from the role of the regular classroom teacher. Explaining the coaching role and informing parents of steps being taken to improve the schools their children attend are methods of promoting public relations and keeping parents involved in the life of the school.

Second Three Months: Adaptations

By the fourth month of school, the school year is in full swing. The new coach should have established several routine practices by this point. One of the practices worthy of continuing is the publication of a regularly issued newsletter. Keeping teachers apprised of the coach's endeavors throughout the building, offering tips on topics of interest to teachers, providing summaries of timely journal articles, and announcing regional workshops or seminars are newsworthy content in a coach's newsletter.

The new coach should also continue to meet with the school principal on a regular basis to continue discussions focused on schoolwide literacy instruction and assessment. If meetings were initially held weekly, they might be held every three or four weeks during this period. It is also advisable to continue to meet with other administrators and with other literacy coaches if possible.

During this segment of the year, the literacy coach should increase the frequency of observations and conferences (both pre- and postobservation) of classroom teachers for whom she has coaching responsibilities. This is the heart of the coach's work. In addition to the important one-on-one sessions with teachers, the coach should continue to conduct meetings that are helpful to small or large groups of teachers. Adaptations may need to be made based on the coach's assessment of needs.

The literacy coach should continue to make presentations at faculty meetings. However, a shift in the type of presentations should be made at this time. The presentations at faculty meetings should become professional development opportunities at which the coach shares the ideas and techniques that she has observed in teachers' classrooms. Faculty meetings are also the appropriate place to introduce data from the prior year's standardized tests that impact current practices and suggest needed change. In addition to interacting with the faculty, the literacy coach should continue to stay in contact with parents, so attending parent meetings remains important at this part of the year.

Additionally, the literacy coach should continue to plan and implement professional development sessions for which he is responsible (these may now include interschool sessions or districtwide sessions). It is also vitally important for the literacy coach to continue to participate in regular self-reflection and note making. Doing so will help the coach to analyze the literacy issues of the school as well as the interrelationships of the staff as they impact the issues. Reflection will also help the coach analyze his or her own beliefs and the status of his or her impact on literacy teaching and learning in the school.

A new task for the coach during this time frame is to initiate a staff survey regarding their perceptions, expectations, and suggestions related to the role of the coach in the school. If grade-level or schoolwide committees related to curriculum or instruction need to be formed, the survey may be the place to solicit volunteers for committee work.

Third Three Months: Assessments and Adaptations

Assessments. As the school year continues, the work of the literacy coach increases. The literacy coach should continue developing each of the areas mentioned in the "2nd Three Months" of the time line. Many literacy coaches assist in the administration and monitoring of schoolwide assessments during this part of the year. Data from in-house assessments can be gathered and analyzed almost immediately. Results of state-mandated tests or other standardized tests may not be readily available because they are often mailed out to companies contracted to score tests and produce summary information.

At this time of the year, the literacy coach should review and reflect on the information from the recently administered staff survey. The information should be shared in a professional manner with those who are able to render focused insights and help the new literacy coach move forward in improving overall literacy teaching and learning in the school. The coach should ensure that the focus of staff development planning and implementation remains consistent with that started earlier in the year.

Adaptations. The literacy coach should be flexible and adapt constantly to the additional layers of work that are part of her responsibilities while working within the same (rather than increased) time allotments. Coaching is a dynamic enterprise. Therefore, being adaptable to both the expected and unexpected is certainly part and parcel of the literacy coaching role. But let's be clear: being adaptable does not mean being erratic or unreliable. As stated several times throughout this text, one of the most significant commitments a literacy coach makes is to the classroom teacher who will be observed and provided feedback. Keeping those appointments with the classroom teacher is vitally important to the improvement of literacy instruction as well as to the relationship building the coach is doing throughout the school.

Fourth Three Months: Assessments and Priorities

Assessments. The last portion of the school year should include the continued work in each of the areas mentioned in both the "2nd Three Months" and "3rd Three Months" segments of this time line.

The literacy coach should review assessment data when they become available. If possible, he should present a year-end summary of assessment results to the faculty. The principal may request additional presentations for parents and administrators. Sometimes the literacy coach is asked to prepare a written summary of assessment results as part of the school's documentation of student achievement.

It is important that the literacy coach continue regularly to self-reflect and note make. The coach needs to review the notes made all year for a cumulative review of her first year's experiences. She should use the reflections to analyze steps that will be part of ongoing practice and decide which steps will be eliminated or changed for the following year.

Priorities. The final portion of the year is a time of self-assessment and assessment of schoolwide literacy program and tests over the course of the year. It is the time for both looking back (analytic reflection) and looking forward (planning). The coach's individual goals should be aligned with schoolwide goals for continued improvement. When both sets of goals are accurately aligned, the coach and any other professionals on the literacy team should be able to state accurate priorities for the next year.

The coach's self-assessment should definitely involve the thorough review of notes made throughout the year. It may also involve reflection on feedback received from the principal's observations of the coach as well as any written documentation the principal must formally submit as part of supervisory responsibilities. If other administrators have direct supervision of or interaction with the coach, their comments (whether formal or informal) should also be considered as part of the reflective process. In addition, coaches may want to speak with several teachers or other coaches they respect to gain some insight about their practice. They should compare the remarks of others with their own notes from throughout the year to reflect on what changes should be implemented in the future.

Assessment, like learning, is a process. As the new coach proceeds from the first year to the second, self-assessments, school testing data, and carefully analyzed assessment of the school's instructional practices should help the coach develop an action plan for continued strategic coaching.

AN EXPERT'S THOUGHTS: DR. ROGER FARR

Roger Farr, a nationally known expert on both reading instruction and reading assessment, is the Chancellor's Professor of Education and the director of the Center for Innovation and Assessment at Indiana University. He is a former president of the International Reading Association and was inducted into the Reading Hall of Fame in 1988. Dr. Farr proudly boasts that he has taught every grade from kindergarten through graduate school.

We asked Dr. Farr to provide some advice for new literacy coaches. His insightful comments are presented here.

Q: What advice do you have for literacy coaches who are new to the role?

A: At the end of each day, ask yourself what you learned that day about being a better teacher. Write down the things you learned and the things you just don't seem to understand about the students and how to teach them. Do that every day! Keep a notebook and date the entries. It might only take 10 or 15 minutes at the end of each day to do this. However, no one should be a teacher who is not learning about learning. You need to spend your entire professional career focused on becoming a better teacher. I have been trying to teach for about 50 years, and I am proud to say I have learned a great deal about teaching, but I am prouder to say that I am amazed at how little I truly understand and how much I need to keep learning. All teachers and coaches should adopt as their prime understanding a phrase I picked up at President Jimmy Carter's establishment of the U.S. Department of Education as a newly created cabinet post. That phrase is simply this: "Learning Never Ends."

The accountability emphasis in education will not wane for at least a decade, and the misunderstanding of assessments will increase. There is no question that schools test too much and assess too little. Assessment, as opposed to testing, ought to be more consistent across the grades. We need to learn how to assess what we believe is important and to share this information across grades and among the teachers working with a particular child.

Too often, we treat reading as an act unto itself, but reading is not something that someone does just to read. One reads for a particular purpose, about a particular topic, and at a particular time. Too many teachers and coaches treat reading as if it is an act engaged in for the sheer pleasure of reading. That is nonsense. Reading is thought guided by printed symbols.

If a coach/teacher can determine a student's functional reading level in all its manifestations, teaching a student to read becomes much easier. Learning to read is developed by reading. Find out what, why, and when someone wants to read, and you will achieve success.

Source: Dr. Roger Farr, Indiana University.

THE COACH'S ASSIGNMENT

Whether the coach is new to the school or the school is new to the coach, the specifics of the coach's assignment need to be established. Observing and mentoring teachers is a given. However, the coach could be assigned to specific grades rather than to the entire teaching staff. The assignment may involve committee leadership and participation that occur after school hours, and it may involve district-level meetings that take place outside of the building.

Typically, some uncertainties come with any new position. The uncertain aspects of coaching are generally found within two areas: human dynamics and the evolution of new projects. The initial responsiveness to coaching by individual and collective teachers depends on their assumptions and their expectations of the position. Teachers will respond positively to a coach who has proven to be professional and committed to them and their school as the coaching process continues throughout the year.

As coaching continues throughout the school year, a new project may emerge that requires the literacy coach's facilitation. For example, after working with teachers in the building, the coach may see a need for a project that involves development of writing instruction. The need may be evident in the coach's classroom observations, several teachers' comments to coaches about writing instruction in feedback sessions and meetings, and in the work samples of students. The coach may determine that professional development focused on writing instruction should include conducting mini-lessons, conducting writing conferences, domain scoring of writing, meeting state writing standards, and identifying exemplars of writing for each grade level. Such a professional development project is no small task to organize and implement and can't be done in one or two sessions. It will be a *project* in every sense of the word, and it will be a long-term process that requires a skilled facilitator as well as the cooperation of dedicated participants.

In this situation, the coach's role as a social agent will emerge. Coaching is inherently a social enterprise because the coach rarely works alone. Interactions with others should be characterized by professionalism, commitment, and good will. Some coaches, whether new or seasoned in the position, will find themselves working with staff in a new school. Other coaches will remain in the same school; although the role of coach may be new to them, they will already be familiar with the curricula, school routines, teachers, and administrators.

Coaching is also inherently both rewarding and challenging. As part of a vision, it has the capability to drive national reform. That vision uses coaches to improve teaching in every classroom in every school.

New School and Staff

Like Marguerite Floyd, the coach described in the scenario at the beginning of this chapter, many coaches leave a position in one building to begin coaching in a new school. Of course, working in a new school means working with a new teaching staff. Toll (2005) views the coach's first interactions with the school staff as "the foundation for future work together" (p. 43). Relationship building takes time and effort, but the coach's reward is usually worth the investment.

Teachers who feel that they are acknowledged and appreciated will respect the coach as a colleague and collaborator. This chapter's recommended time line of events will help the new coach gauge time for getting to know the people and the place. Trying to do everything right away is likely to be overwhelming for both the coach and the staff. An important notion for the coach to keep in mind at all times is that *she* is now a member of the staff. The coach must reflect upon her interactions with the staff and their feedback and responses to her. The coach is a learner, and a coach in a new school with a new staff has much to learn about the culture and dynamics of the school before she can be effective in her work there.

Same School and Staff

Some coaches begin coaching in the same building in which they held a teaching position. They are familiar with the staff, students, and parents, as well as school policies and curricula. Although they remain a colleague to the staff, the new role they assume may cause anxiety or mixed feelings for the staff (and maybe even for the coach). Bean (2004) cites three crucial characteristics of effective coaches: "know your stuff," "experience," and "ability to work with adults" (p. 101). When a coach is assigned to the building in which he has worked, the teachers generally have a good sense that the coach knows "his stuff" and has had successful experience as a teacher. The unknown element is how well the coach will work with the teachers as adult learners.

As a classroom teacher or reading specialist in the building, the new coach surely had a reputation as someone who worked well with children and provided sound instruction to them. Working with adults as learners can involve different challenges, however, and affect collegial relationships, even though those involved have known each other for some time.

Staff Survey Regarding Literacy Coaching

Part of the data collected about literacy coaching should come from the teachers who are coached. A staff survey is an efficient way to collect information. The coach should distribute the survey at a faculty meeting and establish a date for submitting the completed survey. The coach should consider the advantages and disadvantages of anonymous submission and decide if she prefers anonymity of teachers' input.

Two types of surveys may be used: an open-ended survey and a Likert-rated survey. One or the other, not both, should be used within the school year. Open-ended surveys may be found in Resource E (for elementary school) and Resource F (for middle and high school). Likert-rated surveys may be found in Resource G (for elementary school) and Resource H (for middle and high school). Once the survey type is chosen, the survey should be given to the staff. The completed survey information should then be reviewed thoroughly by the coach. The principal may also want to review every survey form personally, or the principal may ask the coach to compile the information into a summary report for review. If an open-ended survey is used, the coach may want to code or sort information to cluster ideas and suggestions. A rated survey can be tallied so that the reviewer(s) can see which items were consistently rated similarly by the staff and which were more differentiated.

RESOURCES AND ASSISTANCE AVAILABLE TO LITERACY COACHES

University Partnerships With Schools

Hopefully, somewhere within the vicinity of your school district is a valuable resource that is very accessible: a university with a teacher education program. University partnerships offer school districts a set of professional advisors, expertise, and supply of knowledge at usually no cost. Universities usually have extensive professional libraries and may have some reading journals for which you do not have a subscription. Our university, for example, has a librarian who is devoted exclusively to assisting education students and faculty. She is most willing to find resources and to provide help in searching the Internet.

As professors in reading education, we have had former undergraduate and graduate students e-mail questions about their classrooms. We have answered questions about reading topics from *A* to *Z*. Our wealth of experience as former classroom teachers, reading specialists, principals, and supervisors has served us well in our positions in higher education. Other professors in our university and other universities are willing to provide their expertise to school districts as well.

Since both of us teach reading diagnostic classes, we have a variety of samples of different types of reading tests available. Sometimes, former students have returned to our offices to review these tests and ask our opinion about which test(s) might be best for their particular testing situation. Thus, we serve as a resource to the students in our program.

University professors have expertise in different areas and are usually very willing to share expertise with local school districts. For example, our university has hosted local schools for special workshops on children's poetry, history day activities, and science workshops. It may behoove the literacy coach to initiate requests for support from a local university for curriculum-related events as well as consulting when expert guidance is needed in the school.

Walpole and McKenna (2004) suggest that university doctoral students are a hidden treasure. Doctoral students are usually knowledgeable concerning the latest research and are most willing to share their expertise. The literacy coach may find it beneficial to contact a university that has a doctoral program in reading. He could ask a professor to solicit help from the doctoral class when the coach needs assistance for action research projects or other reading program needs.

Coach as Liaison

Our university, like many others, has a partnership with a local school district. We provide inservice for the school district, and in return, the school district provides field placements for our undergraduate students. The literacy coach can be a liaison in such instances because she also serves in the role of educating adults concerning teaching methods. She can offer assistance in bridging the gap between theory and practice as she meets with university professors concerning the planning of inservice meetings.

As liaison, the coach may be able to arrange for on-site graduate courses in the school or district. The coach, along with university personnel, should meet to discuss the needs of teachers in the district, which could involve providing a few specific courses in the teaching of reading and writing or a full program for degree or certification. The convenience of having class right in the building at the end of the school day is very appealing to teachers. In some states, graduate course hours are used to renew teaching certificates. The partnership relationship can be beneficial to everyone involved.

Mentoring

Erickson (1995) states that mentoring relationships are essential to the professional development of teachers, especially when they are in the process of change. A mentor provides support, guidance, and a safe place for discussion to take place. Literacy coaches who serve in the role of a mentor can support new teachers as well as veteran teachers.

Although the literacy coach is called a coach, he may still function in the mentoring role to teachers and even to the principal. For example, one of the students in our reading doctoral program mentioned that she is serving as a literacy coach in a building where the principal is new. Although the principal had access to student test scores and other resources, she was able to orient him to the needs of the teaching staff and students at the beginning of the year from an "insider's" perspective.

The coach is likely to mentor teachers within her own district. Another mentoring relationship may exist, however, when a veteran coach mentors a new coach. The two coaches may or may not work in the same district. The mentor should listen carefully to learn the new coach's most relevant concerns. The two coaches can discuss efficient use of time as well as effective strategies to use when interacting with adult learners on a one-to-one basis or in group settings.

Study Groups

Literacy coaches may facilitate study groups within their own schools. They may also participate in study groups centered on a common theme related to coaching. A study group, dedicated to collegial study and action, is a wonderful means of dispelling the feeling of isolation that occurs when many teachers experience instructional difficulty in their classrooms and of exploring a literacy topic in depth.

Study groups can be formed in one of two ways. The first type of formation occurs when a topic evolves from a common interest or concern. The topic is proposed by one or more members of the group. Another type of formation occurs when a school leader, such as the literacy coach, suggests a topic and encourages teachers to enroll in the group. Coaches should help teachers form a shared understanding of what good teaching and learning of literacy looks like within their school. Study groups are a venue for bringing teachers together for such meaningful discussions. Each of the four aspects of the role of the literacy coach discussed throughout this book (collaborator, colleague, facilitator, and learner) is utilized and integrated when the literacy coach facilitates study groups. This is a true picture of literacy coaching in action.

According to Lefever-Davis and Heller (2003), teacher study groups (TSGs) "are formed across the United States as teachers approach professional development . . . to learn about teaching and learning through conversation" (p. 782). TSGs are developed by volunteers who identify a problem or topic they wish to investigate. These groups support collaborative learning and promote positive change in classrooms. Lefever-Davis and Heller are explicit about the many benefits of these groups. TSGs focus learning on "growth and change with support" (p. 783).

School-based study groups often require all faculty members to participate. The faculty determines what the group will study. Study topics are usually related to student learning and the learning environment. According to Murphy (2002), whole-faculty study groups use data to generate a list of student needs, prioritize the needs, and organize study groups around them. Eventually, an action plan is created and implemented. After allowing sufficient time to enact the plan, the groups come together to evaluate the plan and the impact the study group effort had on student performance. Murphy suggests that whole-faculty study groups use logs or sharing sessions to communicate their work. Providing sharing time during faculty meetings is an effective way to communicate the progress and challenges of the groups.

Sometimes, the coach may participate in a study group and not play a role in facilitating it. For instance, a local reading council in southeastern Pennsylvania convened a study group on literacy coaching for teachers throughout the region. The group met several times over two years. Some of the group members were practicing coaches, and others were not. All of the group members were interested in coaching and how it might impact their schools. Common books and articles were read by all of the participants. The content and implications of the reading material were discussed at group sessions. Actual coaching practices, both successes and difficulties, were also discussed. No formal action plan was established as a result of the group, but several participants implemented suggestions they read or heard about as part of the study group conversations. When coaches participate in study groups with others from outside their own schools, they develop new insights and perspectives on their role, network with others in similar roles, and garner suggestions for possible action plans or strategies in their own schools.

Finding and Writing Grants

There is always a need for additional funding in any school district. Grants can be a source of extra funds that the school district is unable to provide. Walpole and McKenna (2004) remark that grantwriting involves a commitment to conducting research, devoting time to writing, and acknowledging and including scientifically based practices in the application.

Many university professionals are willing to collaborate with other professionals in developing grants. Universities offer research classes, and students in the class are expected to write research proposals; perhaps one of the graduate students would be willing to write a proposal for your school or district.

Sources for grant funding include the following institutions: the government (federal, state, local), private corporations, professional organizations, and philanthropic organizations. Most of these sources have Web sites regarding the specifics of grant awards as well as their grantwriting requirements. In addition, large libraries contain books of resources for grant-funding institutions.

Vogt and Shearer (2003) suggest some basic guidelines for writing grants that the coach might want to consider:

- Write about the problem or need first.
- Provide data to support the need.
- Find current research to support your project.
- Provide an assessment for every objective in your project.
- Review other grants that have been awarded from your funding source or attend workshops that are provided by the funding source.
- Inform the administration concerning your proposal. You may also need to make a list of "in-kind or matching funds" from your district.
- Make certain that you have followed all of the grant application guidelines and double-check them to see that everything that is required is included.
- Ask an outsider to read your proposal and comment.
- Provide concise information and make certain that you have followed your goals or outcomes. This will also serve as a basis for collaboration.

If you can solicit input from the teaching staff in developing the grant activities, you will have a stronger base for the application and evaluation procedure required after funding has been awarded.

Technology and Web Sites

The use of computers and technology is a fact of life in the classroom today. Even kindergarten classes infuse computers into daily curricular activities. Bean (2004) states that technology should be employed by teachers to enhance the literacy program in their classrooms. However, hardware and software programs are updated so frequently that it is challenging for school districts to keep current (Vogt & Shearer, 2004). Fortunately, districts often have technology specialists that can give guidance concerning software and hardware selection. The literacy coach should collaborate with the technology personnel as well as the teachers regarding the use of technology in the reading curriculum. If the school district does not have a technology specialist, the local university may have someone on the faculty who would be willing to assist.

The Internet is another resource for teachers and students. Lesson plans, unit themes, ideas for teaching, and other resources can be found on Web sites. However, Vogt and Shearer (2004) caution teachers about what can be found on the Web because some of the sites are not safe for children.

Web sites may not always contain accurate information, either. While the Internet can be a wonderful tool for research, it also has drawbacks.

Technology resources can be found in Resource I. Coaches should review them in terms of the specific learning needs that teachers have in their classrooms.

As mentioned in Chapter 2, the Literacy Coach's Clearinghouse, a joint project of the International Reading Association (IRA) and the National Council of Teachers of English (NCTE), is a wonderful resource. It includes a section that helps schools develop coaching programs. It also has briefs, a library, a blog, and links as permanent features. The site can be accessed at www.literacycoachingonline.org.

AN EXPERT'S THOUGHTS: DR. SHELLEY WEPNER

Dr. Wepner is the dean of the school of education at Manhattanville College in New York. She is the author of several books and a presenter at local, state, national, and international conferences. In addition to her expertise on technology, Shelley Wepner has focused much of her recent work on the role of the literacy coach. She was interviewed because of her expertise in both areas. The advice she offers here is very practical and applies to both the new and the seasoned coach.

Q: How has the integration of technology impacted instructional practices in reading/language arts over the past decade?

A: Although many articles have been written on *how* to implement technology, few have been written on how it has impacted instructional practices with literacy. Coaches and other literacy leaders should review the research concerning the impact on practices for which they have particular questions or concerns.

Q: How can reading specialists and literacy coaches best evaluate software to ensure instructional worthiness?

A: Actually, software is not the wave of the future; the Internet is. The best way to determine the worthiness of software is to use it with children. Another way is to use an established criteria list, such as in *Linking Literacy* (Wepner, Valmont, & Thurlow, 2002).

Q: How do you think literacy coaches might incorporate technology "do's and don'ts" into the professional development they provide for teachers?

A: It depends on what technology is available, so you just can't have a blanket list of do's and don'ts. The decision will be very context based. Specifically, literacy coaches need to know (1) what technology is available and (2) what teachers have done so far with technology and what they are willing to do. Literacy coaches need to be willing and able to demonstrate lessons in classrooms that integrate technology with reading/language arts.

Q: How might literacy coaches and district technology coordinators work together so that they both effectively align curriculum and meet standards?

A: Teachers run the gamut from having no interest in technology to using it all the time, so the literacy coach needs to do homework in this area. For example, a teacher may do a nice job using software only but may never use the Internet. The literacy coach should help these teachers move forward to another level. When there isn't a standard curriculum for technology integration, it makes the task difficult. The literacy coach almost needs a master's degree in technology to be really effective.

Q: How would you compare the following criteria when considering basal anthologies and leveled books versus software programs: price, utility, and teacher training?

A: I'd prefer not to compare these two types of materials because I feel there should be a balance of these resources in the classrooms. Those who decide on these resources need to ask themselves, "What do we want to accomplish by using them to instruct students?"

Q: What would you recommend literacy coaches do to keep current with technology for their own professional use as well as for use in professional development endeavors?

A: There are several things I'd recommend: take courses, practice often using the technology, collaborate with technology coordinators or technology support staff, and collaborate with teachers who show interest in specific uses of technology for their instruction.

Q: What about teachers who are resistant to integrating technology in their classrooms? What suggestions do you have for literacy coaches working with them?

A: First, the literacy coach should make sure the teacher has current, useable technology. Then, the coach should do a demonstration lesson. It will be important for the literacy coach to desensitize the resistant teacher so she helps the teacher move through the following stages: (1) fear of technology, (2) somewhat embracing technology, (3) fully embracing technology. Secondly, the literacy coach could find teachers who are using technology well in their classrooms and see if they will work with teachers who are struggling. Perhaps they could "experiment together" with using technology.

Q: Are there any other suggestions or recommendations regarding technology that you would make for literacy coaches, especially those coaches who are new to the position?

A: Literacy coaches should continually self-assess their own knowledge of technology. It would also be wise if the literacy coach knew what expertise or lack of expertise that the building principal had with technology.

Source: Dr. Shelley Wepner, Dean, School of Education, Manhattanville College.

SUMMARY

Literacy coaching is a process requiring skill. Skills, acquired over time, depend on school culture and context. A major thrust of this chapter was the impact of change on the school environment. Both positive and negative aspects of four key elements were discussed as they relate to change: school culture, the principal's leadership style, parent involvement, and staff interactions.

This chapter addressed first-year coaching by offering practical information, such as a time line and staff survey. Resources, such as university-school partnerships, technology and Web sites, and grants, were discussed. In addition, the benefits of participation in study groups was reviewed.

TOPIC EXTENSIONS FOR CLASS
SESSIONS OR STUDY GROUPS

1. Choose a portion of the time line offered for the first year of coaching and extrapolate the duties mentioned. What practical steps could the new coach take to ensure efficiency in the selected portion(s)? What issues or concerns might evolve during this particular time? What adjustments might you make to the time line?

2. Review the "do's and don'ts" of technology offered by Dr. Shelly Wepner in the interview section of this chapter. What can be added to her suggestions? Apply Wepner's suggestions as well as your additions to your current instructional situation.

3. With a colleague, discuss the questions that Marguerite posed in the scenario in this chapter. Can you add any questions that a new coach might consider? How do Marguerite's questions compare with those of a new coach you know?

4. Take on the persona of a new coach in a new building and create your introductory newsletter to the staff.

RESOURCE E: OPEN-ENDED SURVEY
FOR ELEMENTARY TEACHERS

Please comment on each of the areas related to literacy coaching. Your statements will help the coach reflect on what has taken place with coaching practices in the school this year and to plan for next year.

Part I: For items 1 through 4, please make a general statement and/or comment on each of the descriptors.

1. How do you view the coach in the classroom? (Please include your thoughts about any or all of the following: as observer and mentor, as one who interacts with students, as a model/demonstrator of instructional techniques.)

2. How do you view the coach as a facilitator of meetings? (Please include your thoughts about any or all of the following: grade level, building, and districtwide meetings; study groups; committee meetings.)

3. How do you view the coach as communicator? (Please include your thoughts about newsletter and/or other written communications.)

4. How do you view the coach as a colleague? (Please include your thoughts about the following: interpersonal skills, resource to teachers.)

Part II. For items 5 through 8, please complete the statement with a sentence or two. Your input is valued as we work together to create the best instructional program possible.

5. A suggestion I have is . . .

6. A question I have is . . .

7. Something I'd like to see retained for next year is . . .

8. Something I'd like to see changed for next year is . . .

Name _____   Date _____

Please return this survey by _____.

RESOURCE F: OPEN-ENDED SURVEY
FOR SECONDARY TEACHERS

Please comment on each of the areas related to literacy coaching. Your statements will help the coach reflect on what has taken place with coaching practices in the school this year and to plan for next year.

Part I: For items 1 through 4, please make a general statement and/or comment on each of the descriptors.

1. How do you view the coach in the classroom? (Please include your thoughts about any or all of the following: as observer and mentor, as one who interacts with students, as a model/demonstrator of instructional techniques.)

2. How do you view the coach as a facilitator of meetings? (Please include your thoughts about any or all of the following: team meetings, department meetings, building faculty meetings, districtwide meetings, study groups, committees.)

3. How do you view the coach as a communicator? (Please include your thoughts about the newsletter and/or other written communications.)

4. How do you view the coach as a colleague? (Please include your thoughts about the following: interpersonal skills, resource to teachers.)

Part II. For items 5 through 8, please complete the statement with a sentence or two. Your input is valued as we work together to create the best instructional program possible.

5. A suggestion I have is . . .

6. A question I have is . . .

7. Something I'd like to see retained for next year is . . .

8. Something I'd like to see changed for next year is . . .

Name _____   Date _____

Please return this survey by _____.

RESOURCE G: LIKERT-RATED SURVEY FOR ELEMENTARY TEACHERS

Please rate each of the following items from 1 (lowest) to 5 (highest). Your statements will help the coach reflect on what has taken place with coaching practices in the school this year and to plan for next year. Your input is valued as we work together to create the best instructional program possible. Please return this survey by _____.

Classroom Observations

1. The coach spent ample time observing and conferring with me.	1	2	3	4	5
2. The coach's feedback was relevant, appropriate, and timely. The feedback helped me to set goals and reflect on my teaching.	1	2	3	4	5
3. The observations helped me reconsider room arrangement or visual display of postings.	1	2	3	4	5
4. Appointments for observations were kept.	1	2	3	4	5
5. The coach provided helpful demonstration lessons.	1	2	3	4	5
6. The literacy coach observed several types of language arts instruction in my classroom (instructional reading, guided reading, writing, word work).	1	2	3	4	5
7. I tried new or varied teaching techniques as a result of the coach's work in my classroom.	1	2	3	4	5
8. The literacy coach provided information regarding alternative strategies for diverse learners (ELL, gifted, and special education students).	1	2	3	4	5

Meetings

9. The coach facilitated practical grade-level meetings.	1	2	3	4	5
10. Large meetings (building and/or district meetings) were efficiently facilitated and beneficial to the participants.	1	2	3	4	5
11. I voluntarily participated in meetings such as study groups, committees, or councils that were initiated by the literacy coach.	1	2	3	4	5
12. I felt the coach kept me informed about the content of meetings at which my attendance was not required.	1	2	3	4	5

Resources and Information

	1	2	3	4	5
13. I felt comfortable approaching the coach with questions or comments.	1	2	3	4	5
14. The coach provided resources for me to read, borrow, display in my room, etc.	1	2	3	4	5
15. The coach explained assessment data clearly.	1	2	3	4	5
16. I feel confident administering and scoring assessments as a result of being coached.	1	2	3	4	5
17. The coach provided technology training or suggestions for technology use in my teaching.	1	2	3	4	5
18. The coach shared timely information about curriculum mandates and/or initiatives with me.	1	2	3	4	5

General

	1	2	3	4	5
19. I feel the coach was consistently professional in our interactions.	1	2	3	4	5
20. I feel the faculty discusses instructional issues in a professional, collegial manner under the coach's leadership.	1	2	3	4	5
21. I feel the faculty's input regarding professional development topics and presenters is honored by the literacy coach.	1	2	3	4	5

Other Comments (Optional)

22.

RESOURCE H: LIKERT-RATED SURVEY
FOR SECONDARY TEACHERS

Please rate each of the following items from 1 (lowest) to 5 (highest). Your statements will help the coach reflect on what has taken place with coaching practices in the school this year and to plan for next year. Your input is valued as we work together to create the best instructional program possible. Please return this survey by _____.

Classroom Observations

1. The coach spent ample time observing and conferring with me.	1	2	3	4	5
2. The coach's feedback was relevant, appropriate, and timely. The feedback helped me to set goals and reflect on my teaching.	1	2	3	4	5
3. The observations helped me reconsider room arrangement or visual display of postings.	1	2	3	4	5
4. Appointments for observations were kept.					
5. The coach provided helpful demonstration lessons pertinent to my content area.	1	2	3	4	5
6. The literacy coach observed several types of content area vocabulary, study skills, and comprehension skills instruction in my classroom.	1	2	3	4	5
7. I tried new or varied teaching techniques as a result of the coach's work in my classroom.	1	2	3	4	5
8. The literacy coach provided information regarding alternative strategies for diverse learners (ELL, gifted, and special education students).	1	2	3	4	5

Meetings

9. The coach facilitated practical department meetings.	1	2	3	4	5
10. Large meetings (building and/or district meetings) were efficiently facilitated and beneficial to the participants.	1	2	3	4	5
11. I voluntarily participated in meetings such as study groups, committees, or councils that were initiated by the literacy coach.	1	2	3	4	5
12. I felt the coach kept me informed about the content of meetings at which my attendance was not required.	1	2	3	4	5

Resources and Information

13. I felt comfortable approaching the coach with questions or comments.	1	2	3	4	5
14. The coach provided resources for me to read, borrow, display in my room, etc.	1	2	3	4	5
15. The coach explained assessment data clearly.	1	2	3	4	5
16. I feel confident administering and scoring assessments as a result of being coached.	1	2	3	4	5
17. The coach provided technology training or suggestions for technology use in my teaching.	1	2	3	4	5
18. The coach shared timely information about curriculum mandates and/or initiatives with me.	1	2	3	4	5

General

19. I feel the coach was consistently professional in our interactions.	1	2	3	4	5
20. I feel the faculty discusses instructional issues in a professional, collegial manner under the coach's leadership.	1	2	3	4	5
21. I feel the faculty's input regarding professional development topics and presenters is honored by the literacy coach.	1	2	3	4	5

Other Comments (Optional)

22.

RESOURCE I: TECHNOLOGY RESOURCES

Helpful Professional Web Sites

Alliance for Excellent Education	www.all4ed.org
Association for Supervision and Curriculum Development	www.ascd.org
Center for the Improvement of Early Reading Achievement	www.ciera.org
Children's Book Council	www.cbcbooks.org
Classroom Connect	www.classroom.com
International Reading Association	www.reading.org
Literacy Coaching Clearinghouse	www.literacycoachingonline.org
National Association of Elementary School Principals	www.naesp.org
National Association of Secondary School Principals	www.nassp.org
National Council of Teachers of English	www.ncte.org
National Staff Development Council	www.nsdc.org
Pennsylvania High School Coaching Initiative	www.pacoaching.org
Reading First	www.readingfirstsupport.us
Read-Write-Think	www.readwritethink.org
Striving Readers	www.ed.gov/programs/strivingreaders/
WebQuest	http://edweb.sdsu.edu/webquest/index.html

Online Stories, Books, and Magazines (for Classroom or Home Use)

Aesop's Fables: K–8	www.umass.edu/aesop/
Antelope Publishing: K–8	www.ongoing-tales.com/contents.html
Awesome Library: K–12	www.awesomelibrary.org
Bedtime-Story: K–6	www.the-office.com/bedtime-story/
Books to Download: K–5	www.learningpage.com
Children's eLibrary	http://childrenslibrary.com/welcomeback.php

Online Children Stories	www.ucalgary.ca/~dkbrown/stories.html
Clifford Interactive Storybooks	http://teacher.scholastic.com/clifford1/
Enchanted Learning	www.enchantedlearning.com
Fable Library: K–3	www.fablevision.com/place/library/index.html
Family Education Network	www.familyeducation.com/home/
Goodnight Stories: K–5	www.goodnightstories.com
KidPub: K–5	www.kidpub.com
Literacy Connections: K–12	www.literacyconnections.com
Lil' Fingers: K–1	www.lil-fingers.com
McBookWords: K–12	www.mcelmeel.com/curriculum/authorlinks/index.html
Children's Storybooks Online: K–2	http://magickeys.com/books/index.html
Mother Goose on the Web, Internet Public Library	www.ipl.org/div/kidspace/storyhour/goose/
Online Literature Library	www.literature.org
Poetry4Kids: K–5	www.poetry4kids.com
Reading A–Z: K–5	www.readinga-z.com
Starfall: K–2	www.starfall.com
Storybook Online: K–8	www.storybookonline.net
StoryPlus	www.storyplus.com
This Is True	www.thisistrue.com/samples.html
Stories to Grow By With Wootie Owl	http://storiestogrowby.com

The Schools in Which We Work   **4**

INTRODUCTION

The Reading First initiative has helped the role of the literacy coach achieve prominence in American primary classrooms. Literacy coaches also collaborate with teachers in other grades, but the current emphasis on coaching support seems to be in the early grades. This emphasis is due to the funding provided by the Reading First legislation. Whether a literacy coach has worked in the role for several years as a primary, middle, or high school coach, she needs to be acutely aware of the specific characteristics of the school as a whole, individual classrooms in particular, and the learners who work and grow in those settings.

This chapter examines the characteristics of primary/elementary, middle, and high schools and special education. It relates those characteristics to the knowledge base literacy coaches need to have and the skills they need to use to focus on instructional improvement.

SCENARIO

Maureen Kulp is a well-respected teacher and reading specialist who has worked for Central School District for 17 years. Last spring, Maureen interviewed for and was selected for the position of literacy coach in the district's 9–12 high school. Maureen spent the first three months of the new school year carefully observing in classrooms, meeting with the principal and department heads, and attending regularly scheduled meetings with the district administrator who supervises both literacy coaches and reading specialist. Because Maureen's position is new and there is only one high school in the district, she is the only coach assigned to a secondary school; eight other literacy coaches work in the district's seven elementary schools and the one middle school.

In meetings with her supervisor, there is time for dialogue in which strengths and issues are discussed. Professional readings are shared and discussed, and live or video presentations are made. However, Maureen has noticed that all of the meetings have had an elementary focus; secondary literacy issues have been absent from coaching meetings.

Generally, the middle school literacy coach seems to address most of the same strengths and issues as the elementary coaches. Maureen has attempted to talk about issues specific to the high school but finds that her remarks are often dismissed as insignificant or are quickly overshadowed by the elementary topics. Maureen is very much satisfied with the work she is doing at the high school and enjoys the change from her previous position. However, the meetings she is required to attend are a consistent source of frustration for her.

Choose one of the following roles to respond to Maureen's situation:

a. As Maureen, request a meeting with the supervisor in charge of the meetings. Create a list of pros and cons about the meetings and a way to present them to the supervisor in a professional and proactive manner. What suggestions would you make?

b. Maureen has an excellent relationship with the high school principal. They respect each other and are able to share confidences about staff concerns. After the last meeting, Maureen decided to talk with the principal about the high level of frustration she is feeling. As the high school principal, what advice would you offer Maureen? How might you help her to change the situation? What would you suggest she do? What would you suggest she not do?

PRIMARY/ELEMENTARY SCHOOL SETTINGS

Characteristics

Primary/elementary schools typically provide education for children from kindergarten through fifth grade. However, there may be different configurations: prekindergarten through fourth grade, kindergarten and first grade only, and so forth. In some districts, kindergarten children from throughout the district are educated in one building, a school specifically devoted to kindergarteners' development and readiness for first grade. Teachers in these schools are often certified in Early Childhood Education rather than, or in addition to, Elementary Education.

In some schools, you will find ungraded primary classrooms, and in others, you may find multiage classrooms that include a three-year span of ages (Miletta, 1996). Regardless of the way in which the primary/elementary school is organized, diverse learners, such as English language learners, children with disabilities, and gifted students, are likely to be included.

Urban, suburban, and rural classrooms are found in almost every state in the country. Although the location may vary, urban schools are generally characterized as having large buildings (many in need of repair) with overcrowded conditions. Urban schools rarely have sufficient school-yards. In major cities, schools that serve primary/elementary students may have small, inadequate playgrounds or no play areas at all. Suburban schools are sometimes characterized as buildings that are in good physical condition and are attractive both inside and outside. Suburban primary/ elementary schools often have play yards with equipment that is specifi-cally designed for the use of small children. Many suburban schools also have manicured lawns with trees and others shrubs in addition to the play areas. With this patchwork quilt of school buildings in various settings across our country, we may find the literacy coach's "office space" within a building to be anything from a transformed closet to a section of a hall-way with partitions or even an actual room. Wherever the coach has a base of operations his role is to promote instructional achievement through a strong understanding of early literacy and developmentally appropriate practices in the primary/elementary school.

In addition to the variations in school buildings, there are great differ-ences in the sizes of primary/elementary classrooms across America. According to the National Center for Educational Statistics (2003), the populations of elementary classrooms range from 17 to 25 students. Primary and elementary classrooms are designed to meet the needs of the young children who work there; the physical space is filled with small desks, tables, sinks, and bookshelves. While there is accommodation for the physical size of the child, accommodation also should be made for the emerging learning needs of the child. Certain common elements in pri-mary classrooms should be seen, no matter what the classroom size: many books for the children to handle and read; word walls; learning cen-ters; display areas covered with children's work; carpeted areas for story time or any whole-group lesson; and uncarpeted areas for art, science, and other activities that may involve spills. Both the physical organization of the classroom and appropriate teaching are contributing factors in how the youngest learners in our schools achieve (Morrow, 2003).

Curriculum in the Primary/Elementary School

The purpose of curriculum in any primary/elementary school is to provide beginning literacy instruction effectively. According to Radencich (1995), analysis and improvement of the curriculum are tasks that cannot be underestimated. Teale and Yokota (2000) cite seven points from research concerning the characteristics of beginning reading instruction: (1) emergent literacy provides a foundation for all learning, (2) comprehension instruction is a core feature, (3) a multifaceted word study program is essential, (4) writing—integrated and separated—is central, (5) reading fluency must be developed, (6) children need to practice by reading connected text, and (7) the early literacy program is conceptualized as developmental.

Common occurrences in the literate environment in primary/elementary classrooms promote reading and writing in developmentally appropriate ways when they are incorporated into the daily schedule within the classroom (Morrow, 1997; Pressley, 2002; Taylor, Pearson, Clark, & Walpole, 2000). Many of these common occurrences are found when curriculum is integrated with content area learning:

- Reading quality literature aloud to children
- Language experience activities
- Both whole-group and small-group instructional settings
- Word-building opportunities
- Writing (journal writing, responding to literature, shared writing, dictated writing)
- Opportunities for children to select easy reading materials for independent reading from a classroom library
- Opportunities for children to talk about what they are learning with their teacher and with each other

The literacy coach, reading specialist, principal, and primary/elementary teacher should be aware of these salient points when delivering the curriculum and if they are involved with writing the curriculum for their school.

The Coach's Role in Achieving Instructional Excellence in the Primary/Elementary Grades

Assisting the primary/elementary teacher and students requires that the coach act as a facilitator, observer, colleague, and learner (often simultaneously). These classrooms are usually nurturing places where interactions are pleasurable and visitors are welcome. As the literacy coach observes and interacts in the primary/elementary classroom, it is crucial for her to be aware of balanced literacy approaches and early literacy tenets previously discussed. Occasionally, a literacy coach may find a situation in which a teacher omits one or more of the important instructional techniques that should be a part of the daily routine, such as reading aloud to children or providing writing instruction. This teacher's instruction is not within a balanced literacy framework. The literacy coach, cognizant of these omissions, would need to coach the teacher about the importance of these components and help him find the time and techniques to include them in daily instructional practices. Demonstration teaching by the literacy coach may also be warranted.

The literacy coach in the primary/elementary school assists teachers in integrating curriculum so that children are reading, writing, and talking about the topics of study in science, social studies, math, and health. Each of these curricular areas can be enhanced with language experience stories, journal entries, self-selected writing, a variety of easy reading texts such as leveled texts, and guided discussion groups. According to Au, Carroll, and Scheu (1997), integrating the language arts with content area subjects is a "natural link in a balanced literacy program" (p. 72). The literacy coach's expertise must span her observations in classrooms, her ability to help teachers plan integrated lessons, and her repertoire of strategies for encouraging modeling skills and guiding learning for balanced instruction.

The integration of the language arts with the content areas in the primary/elementary grades not only saves time needed for instructional planning and implementation but also provides opportunities for students to engage in hands-on activities and surround those activities with student talk and literacy. Therefore, literacy development can occur throughout the day as part of experiences that are connected to both the formal curriculum and informal activities (Pressley, 2002).

Working With Paraprofessionals

In addition to working with teachers, literacy coaches may have contact with (and possibly coaching responsibilities for) paraprofessionals in the primary/elementary school. Since the youngest learners in schools do not have the level of independence to work alone or in pairs, their classrooms often have a paraprofessional assigned for at least part of the day. When paraprofessionals have instructional duties with individual children or even small groups of children, it is incumbent on the literacy coach to be observant of their instructional practices. The practices need to be assessed to determine if they are aligned or misaligned with the school's curriculum and the teacher's mode of instructional management.

If the literacy coach and/or classroom teacher has concerns about the paraprofessionals, there are several alternatives to handling the situation. The first alternative is to schedule an informal meeting with the teacher and the paraprofessional to discuss a particular literacy topic or technique. This meeting may be especially helpful if the teacher is unable to persuade the aide to interact with the children in a certain way or use materials more appropriately. When the literacy coach meets with both the teacher and the paraprofessional at the same time, the message is presented that this type of instruction is an important expectation for all of the primary students in that particular grade.

A second alternative is for the literacy coach to ask a reading specialist assigned to the primary/elementary grades to work with him to create a training session, or even a series of workshops, specifically designed for the paraprofessionals who work in those grades. Literacy-related topics such as invented writing, read-aloud techniques, echo reading, and word recognition skills should be included in training for those who assist in primary/elementary classrooms.

A third alternative is to provide one or more demonstration lessons with the paraprofessional as an observer. Then the literacy coach should process the whys and hows of the lesson with the paraprofessional.

A fourth alternative is to teach the majority of the class so that the classroom teacher is free either to provide a demonstration lesson with the paraprofessional as an observer or to observe closely the aide working a small group of children. Feedback is then provided to the aide.

Finally, the goal of the literacy coach is to improve instruction. When instruction is provided by others in addition to the classroom teacher, the literacy coach needs to be cognizant of the quality of the instruction others are providing and able to enact an action plan for improvement if the instruction is below standard. Literacy coaches need to "use their knowledge and performance skills to make a school-wide impact by demonstrating lessons and communicating and collaborating with classroom teachers and paraprofessionals" (Shaw, Smith, Chesler, & Romeo, 2005, p. 6).

Parents and Families

Although the primary responsibility of the literacy coach is to work with classroom teachers, on occasion, the coach may be asked to work with parents and families. For example, if a reading program has a home component that needs specific procedures followed (fluency checks, repeated readings, prewriting brainstorming forms), the literacy coach may be asked to meet with families to ensure compliance with procedures. Of course, reading specialists have always worked closely with parents and families. They could certainly provide parents with the sessions described here by themselves or in partnership with the literacy coach.

MIDDLE AND HIGH SCHOOL SETTINGS

Characteristics

Middle schools typically educate children in grades six through eight. High schools generally educate children in grades 9 through 12. Variations include grades five through eight or grades six through eight. In addition, some districts have schools that house both the elementary and middle grades (K–8 schools). Whatever the configuration, middle and high schools are considered secondary schools.

Because of the developmental stage of the learner, middle schools often cluster a certain number of students together in a "team" or a "house." Clustering students enables a few teachers (perhaps three or four) to get to know well a portion of the students in a particular grade level. For example, if there are 500 students in sixth grade, the class may be divided into five groups of 100 students each. One of the groups will be named as a team or house, for example the "Millennium Team." The Millennium Team will work with four teachers of the major subject areas of language arts, math, science, and social studies. The teachers become familiar with the students and collaborate with other team teachers during a common planning time. During the common planning periods, teachers can plan projects and lessons that are integrated across the curricular areas. They can combine classes for special events and presentations. Another advantage of this teamwork is that teachers discuss concerns about particular students when they meet together. Also, they can set a schedule of major assignments and tests so that there is no overlap for the students. Middle school teachers and students get to know each other well when such a teaming model is in place.

When there is a common planning time, middle school teachers can set aside one period a week for meeting with specialists such as the counselor, principal, reading specialist, or literacy coach. Whether the literacy coach attends the meetings as a regularly scheduled participant or as an occasional invitee, she has the opportunity provide professional development as part of the meeting, schedule times for individual teacher meetings, and arrange for demonstration lessons or observations.

According to the National Center for Educational Statistics (NCES, 2003b), the normal range of class size in the United States at the secondary level is from 19 to 26 students. Urban secondary schools, like urban elementary schools, generally have larger class sizes than the average suburban school. When class size is large, individualizing instruction is difficult. In high-poverty middle and high schools, students continue to read on average two to three years behind grade level (NCES, 2003a).

Depending on the number of daily classes a teacher must teach, the teacher may be responsible for the instruction of 125 to 150 students each day. Teachers at the secondary level are often certified in one major area, the area for which they have major teaching responsibility. Some teachers are dually certified, meaning that they may hold credentials in two curriculum areas, such as science and social studies.

The length of classes varies in secondary schools. Some schools allot 45 minutes per period or class. Others allow 75 minutes. Even though American secondary schools are as varied as the 50 states, they share the common purpose of providing a sound education that will enable students to thrive as literate, thinking beings in a global economy. The variations in class size, daily teaching schedules, and variety of subjects taught are challenges that the literacy coach must take into account when working within the secondary school setting.

Curriculum in the Secondary School

The diversity of young people attending American secondary schools at the beginning of the 21st century means that a much more comprehensive education is needed than was required by any previous generation (Sturtevant, Linek, Brozo, Hinchman, & Boyd, 2005). The education of secondary students must include development of a strong base of knowledge across many content domains as well as advancement in reading and communication skills. The impact of technology on teaching and learning has changed the face of education, particularly for secondary students who have a level of independence in technology use. Unfortunately, the overall reading achievement of adolescents is not keeping pace with the demands of a technological society (Alvermann et al., 2002).

In secondary schools where lecture-style presentations remain the prominent mode of instruction, the intention is to convey a large quantity of factual information in the limited time allotted for the class. Teachers continue to use a lecture mode, assuming that their pace of instruction allows them to deliver the full content of the required curriculum. Secondary students who attend large classes with minimal class time for seven, eight, or nine daily classes participate in a factory-type model of schooling, which is incompatible with teaching or utilizing content area literacy strategies known to improve student content learning.

Students need time to read thoughtfully, to write cogently, and to participate actively in class discussions and experiments. Teachers need time to assess students' needs, answer individual questions, and troubleshoot learning difficulties. Moxley and Taylor (2006) indicate that high expectations should be included in daily practice for middle and high school students. These students should have equal access to their content curriculum while learning vocabulary, developing fluency, and adequately comprehending their content texts.

The Literacy Coach's Role in Achieving Academic Excellence in the Secondary School

Bean (2005) notes that although there is much to recommend about literacy coaching as an approach for improving instructional practices, the potential may not be realized due to a too-narrow definition of *coaching*, a lack of pedagogical content knowledge or leadership skills, or a lack of enough coaching time to make a difference. The literacy coach working in a secondary school may encounter some common misconceptions among teachers about the role of literacy in the content areas. Content area teachers are specialists in their area. Some secondary teachers believe that teaching literacy skills subtracts from the teaching of important concepts in their content disciplines. Others believe that teaching reading and writing is not their responsibility but rather resides only in the province of English or language arts teachers. According to Sturtevant et al. (2005), effective professional development can alleviate these misunderstandings by building essential knowledge among teachers about the important role all of them perform in developing reading and writing skills of middle and high school students. The literacy coach who provides professional development in the secondary school can help teachers understand that their students can develop content knowledge at the same time that they are improving literacy skills. Secondary administrators may also need to be included in these professional development sessions if they share the same misconceptions about literacy learning. It is important that administrators support the literacy program of the school.

As literacy coaches work with secondary teachers, the strategies that they present and recommend should follow from the district's comprehensive framework. For example, when working with teachers from a high school social studies department, a literacy coach could assist the teachers as they plan the development of a major research project for their students. The coach needs to become familiar with the text and any primary resource documents that the teachers will have students use. Becoming familiar with these materials will help the literacy coach collaborate with the teachers in determining vocabulary and concepts that need explicit instruction. Also, the coach can suggest (and even model) strategies that can help make the instruction clear and the learning proficient. The coach may even suggest a particular semantic organizer or note-making procedure. The literacy coach should help these teachers embed the use of technology as a criterion for the students' research. Recommending specific Web sites for content information as well as a software program for formatting the written portion of the project will assist the department's teachers in enhancing the projects by raising their expectations of students' research. The use of specific Web sites could also make students accountable as researchers and self-monitors.

When teachers recognize the fit of literacy teaching with their content area, they are generally more willing to implement strategies that promote student learning. One of the chief roles of the literacy coach in the secondary school is to model and guide teachers in using appropriate strategies. The growth of a collaborative teacher culture is marked by increased teacher willingness and ability to collaborate, peer accountability, and individual teacher knowledge about other teachers' classrooms (Symonds, 2003b). An equally important role for the secondary school literacy coach is to observe in content area classrooms. Frequent observations, whether live or videotaped, provide opportunities for individual teacher-coach sessions in which feedback can be shared. Observations also inform the literacy coach about what needs and issues can be addressed in department or full-faculty professional development days. Moxley and Taylor (2006) describe observations done by the literacy coach as "the glue between coached collaboration sessions and classroom practice" (p. 15).

It seems that for the secondary literacy coach to have a major impact on academic excellence, she needs to have a complete and thorough knowledge of the curriculum from several vantage points: the written curriculum, the pedagogical practices of teachers as they implement the curriculum, and how the students' knowledge of the content of the curriculum is evaluated by teachers. The literacy coach must reflect on the consistencies or inconsistencies across these areas. This knowledge base and appropriate leadership skills should empower the literacy coach to function as a change agent for instructional improvement. Acquiring this knowledge takes time. Observing in classrooms and collecting pedagogical data also takes time. Achieving excellence in secondary schools depends on quality instruction. Excellent coaching can do much to raise the bar for instruction in individual classrooms and in entire schools. As Bean (2004) reminds us, "enough coaching time" is an essential component if literacy coaches are to make a significant difference in secondary schools.

SPECIAL EDUCATION CLASSROOM SETTINGS

Characteristics

Difficulty with learning to read is a primary characteristic of children placed in special education programs (Walmsley & Allington, 1995). These students may require special strategies or specialized equipment to enable them to learn. Their disabilities usually demand that teachers provide instruction below the student's age-appropriate grade level.

Some special education students are removed from the general population of students and placed in self-contained special education classes because they have exceptional learning needs. These students are usually grouped by age or grade level and remain in special education all day throughout the school year.

Other special education students attend some of their classes in a resource room and the remainder of their classes in the regular education classroom. The resource room teacher, a teacher certified by the state as a special education teacher, provides instruction to the student in the curriculum area for which the child has been identified as disabled. The resource room is an example of a pullout model of instruction. For example, if an eighth-grade child is diagnosed with a math disability, he will receive his math instruction in the resource room and instruction in all other areas of the curriculum in the regular eighth-grade classroom. If a third-grade child is diagnosed with a reading disability, she will receive her reading instruction in the resource room and all other instruction in the regular third-grade classroom.

Many, but not all, special education students may be delayed developmentally or socially in addition to their specific learning disability. Specific disabilities such as autism and Asperger's syndrome are included in the special education categories. Students with these conditions may be taught in either self-contained classes or resource rooms. Because of the many needs of special education students, paraprofessionals are usually assigned to their classrooms. Small student-adult ratios are very important to children who need a great amount of individual attention as they learn in school.

Students with multiple severe disabilities are often placed in self-contained classes that receive labels such as "life skills classes." The purpose of these classes is to teach the students to function self-sufficiently in the home and the school and, eventually, at some level of independence in the workplace. These students generally attain only minimal literacy skills because of the severity of their neurological impairments.

Each of the special education classes described here is typically found in schools throughout the country. Literacy coaches may work in these classrooms as a part of their responsibilities within the school.

Curriculum in the Special Education Classroom

Special education teachers in self-contained and resource room classrooms provide instruction that is aligned to the curricular standards of the school. According to Walp and Walmsley (1995), there will always be limits on the progress at-risk children can make unless a strong core curriculum is in place.

In special education classrooms, the instructional level of the student is not equivalent to his age-appropriate grade level. For example, a student who is nine-and-a-half years old would typically be in the fourth grade. A special education student of that age usually will not receive instruction in reading and math at that grade level. The student's individual progress is the determining factor in advancing in leveled material or to more difficult curriculum content. As special education students transition to regular education classes (either on a daily basis or at the discontinuation of their self-contained instruction), the literacy coach can provide awareness of curriculum content and learning demands at that level for the special education teacher.

Special education students are often required to take standardized tests as part of gathering assessment data at the school or district level. Some states require special education students to take mandated tests at grade level even though the students do not receive instruction at grade level. Consequently, students with the most severe disabilities are either exempt from state tests or take individually administered tests with adults who are permitted to read directions to the students. Literacy coaches may be asked to assist in this manner.

Certified special education teachers have a high knowledge of specific disabilities as well as the attending and behavioral issues of their students. However, Strong and Traynelis-Yurek (2006) found that in a survey of more than 600 special education teachers in the mid-Atlantic states, only one-half of the special education teachers reported that they had taken more than one or two reading courses in their graduate or undergraduate training program. Many special education teachers in the mid-Atlantic states have minimal knowledge concerning the teaching of reading. (The IRA standard is three courses.) Literacy coaches can fill the gap because they can supply resources and models for special education teachers. Literacy coaches can provide reading or writing demonstration lessons or conduct professional development sessions for the special education staff.

Response to Intervention

The reauthorization of the Individuals with Disabilities Education Act in 2004 (IDEA), an act forged largely from NCLB, includes the concept of a preidentification strategy called *response to intervention* (RTI). IDEA specifically states that "lack of appropriate instruction in reading" cannot result in the diagnosis of a learning disability. However, it does allow schools to use 15 percent of their special education funds toward the early interventions implemented through RTI models. States now have the option of using RTI criteria rather than IQ-achievement discrepancy formulas to identify students in need of special education (Klinger & Edwards, 2006).

RTI is a three- or four-tiered model delineating when intensive intervention is needed for children who fail to learn from (or be responsive to) the instruction provided as part of the regular classroom program. Academic intervention changes at each tier. The first tier is regular classroom instruction. The middle tier(s) involves an intensive intervention model, and the last tier is usually special education placement. As a student moves from one tier to the next, the intervention becomes more intensive. According to Fuchs and Fuchs (2006),

> increasing intensity is achieved by (a) using more teacher-centered, systematic, and explicit (e.g., scripted) instruction; (b) conducting it more frequently; (c) adding to its duration; (d) creating smaller and more homogenous student groupings; or (e) relying on instructors with greater expertise. (p. 95)

RTI has strong implications for literacy coaches and others who are responsible for both regular and special education. Using RTI models necessitates training for preservice and inservice teachers through professional development sessions, since IDEA "has numerous references to the professional development of teachers, both special and regular educators" (James, 2004, p. 3). Currently, it is the responsibility of the school district to "measure and define nonresponsiveness" in the special education identification of students (Fuchs & Fuchs, 2006). This responsibility is significant and can only be carried out effectively if curricular decisions and delineations between the first tier (regular classroom instruction) and the next tier (a specified intervention) are seamless. However, serious challenges may become evident if a plethora of RTI assessment methods are sporadic and inconsistent.

RTI is an attractive model because it provides funding and autonomy to school districts. Planning for careful implementation of RTI should be coordinated by a team of experts that includes the literacy coach and the reading specialist. The team should then follow through with monitoring the other stages of the model: implementation of the intervention, data collection, and analysis. The team can also be instrumental in the referral process for special education placement.

James (2004) indicates that "implementing the RTI model across the nation to guarantee better results for all students will likely be a much lengthier process requiring extensive scientific research on many aspects of a pre-referral model of intervention" (p. 5).

The Literacy Coach's Role in Achieving Academic Excellence in Special Education Classrooms

Observing in special education classrooms provides pedagogical information about the teacher's and the paraprofessional's instructional interaction with students. The literacy coach's observations give him opportunities to supply feedback and resources to these instructors.

One strategy that the literacy coach might use is to invite the special education teacher to attend specific grade-level meetings or study groups that would be beneficial. Another strategy that the coach could use is to lend the special education teacher a videotaped lesson that she feels has relevance for that teacher. After the tape has been viewed, the coach could facilitate a discussion with the teacher about pertinent happenings within the videotaped lesson. A third possible strategy is that the coach schedule a time when the special education teacher can accompany the literacy coach to a regular education classroom to view a demonstration lesson. The lesson can be conducted by either the coach or another exemplary teacher in the building, and discussion of the lesson should follow.

The dialogue that occurs between the coach and the special education teacher provides a valuable step in improving instruction in special education classes. Reporting on a case study of collaborative literacy teams, Lyons (2001) states that special education teachers were extremely pleased that they had observed and learned new teaching techniques for helping students learn how to read and write. The coach and other staff with professional development responsibilities should consider and identify philosophical issues surrounding congruence between literacy instruction in regular classrooms and literacy instruction in special education classrooms (Walmsley & Allington, 1995).

Literacy coaches need to internalize the tenet that special education teachers should be included regularly in professional development. This inclusion extends the opportunity for processing information about curriculum or pedagogy among the special education staff and between the special education teachers and their colleagues in regular education classes. Exemplary special education teachers should also be encouraged to share their tips and techniques with staff at professional development sessions.

After classroom observations, it may become apparent to the literacy coach that a group of paraprofessionals working in special education classrooms needs inservice training on a particular topic (e.g., prewriting techniques, use of the word wall, fluency checks). After acquiring permission from the principal to conduct the inservice, the decision should be made whether the coach or a reading specialist in the building should conduct the training sessions.

Ensuring consistency in instructional quality within a school is a major job responsibility of the coach. Embracing the special education staff by offering them the same coaching services offered to the rest of the staff can do much to meet this goal.

TWO EXPERTS' THOUGHTS: DR. RICHARD VACCA AND DR. JOANNE VACCA

This interview was a double pleasure! Dr. Richard and Dr. JoAnne Vacca, experts in content area literacy and adolescent literacy, were gracious enough to be interviewed together and respond to questions regarding the literacy coach in secondary schools today.

This husband-and-wife team has spent a lifetime working with secondary teachers. They have published several books on the topic of content area literacy. Richard Vacca is a past president of the International Reading Association. In their interview responses, they provide sound insights and make a strong case for the position of the literacy coach in every secondary school in the country.

Q: In your opinion, what professional development tasks should the literacy coach perform in secondary schools today?

A: To meet the literacy needs of adolescents, school districts throughout the United States are creating instructional support positions known as "literacy coaches." The main role of the literacy coach is to provide continuing professional development for content area teachers. In some respects, the literacy coach is similar to the role that some reading professionals held in secondary schools in the 1960s and 1970s, when schools with federal grant funds hired "reading specialists" to provide "resource" assistance to other teachers. However, today's literacy coach often has a more multifaceted role than yesterday's reading specialist. Literacy coaches in middle and high schools are viewed as teacher leaders whose main professional development tasks are to mentor individual teachers, model effective instructional practices and strategies and observe in classrooms, work with study groups and teacher teams, lead a schoolwide literacy council, advise administrators on the school literacy program, collaborate with literacy coaches in other schools to ensure best professional development practices, administer and monitor literacy assessments, and work with parents or community groups.

Q: What do you think should be done to elevate the importance of the role of the literacy coach in secondary schools (as it is in the elementary schools)?

A: If the role of the literacy coach is to be elevated in middle and high school, then literacy coaches must be viewed in school districts as "teacher leaders" whose main responsibility is to work within a professional development context with middle and high school teachers. Their roles cannot be viewed as "add-ons" to an instructional staff, nor can their roles be spread too thin. For example, the role of the literacy coaches should not be confused with that of reading specialists, who, traditionally, have worked primarily with small groups of struggling readers in pullout programs and, secondarily, with teachers in a professional development context. While some middle and high school literacy coaches do indeed work with small groups of students on a limited basis, we believe that having a regular class schedule should be discouraged by many programs, since this can prevent coaches from working effectively with teachers due to time and scheduling constraints.

Moreover, the potential roles for a coach are so numerous that coaches who are asked to do too much too quickly can easily feel overwhelmed and ineffective. School leaders, in consultation with literacy coaches, can elevate the importance of the literacy coach by developing long-term plans that do not attempt to accomplish everything in the first year or two.

Finally, we believe that the role of the literacy coach can be elevated in middle and high schools if school districts seriously consider implementing the Alliance for Excellent Education's (www.a114ed.org) recommendation that a school district hire one literacy coach in a school for every 20 teachers. The list of potential responsibilities for literacy coaches can be overwhelming, especially when one considers that middle and high schools with hundreds, even a thousand or more students, often have only one coach.

Q: How can literacy coaches help content area teachers embed sound reading/writing strategies in their classes?

A: Nothing can be more challenging than working with content area teachers on the development of literacy practices and strategies. It's not enough for the literacy coach to know his or her stuff. Literacy coaches must put into play sound principles for professional development. They must, in fact, become effective staff developers. By this we mean that they must be able to demonstrate effective process strategies for "content delivery," which include techniques for group participation, role-playing, and small-group interaction. Not only must they work with small groups of content teachers on content literacy practices and strategies, but they must also be ready to provide demonstrations on the strategies in actual classroom situations.

Q: How can the literacy coach help secondary schools provide curricular congruency between the special education classes and the regular education classes?

A: Literacy coaches must provide leadership for schools to address the needs of all learners, including those who have been identified as learning disabled in special education or mainstreamed classes. To accomplish this, we support the organization of "literacy leadership teams," as recommended by the National Association of Secondary School Principals (NASSP). Not only can the literacy leadership team conduct a needs assessment about the overall literacy achievement and needs of different groups of learners (in both special education and regular education contexts), but it can also systematically plan ways to support both student and teacher learning. While special education learners are a diverse group and can be defined in a wide variety of ways, all students in middle and high school who struggle to meet course expectations due to difficulties in reading need special attention in the school literacy plan.

Moreover, the literacy coach can organize workshops and study groups to help teachers understand the variety of reasons special education students may struggle with reading in the content area classes. Understanding the learner and the nature of the reading tasks required in content courses is a first step toward providing curricular congruency between special education classes and regular education classes

Source: Dr. Richard Vacca and Dr. JoAnne Vacca, Professors Emeriti, Kent State University.

SUMMARY

This chapter presented the characteristics of primary/elementary, secondary, and special education classes with which the literacy coach should be familiar. Curriculum concerns for the various levels of compulsory education were discussed regarding their relevance to providing effective instruction. Recent RTI tenets were explained. Specific suggestions were made to assist the literacy coach in recognizing and achieving excellence in his school.

A scenario about an experienced literacy coach who is newly appointed to a high school is presented at the beginning of the chapter. It is offered as a starting point for readers to discuss the situations in which the coach may find herself and to reflect on how they might deal with them.

The interview of Vacca and Vacca gets at the heart of this chapter, addressing the role of the coach in secondary schools and the need for coaching of special education teachers as well as regular education teachers.

TOPIC EXTENSIONS FOR CLASS SESSIONS OR STUDY GROUPS

1. Use the research-based items regarding effective early literacy instruction (mentioned in the section on curriculum of "Primary/ Elementary School Settings" in this chapter) to create a checklist of the strengths and weaknesses of early literacy instruction in your school or district. How can the checklist be helpful to a literacy coach?

2. Respond to the scenario regarding Maureen Kulp at the beginning of the chapter. Share your ideas with others to both options given for the scenario.

3. As a literacy coach, what issues regarding curriculum congruency do you think are vital components that should be shared between a school's regular education and special education language arts curricula?

The Communities   **5**
in Which We Work

INTRODUCTION

The literacy coach often extends the use of her leadership skills beyond working with classroom teachers during the regular hours of the school day, perhaps to outside entities in the community. Research (Benjamin & Lord, 1996; Come & Fredericks, 1995; Enz & Searfoss, 1996) suggests that quality reading programs emanate from strong leadership within the school as well as from sincere efforts by school personnel to reach out and involve all members of the family and the community.

This chapter focuses on community connections outside the realm of the school environment. It discusses the implementation of the coach's leadership skills in two major areas: parent involvement and professional organizations and agencies.

SCENARIO

Joanne Bradley is student teaching for the spring semester in Ms. Cardelli's second-grade classroom in Edgewood School. Joanne is working hard to prepare her lessons as she acquires more teaching responsibility. She has been professional and personable in her interactions with students, teachers, and parents. Ms. Cardelli is very pleased with Joanne's teaching abilities and classroom management. The two women get along well and have formed a friendship.

Joanne has attended two home-and-school meetings since starting her student teaching. She has attended the faculty meetings conducted by the principal and heard a number of presentations by the school's literacy coach. At this month's meeting the literacy coach announced that the regional International Reading Association's meeting would be held in the fall in a nearby city, just 20 miles from Edgewood School. The literacy coach distributed some information about the regional meeting and encouraged teachers to attend. The principal stated that he would provide funding for registrations of the first three teachers who expressed an interest in attending.

After the meeting adjourned, Joanne approached the literacy coach and asked her what IRA was, saying she hadn't heard of it before today's meeting. The coach invited Joanne to her office to share some further information. She told Joanne about her own membership in IRA, the state's reading council and the local reading council. She explained that she was an officer of the local reading council and discussed the advantages of professional development and networking from her participation. She showed Joanne journals produced by both IRA and the state council and told her how valuable they could be for her own learning and for sharing current information on language arts teaching and learning with the staff. She provided Joanne with student membership forms for IRA and told her how to access forms on the Internet for the state and local councils.

When Joanne returned to Ms. Cardelli's classroom, she told Mrs. Cardelli how much she had learned from the literacy coach about professional organizations. Ms. Cardelli told Joanne that she is also a member of the three organizations as well as the National Association for the Education of Young Children (NAEYC). She stated that she felt the memberships have done much to help promote her professional growth. She, too, encouraged Joanne to join IRA and the other groups and to note her membership on her resume as she applied for teaching positions. Joanne was glad for the advice she had received from the literacy coach and her cooperating teacher. She had never heard about these important organizations before. Why hadn't she heard about them at the state university? She knew she would enter graduate school in the near future. How would she have time to teach, go to graduate school, and participate in professional organizations?

PARENTS: GROUPS AND INDIVIDUALS

The Coach's Role in Assisting Parents of Public School Children

The primary role of the literacy coach is to work with teachers to improve instruction. However, sometimes the literacy coach may also work with parents. Literacy coaches need parents' support, and parents should be afforded the opportunity to have the coach share his expertise with them. According to Toll (2005), wise coaches will develop strategies to help them become visible and accessible to parents.

The coach's involvement with parents is usually within group meetings. Individual coach-parent meetings may be requested by the principal or classroom teacher when there is a special concern about a child's progress in school or an issue about how to help a child at home.

The coach's involvement with parents could consist of any of the following types of meetings:

- Addressing parents attending a PTA or home-and-school meeting about a specific topic
- Training parent volunteers to assist in regular and special education classrooms
- Giving a presentation at a school board meeting about test data, curriculum renewal, or new technology programs related to literacy learning. In addition to giving the presentation, the literacy coach may respond to questions parents pose at these meetings.
- Demonstrating a technique (reading aloud, fluency checks, echo reading, brainstorming a writing topic) at a schoolwide literacy fair or family literacy night.
- Participating in a child study team meeting and addressing parents' concerns
- Writing a grant that requires teacher and parent input

Parent Workshops

Both reading specialists and literacy coaches are frequently asked to provide workshops for parents. The expertise of the professionals concerning the developmental stages of reading and writing as well as the theory-practice connections for teaching the language arts makes them credible presenters for parent workshops. Parent workshops are commonly held for parents of children participating in Title I or other remedial programs. Workshops are also advertised for introducing parents to new programs that the school is using, particularly those involving technology (Au, Carroll, & Scheu, 1997; Pressley, 2001). Literacy-based technology is a topic that can be shared with parents so that they gain awareness of both valuable and valueless Web sites and commercially produced software packages. Parents generally appreciate the recommendations educational experts make regarding what may help their children at home when they use the computer.

In addition to being a presenter at parent workshops, the literacy coach could organize an event for which several workshops are offered at one time (Moxley & Taylor, 2006; Toll, 2005). Since Title I directors are required to provide parent workshops, a director may ask the literacy coach to assist in planning and organizing the event. The school or district could also sponsor parent workshops several nights throughout the school year. A single literacy coach or several coaches together may be asked to plan, advertise, solicit presenters, and purchase supplies and materials for the workshops.

Meeting With Parents Individually

Literacy coaches rarely meet with parents individually as a part of their job requirements. However, such meetings could occur in both planned and unplanned instances. Planned meetings occur when a classroom teacher asks the literacy coach to join her in a meeting with a parent. Typically, the reading specialist would meet with the teacher and the parent. The literacy coach, however, may be asked to meet with individual parents in the absence of an available reading specialist. In this situation, the teacher calls upon the coach's expertise to explain a new intervention for the parent's child or to provide a clear overview of recent testing individually administered to the child.

Sometimes the literacy coach is the best resource for providing information to a parent. For example, a family whose children enter school midyear may be confused by the teaching methods, curriculum, or text materials used in the new school as opposed to the prior school. If the new school's curriculum is thematically based, the literacy coach may be asked to meet with the parents to explain how and why the integrated curriculum is implemented. The coach could provide the parents with handouts, a video, or a DVD about the topic.

Unplanned meetings with individual parents may occur incidentally. For example, the literacy coach encounters a parent in the school hall or office. The parent directs this question to the coach:

Why are you spending so much time in my son's classroom? Is everything OK? My son tells me that you have been in his classroom five times over the past two weeks. I asked him if you were teaching, and he said that you weren't.

To answer the parent's question, the literacy coach explains his role and the importance of observing in the classrooms to provide consistency in the delivery of the curriculum. The coach should not reveal any specific details of his work in the boy's classroom, especially if there are concerns regarding instructional improvement. It is a good idea for the coach to have a handout that can be given to parents when they inquire about the role of the literacy coach. Although the professional staff may be aware of the need for this expert position, some people outside education do not fully understand the roles of those who are not regular classroom teachers (including reading specialists and math coaches).

In addition to chance meetings in the school, the literacy coach could encounter parents outside of school. Perhaps a parent will meet the coach while shopping or even at a social event. Although these meetings are informal, the coach should maintain a professional demeanor in responding to comments and questions that the parent may generate. She can provide definitions of her role as explained in her job description.

Assisting Parents With Homeschool Programs

Many American parents opt to educate their children at home rather than send them to local public or private schools. Homeschool programs must meet local and state requirements. According to the Education Commission of the States (2006), regulations regarding homeschooling vary from state to state. Some states, including Oklahoma, Missouri, and New Jersey, have only minimal requirements. Other states, such as New York, Rhode Island, and Pennsylvania, have several mandates, such as parental notifications, state tests, professional evaluations, and curriculum approvals. The states that have several mandates typically require parents to meet with school officials to learn about curriculum requirements and state standards. The states ask homeschooled children to take district and state tests that are required at certain grade levels.

Although the literacy coach usually does not have the role of making the first contact with homeschooling parents, she may eventually interact with these parents. In her role as the literacy coach, she can invite homeschooling parents to attend parent workshops. The coach may also be designated as the school representative who will explain test results to homeschooling parents. If a homeschooling parent decides to transition his children to the school, the principal may ask the literacy coach to meet with the parent to explain the school's language arts program.

LINKING TEACHERS TO PROFESSIONAL ORGANIZATIONS

Joanne Bradley, the student teacher in the scenario offered in this chapter, knew little about professional organizations that may prove invaluable to her as she moves along her career path. Since the literacy coach's primary role is to assist in instructional improvement, encouraging teachers to join professional organizations can be a major impetus to such improvement. The literacy coach should be aware of the organizations mentioned in Figure 5.1. Although this is not a complete list of educational professional organizations, it includes key organizations involved with promoting literacy teaching and learning. Each of these organizations publishes information that reflects current practices in the field. The information can be useful to literacy coaches and the teachers that they serve.

GOVERNMENT RELATIONS

Many professional organizations have governmental relations committees, which inform the organization of current legislation that may affect the members and meet/contact state and federal legislators regarding advocacy issues. The committees are chaired by a knowledgeable member with strong leadership skills. They meet several times throughout the year and disseminate information at the regularly scheduled board meetings of the organizations and through print materials if necessary. Governmental relations committees often work behind the scenes, and those in the general membership may not be aware of the important role and good work these committees do. Both reading specialists and literacy coaches need to be aware of these committees within the organizations to which they belong, as changes in policy and procedure may directly affect educational programs, funding sources, or specific literacy positions within schools.

In a recent article in *Reading Today* (Micklos, 2006), a success story is told about a state reading association whose efforts helped bring about policy change in Pennsylvania. The original state policy was that teachers could add a reading specialist certification to their teaching credential by simply passing the Praxis exam. The state reading association took exception to this policy because it believed that reading specialists should have both intensive and specialized training. The government relations committee led the effort and was supported by the Professors of Reading Teacher Educators (a special interest group of the state association). The organizations worked diligently for two years to effect change. They targeted three key legislators, who received approximately a hundred personalized statements by reading educators in the state explaining why they opposed the current regulations.

AN EXPERT'S THOUGHTS: DR. JESSE MOORE

Dr. Jesse Moore, a professor at East Stroudsburg University in northeastern Pennsylvania, is currently the governmental relations chair of the International Reading Association. He is also the governmental relations

Figure 5.1 Professional Organizations That Promote Staff Development and/or Literacy Services for Children

Organization	Mission	Contact Information	Chief Publications
ASCD (Association of Supervision of Curriculum Development)	Advocates sound policies and sharing best practices to achieve the success of each learner.	1703 N. Beauregard St. Alexandria, VA 22311-1714 www.ascd.org 800-933-2723	Educational Leadership Books and videos are also available
IRA (International Reading Association)	Dedicated to promoting high levels of literacy for all by (1) improving the quality of reading instruction, (2) disseminating research and information about reading, (3) encouraging the lifetime reading habit.	PO Box 8139 800 Barksdale Rd. Newark, DE 19714-8139 www.reading.org 800-336-READ (7323)	Reading Teacher, Journal of Adolescent and Adult Literacy, Lectura y Vida, Reading Online Books, brochures, and videos are also available.
NAEYC (National Association of Educators of Young Children)	Dedicated to improving the well-being of all young children, with particular focus on the quality of educational and developmental services for all children from birth through age 8.	1313 L St. NW, Suite 500 Washington, DC 20005 800-424-2460 www.naeyc.org	Young Children, Early Childhood, Research Quarterly
NCTE (National Council of Teachers of English)	To advance teaching, research, and student achievement in English language arts at all scholastic levels.	1111 W. Kenyon Rd. Urbana, IL 61801 217-328-3870 www.ncte.org	Language Arts, School Talk, Voices From the Middle, English Journal, Classroom Notes Plus, College English, English Leadership Quarterly,
NSDC (National Staff Development Council)	Committed to ensuring success for all students through staff development and school improvement.	5995 Fairfield Rd. #4 Oxford, OH 45056 513-523-6029 www.nsdc.org	Journal of Staff Development

chair of the state reading association in Pennsylvania. Because of his knowledge, enthusiasm, and leadership at both the state and national levels, he has gained the respect of educators and legislators alike. We interviewed Dr. Moore in February 2006, and his responses follow:

Q: What do you see as the strengths of literacy coaching at this time in the United States?

A: The major strengths I see are that it provides continuous professional development that can be directly tailored to a teacher's, school's, or district's needs because it is classroom-embedded. It also opens up the isolated culture of a school and fosters collaboration among professional groups in a school or district. Finally, it places the focus on demonstrable positive changes to teachers' practices that, in turn, are expected to result in greater student learning.

Q: What should universities and professional development experts be doing to ensure quality literacy coaching?

A: Graduate schools of education should be developing programs of study to educate and certify literacy coaches that could be an add-on endorsement to their current teaching certificate. I believe that these coaches should have at least a "reading teacher" or, more preferably, a "reading specialist" certificate prior to beginning such a program of study. The program of study for coaches should include some course work on "instructional leadership" and at least one course on "teaching literacy." It should also involve an extensive field-based component in classrooms that would be closely supervised by both the university and school-based staff.

Q: What do you see as the political underpinnings of literacy coaching? How are these beneficial? How are they detrimental?

A: My "conspiracy theory" says that there is a movement to greatly reduce or eliminate the "reading specialist" position in the schools (i.e., teachers who work with students in their classrooms [push-in] or in a pullout situation with small groups of students or one-on-one). The best bang for the buck is probably thought to be with the reading coach, because she can influence numerous teachers who will become more effective and thus will produce greater student reading achievement.

One bit of evidence that specialists are an endangered species is found in the 2003 *Standards for Reading Professionals* from IRA. There are no reading specialist standards in that document. There are standards for paraprofessionals, classroom teachers, reading specialist/literacy coaches, teacher educators, and administrators. Unfortunately, the reading specialist/literacy coaches column really only describes what literacy coaches do. Reading specialists spend at least 75 percent of their time teaching reading to students, according to a study by Rita Bean. At no place in the reading specialist/literacy coaches column do the words *teach* or *instruct* occur. The words used most often are *support, train,* and *assist* the classroom teacher. . . . Also used are *plan, demonstrate, model,* and *evaluate* for classroom teachers. In essence, IRA has eliminated specialists from the picture. Was that done on purpose? I don't know. Did the standards committee want to imply that reading specialists do the same things as paraprofessionals and classroom teachers as well as all the literacy coaching duties the standards describe? The standards are really quite unrealistic because they state that the candidates should be acting as literacy coaches while completing the requirements for a reading specialist certificate.

Source: Dr. Jesse Moore, IRA Government Relations Chair; KSRA Government Relations Chair.

LINKING TO OTHER LITERACY AGENCIES

Most of the literacy coach's work will be within the school to which he is assigned. However, on occasion, the coach may be involved with other agencies and organizations within the community. Adult education agencies often depend on local school districts for volunteers or teachers. Also, parents and other adults in the community may not be able to read well and ask the school for assistance. The literacy coach is in a position to make a referral to an adult education course for those individuals requesting help.

Adult Education

There is an old adage that says parents are the child's first teachers. However, as their children progress through school, some parents may feel uncomfortable with their own literacy skills and feel that they may be unable to help their children's literacy development as they should. These concerned parents frequently look to the expertise of school personnel, such as the literacy coach, for assistance. Vogt and Shearer (2004) point out that family literacy programs can assist parents in improving their own literacy while also helping them to learn how to work with their children.

The Adult Education and Family Literacy Act, Title II of the workforce Investment Act of 1998, provides funding for programs that work with both individuals and families. The Family Literacy Commission of the

International Reading Association (Morrow, 1997) indicates that the new model of working with parents involves collaborating with them rather than the former model of "training them." Vogt and Shearer (2004) explain that the key to working with parents is to respect and validate languages that are spoken at home; research cultural issues related to literacy; provide assistance in locating medical, legal, and other community resources; and support families as they become more proficient in language and literacy. If the literacy coach is assigned (or volunteers) to become involved with an adult education program offered by the school or community, it is important for her to be aware of these key areas. She will need to implement them herself or find others in the school or community who are able to do so.

In addition to the broad areas mentioned above, specific techniques can be used when educating adult learners. Radenich (1995) developed a list of suggested instructional procedures for working with adult learners:

- Writing workshops (conversational in style and involving writing from their own lives)
- Language experience (especially helpful for English language learner adults)
- Cooperative learning (recognizing the experience and knowledge of each person for whom the teacher is a facilitator)
- Print materials (using everything from wordless picture books to adaptations of classic novels)

Several organizations have been formed to assist adults who lack reading skills and working skills:

- The National Center for the Study of Adult Learning and Literacy (NCSALL) is a federally funded research and development center focused solely on adult learning. (www.ncsall.net)
- The National Center on Adult Literacy (NCAL) is engaged in cutting-edge research, innovation, and training in adult education and technology. (http://literacy.org)
- Proliteracy America, the largest adult literacy organization in the United States, was formed from the merger of the Laubach Literacy and Literacy Volunteers of America in 2002. It provides certification for its volunteer teachers. (www.proliteracy.org)
- Focus On Literacy, Inc., located in New Jersey, is another volunteer organization that provides literacy instruction and assistance to ELL adults. (http://focusonliteracy.org)

Working with adults in literacy is an extension of working with middle and high school students. The literacy coach should be used as a resource in this aspect of community involvement and outreach.

Agencies That Train Literacy Coaches

Literacy coaches may receive training through university courses, in-house district training, or professional research on their own. Some non-school agencies provide training for literacy coaches. Although training of coaches may occur through agencies outside the school, the ultimate goal is for the coaches to work collaboratively within schools.

The Reading and Writing Project housed at Columbia University trains "professional developers" (http://rwproject.tc.columbia.edu). The goal of this coaching model, which provides collaboration with teachers in New York City, is to support expert literacy instruction with the city's schools through research, writing, and professional development of teachers and school leaders.

The Consortium on Reading Excellence (CORE) is an agency based in California that trains both Reading First and non–Reading First coaches for the elementary grades. The agency provides three-day institutes that train not only coaches but reading coordinators, principals, reading teachers, and teacher leaders as well. Site-level support for implementation of reading programs is provided. Topics include essential literacy concepts, coaching skills, data collection and analysis, current research, and best practices.

Children's Literacy Initiative (CLI) is a well-known nonprofit agency on the East Coast that provides services to schools that serve low-income families. CLI hires and trains literacy coaches to provide coaching services in schools. The agency and the school form an agreement (usually a signed contract) for the provision of services for a certain period of time. A coach from one of these agencies may be assigned to a particular school or to a particular grade level within a school district.

AN EXPERT'S THOUGHTS: DR. LINDA KATZ

The following interview of Linda Katz, CLI's executive director, provides a clear picture of the work done and the standards set by a quality nonprofit organization. This organization serves all schools, public, private, and parochial, that serve low-income children in prekindergarten through third grade.

Q: How did CLI originate? What is its philosophy?

A: We started in 1986 with a giant children's book and music fair with 20 Caldecott winners, actor LeVar Burton, and an orchestra performing *Peter and the Wolf*. Pretty flashy start! We evolved by 1988 to an incorporated 501(c)(3) with the idea of bringing great books to children living in high-poverty areas and training their teachers, caregivers, and parents to read aloud to them. We've always used the research on vocabulary development to choose books and how to read aloud. Since then, we have developed into a professional development organization providing books, training, and content coaching (one-on-one, in the classroom) to many teachers in urban school districts. Our work has been studied, most notably by Richard Allington and Anne McGill-Franzen, and shown to make a difference in student assessment outcomes.

Q: Do school districts ever ask for services as part of their federal programs, such as Title I or Title VI? If so, can you talk about what services CLI provides for districts with such federal funding and the expertise of CLI coaches?

A: Schools can use both Titles to hire us. We provide Institutes (3- or 4-day), seminars (full-day), workshops (2 hours), coaching, grade-level meetings, model classroom creation, book collections, and a prekindergarten curriculum (*Blueprint for Early Literacy®*) to schools, teachers, school-based coaches, principals, Head Start, and child care agencies. We serve teachers and caregivers for children aged 4–8. We also provide parent workshops on reading aloud. Our topics are almost all those that relate to effective reading and writing practices.

Q: What characteristics do you look for in hiring literacy coaches?

A: All have bachelor's or master's degrees in elementary education and/or reading specialist. Some are getting their doctorates or teach at the university level.

Characteristics that I look for include the following:
- Has excellent content knowledge of effective reading and writing instructional practices
- Has an enthusiasm and love of children, which is at the heart of why they became a teacher in the first place
- Sees self as a lifelong learner
- Motivated to succeed and has a good work ethic
- Committed to working in urban and/or high-poverty school districts as a mission, not just a job

- Personable and has a positive attitude
- Is a change agent and effective with resistant adults

Q: As coaches from outside rather than inside a school system, what are some common positive and negative perceptions and situations the coaches report back to you as executive director of CLI?

A: Positive: Usually has more authority with teachers; has a good basis of comparison for good teaching; more knowledgeable about current best practices due to constant CLI training and supervision; less willing to adapt to mediocrity.

Negative: Some of the common comments we hear from our literacy coaches are

"Not enough time in any one school" and "Does not have easy access to the principal—to teach and encourage the principal to support good practices and build collegiality."

Many principals are not willing to do the work necessary to sustain any interventions. Teachers often think they are far better practitioners than they are and challenge the coaches to prove that there is more to learn and that their practice can be improved. Many schools think the work will be quick and easy and do not make the investment of time and money to get real results.

Q: When you contract with school districts, how do you provide professional development for administrators? For teachers? For other staff?

A: We start with an Institute to develop enough content knowledge around five important areas (classroom literacy environment, small-group instruction, reading aloud for comprehension and vocabulary development, writing, and Message Time Plus®). We follow up with coaching, grade-level meetings, and seminars as needed. We insist on our clients purchasing book collections to support the work we ask teachers to do.

Q: Do you think nonprofit organizations such as CLI will have a major role in coaching in the future?

A: Yes. There are too many (probably the majority) of teachers in classrooms today who don't know enough about teaching reading to be able to teach all children at high levels of achievement. The best way to reach those teachers is through professional development because teaching is a clinical profession. Just as doctors cannot learn everything needed at college and even medical school, excellent internships and continuing improvement at the work site are necessary.

Q: Do you have any other comments you would like to share with us about literacy coaching?

A: We would like to see higher standards for choosing, training, and supervising coaches. We think that schools [that seek to] hire the best teachers are not necessarily getting the best people or providing them with the training, structure, and materials they need to be successful. This will probably become a field that requires a special degree in the future, which is not necessarily the best solution. Those of us with a great deal of experience in the field need to be consulted about how to train and supervise coaches, what kinds of supports they need, and how to judge their effectiveness.

Source: Dr. Linda Katz, Executive Director of Children's Literacy Initiative, Philadelphia, PA.

SUMMARY

Situations were presented in which the literacy coach may interact with community members (parents of students in the school, parents of home-schooled students, government relations committees, nonprofit agencies). Suggestions were provided for working in each of the situations mentioned in the chapter. The importance of membership in professional organizations for both the literacy coach and all professional educators was stressed.

TOPIC EXTENSIONS FOR CLASS SESSIONS OR STUDY GROUPS

1. Refer to the scenario at the beginning of the chapter and discuss how the literacy coach could have ensured that Joanne (and any other student teachers) would know about the value of professional organizations before a faculty meeting late in the year. What can colleges and universities do to make sure that those embarking on teaching careers are aware of professional educational organizations? What would you tell someone entering the teaching profession about local, state, or national organizations?

2. Explore the Web sites for the professional organizations discussed in this chapter. What information can you find about the history of the organizations as well as their current focus? What Web sites are easy/difficult to maneuver? What links on the Web sites are valuable for a literacy coach?

Literacy Leadership **6**

INTRODUCTION

Lambert (2001) asserts that the core of leadership is about learning together and constructing meaning and knowledge collectively and collaboratively. The literacy coach, an informal rather than a formal leader in the school, plays a major role in helping three distinct groups learn together collectively and collaboratively: the teachers with whom the coach works closely, the students who are part of those teachers' classes, and the administrators who are accountable for curriculum and assessment. It is important that each of these groups accepts the literacy coach as a literacy leader. They also need to realize that they, too, are literacy leaders.

Literacy leadership cannot start and end with the literacy coach. The roles of central office administrators, principals, classroom teachers, and reading specialists are all crucial in promoting literacy skills and strategies of students. This chapter presents information on the interactions between the literacy coach and the building-level and central-office administrators with whom the coach will work.

SCENARIO

When her husband was transferred to a large city in the east, Charlene Martin and her family found their city home and schools quite different from their familiar surroundings in rural Iowa. Charlene, an experienced teacher of 22 years, had worked in both elementary and middle schools as a classroom teacher. The last six years of her career had been spent as a building reading specialist and supervisor of the summer reading and writing program for her school district.

Charlene, hoping to continue her teaching career, sought a teaching position in the city as soon as her family settled in their new home. Although her application stated that she preferred a classroom position or a reading specialist's position, Charlene was offered a position as a literacy coach in a large, diverse inner-city elementary school for students in kindergarten through sixth grade. Charlene's interview was impressive due to the combination of her experience, knowledge, personality, and social skills. The administrative team that interviewed her felt she would be excellent for the new position they had created for the upcoming school year of literacy coach for grades 4, 5, and 6.

Charlene happily accepted the position. It was a short bus ride from her home and just two miles from the high school her sons would attend. Although she was confident about her abilities and felt comfortable being both a leader and a learner in her new position, Charlene had some anxiety about the changes she would face moving from a rural to an inner-city school, working with English language learner (ELL) students, working with new teachers and administrators, and providing professional development sessions for the staff alone at times and copresenting with the literacy coach for the primary grades at other times.

THE LEADERSHIP ROLE

McAndrew (2005) posits that an effective leader capably juggles four roles simultaneously: direction setter, change agent (who encourages risk taking), spokesperson for the organization, and coach. He describes a coach as a team builder who passionately lives the vision and is accepted as a model and mentor. Simultaneously being a team builder, visionary, model, and mentor is a complicated matter. Leadership is complicated since it requires combining elements that do not necessarily fit together easily (Fullan, 2001). Whether serving in a formal leadership position, such as an administrative position (superintendents, curriculum directors, principals), or an informal leadership position, such as literacy coach, leadership responsibility in schools is challenging because it involves constant reflection and critical assessment of practices.

WORKING WITH SCHOOL ADMINISTRATORS

As a teacher in an informal leadership position, the literacy coach inevitably works for, and alongside, the administrative team. Professionalism and collegiality are just as important in interactions with administrators as in the interactions with teachers.

The literacy coach may be asked to attend district meetings with administrators. The meetings may involve overall district concerns that directly or indirectly impact the coach's responsibilities, such as meetings related to the use of technology in instruction, revising a standards-based report card, creating school and district Web sites, forming partnerships with local universities, and increasing parent involvement in the schools. As an active participant in the administrative meetings, the coach informs herself of district plans and initiatives. As a result, she becomes prepared to help teachers adapt to the changes as they filter down to individual classrooms.

Providing professional development for school administrators may be a required task for the literacy coach. Figure 6.1 lists three types of situations in which groups of administrators may need the expertise of the literacy coach. Examples are given for each of the situations.

The coach's interactions with administrators are typically not limited to meetings or other group situations. The coach frequently meets with administrators, especially the building principal, on an individual basis. The following sections address the collaborative nature of the work of the literacy coach when interacting with school administrators.

Principals Are Principal: Building-Level Administrators

A key administrator with whom the literacy coach will work closely is the principal. Both are literacy leaders. The role of the principal is "more important than ever," demanding a sophisticated set of skills

Figure 6.1   Professional Development for Administrators

Situations	Examples
Awareness sessions	• The literacy coach shares information about recent changes in state-mandated testing for particular grade levels. • The literacy coach shares a planned schedule of districtwide inservice sessions related to language arts instruction for the next two years.
Literacy program overview	• The literacy coach shares oral and written information about newly adopted texts, technology, and assessments for the school's reading program.
Explicit training	• The literacy coach demonstrates techniques that principals and administrators should be observing in classrooms. If guided reading instruction is endorsed by the district, the coach could demonstrate through role-play or types of actual guided reading instruction. The training would also include aspects of management, timing, note making, and types of materials used for guided reading.

(Lambert, 2001). The National Association of Elementary School Principals (2001) has published standards for what principals should know and practice to put student and staff learning at the center of their leadership. Meeting these standards can transform principals into literacy leaders. Setting focused goals based on teaching and learning and sharing responsibilities with faculty enables the principal to promote literacy learning (Jay & McGovern, 2006).

As a literacy leader, the principal is uniquely able to initiate and support the work of the literacy coach in the school. The principal needs to be involved in professional development that a literacy coach provides for the teachers (Wepner & Quatroche, 2002). When principals become knowledgeable about reading, they become even more supportive of the total school reading program. According to Jay and McGovern (2006), a "culture of informed collaboration promotes sound curricular decisions about literacy teaching and learning" (p. 52).

The principal must be able to create a professional learning community in the school. According to Fullan (2001), the principal does not simply foster greater learning capacity in the school, she must "cause" it. Fullan suggests that principals should strive to enhance skills and knowledge of teachers, create a common culture of expectations directly related to those skills and knowledge, nurture productive professional relationships among the teaching staff, and hold individuals accountable for their contributions to the collective result. Although Fullan is speaking of teaching and learning in all areas of the curriculum, we find his words closely aligned to the specific needs of literacy leadership within schools.

The principal whose leadership focuses on students' literacy development is able to analyze the research-practice connections in classrooms in terms of utility and development over time. The principal functions as an informed consumer of the research and as an inclusive learner in the professional development phases that are needed to promote quality teaching and learning of literacy skills in the school (Jay & McGovern, 2006). A strong, cohesive working relationship of the literacy coach and the principal is crucial in providing the leadership necessary to create conditions for ongoing professional learning as well as student learning

Central Office Administrators

School Boards

The local boards of school directors are important stakeholders in the school program. Wepner and Quatroche (2002) believe that they should be knowledgeable about what teachers are doing to further the district's goals for the reading program. School boards can support the reading program by making informed decisions about budgets, personnel, and curriculum. The literacy coach should be prepared to make presentations to school boards concerning these issues.

A resource of information for local school boards is the National School Boards Association (NSBA). It publishes a guidebook on adolescent literacy called *The Next Chapter: A School Board Guide to Improving Adolescent Literacy* that provides information on improving reading and writing instruction for middle and high school students. This guidebook can be downloaded for free from NSBA's Web site (www.nsba.org).

Curriculum Supervisors

Many current supervisory practices look primarily at curriculum and instruction: what the student is learning and how the student is learning it (Aseltine, Faryniarz, & Rigazio-DiGilio, 2006). The typical pattern of supervision and evaluation with teachers involves setting a new goal at the beginning of the year, classroom visitation throughout the year with feedback, and the supervisor's year-end evaluation report. All districts have a written plan for how teachers and other personnel will be supervised and evaluated.

The literacy coach is usually one of the faculty members that a reading and language arts supervisor oversees. Since the reading and language arts supervisor has an administrative function, the literacy coach may receive a yearly or biannual evaluation from this professional as well as from the principal. This type of evaluation is especially helpful to the literacy coach because it is content-specific.

However, even the Association for Supervision and Curriculum Development has published only a few books on supervision in the past 40 years (Radenich, 1995). Perhaps supervision's lack of a prominent place in the literature is due to the fact that the role needs more clear definition. Wepner (1989) blames this phenomenon on the fact that school budgets are smaller, federal spending has decreased, and new priorities in education have been established over the past 20 years.

Literacy coaches should regard the supervisor as a valuable partner in the development and progression of the reading program in the school. This partnership is critical to the continuing administrative support literacy coaches receive. To provide documentation of pertinent coaching responsibilities performed between one evaluation and the next, coaches should be prepared to relate information about their duties in a clear and succinct manner. Preparing a checklist of the key areas for which literacy coaches are responsible, as shown in Resource J, can be helpful. Confidences that the coach shares with classroom teachers should not be included as a part of this form or any communication that the coach provides for the supervisor. The form is intended as an overview of the work the coach has done and continues to do. Comments on the form should be brief phrases or bulleted statements. Using the form should help coaches generate a cogent verbal presentation to accompany the checklist. An example of a completed checklist as it pertains to Charlene Martin, the literacy coach from this chapter's scenario, is included in Resource K.

If the coach wishes to provide more detailed information related to the checklist, it may be helpful to include actual documents in a portfolio that is presented to the curriculum supervisor, especially if the meeting between the coach and supervisor occurs only biannually or annually.

Superintendents

As executive officers, superintendents shoulder the responsibility for school district programs and operations. In this role, they are under great stress and cannot always know the particular day-to-day workings of curriculum implementation or professional development. As the executive officer, the superintendent should be equipped with current information to make wise decisions. Sometimes, the literacy coach may need to keep the superintendent informed concerning relevant issues in the reading program.

McKenna and Walpole (2004) indicate that literacy coaches who share their information and knowledge with humility are more likely to be successful at creating positive relationships within the school district. Depending on both the size of the district and the superintendent's wishes, the literacy coach may have direct access to communicating with the superintendent in person or in writing. For example, in large urban districts that have regional superintendents in addition to the chief executive officer, it may be extremely difficult for the literacy coach to communicate directly with the superintendent. The literacy coach should then be cognizant of the line and staff organizations of the school district (Walpole & McKenna). The communication protocol may be particularly important if another central office administrator serves as the direct supervisor of the literacy coach. The supervisor may want all communication to the superintendent to be filtered through him before going, or instead of going, directly to the superintendent.

The literacy coach, like the superintendent and the principal, works more closely with adults than children. Effective communication among the adults within the school system is critical to maintaining a correct flow of information. The following modes of communication are suggested to make the information between the superintendent and the literacy coach flow smoothly.

Communicating in Person. The literacy coach may have several opportunities for direct professional communication with the superintendent. The opportunities may be planned or spontaneous. In either case, the literacy coach should present information as it relates to the well-being of the teaching and learning that occurs in the school.

Some interactions may occur in the following scenarios. First, the literacy coach may extend an invitation to the superintendent to participate in or observe a meeting. An invitation may include attending a districtwide or schoolwide professional development meeting or even a study group session. The superintendent may be able to stay for only part of the meeting, but the opportunity to learn firsthand what is happening in terms of professional development is very valuable. Also, the superintendent's attendance makes a strong statement to the teachers about the importance of their time and effort investments in professional development projects.

Second, the coach may be asked to give a presentation to a group other than teachers for which the superintendent is present. Such events may include school board meetings, principals' meetings, or parent workshops and information sessions. Sometimes, the coach may be asked to be an active member of a committee comprised of both school district personnel and community members. It is likely that the superintendent is either a regular or occasional member of such a committee. These venues give the superintendent another view of the work of the literacy coach and the impact of coaching on the school and community.

Third, the coach and the superintendent may meet by chance in the school or in the administration building. The coach may be able to share some information about alignment of curriculum and assessment or the collaborative relationships that exist between the coach and the teachers. Although chance encounters may be brief, they are another opportunity for the literacy coach to keep the superintendent informed about the advances coaching has facilitated within the district.

Communicating in Writing. Perhaps the literacy coach has no opportunities for direct personal communication with the superintendent. Written communication can provide important information that the superintendent may indeed want to have but may not have the time to acquire in person. Written communication could include newsletters that contain items submitted by the coach. Materials from meetings should also be sent to the superintendent to keep her abreast of professional development; these may include agendas, journal articles shared with teachers, and information about programs being considered for district adoption. E-mail is another form of written communication. However, messages should be sent judiciously to ensure that they will be read rather than discarded because of frequency and lack of substance.

In their leadership role, literacy coaches not only support administrators, but they can attempt to move superintendents and other administrators toward democratic leadership (McAndrew, 2005). Because the superintendent is not in the daily view of the teaching staff, misperceptions can occur. The literacy coach, who is one of the school members closest to the teachers, can help alleviate some of these misperceptions.

AN EXPERT'S THOUGHTS: DR. KEN KOCZUR

Ken Koczur is the superintendent of Pine Hill School District in southern New Jersey. He has been an educational administrator for nine years. His interview about the role of the literacy coach from a superintendent's perspective offers insights on funding for literacy coaches and communication between coaches and administrators. Dr. Koczur's comments are made in conjunction with two members of his administrative team: the curriculum coordinator and basic skills specialist.

Q: Do you think literacy coaching is here to stay and will remain a long-term professional development venue in America's schools? Why or why not?

A: Literacy coaching will remain so long as it is effective in producing results. In order for this to occur, though, it must be properly implemented and fully funded by the federal government.

The responsibilities of the literacy coach should include: serving as a resource and consultant to teachers for effective reading and writing, coordinating the reading program, contributing to the assessment of reading ability of individual students and structuring intervention programs, proactively providing professional development and training aimed at improving the quality of classroom instruction for reading and writing.

Q: In your visits to schools, who do you see coaching classroom teachers besides those designated as "literacy coaches" or "reading coaches"?

A: In the Pine Hill School District, principals, curriculum coordinators, consultants, and teachers themselves also serve as coaches for classroom teachers in need of literacy training. Additionally, the district offers a summer course for any teacher desiring to improve his or her teaching skills.

Q: What should those in leadership positions know about literacy coaching? What should they expect from it?

A: At the local, state, and federal level, those in leadership positions need to be aware of the investment that is needed for the implementation of an effective literacy coaching program. This includes adequate funding for the ongoing training of literacy coaches and teachers. From this, our leaders may expect results that reveal an increase in literacy among the nation's public school students.

Q: What suggestions do you have for literacy coaches when interacting and reporting to administrators?

A: The literacy coach needs to clarify the requirements of the program and update the administration team regularly on student progress. However, it is important that all parties involved (including the teachers) understand that the literacy coach is not to formally evaluate the teachers or even informally report to the administration team on any teacher's progression with the program. A classroom teacher needs to feel comfortable enough with the literacy coach to reveal any areas of weakness in his/her teaching. In doing so, the teacher will be much more open to suggestions offered by the literacy coach on ways to improve.

Q: If districts are fortunate enough to have literacy coaching, do you feel the coaches should focus on a particular level (e.g., elementary, middle, or high school), or do you feel the coaches should be assigned across the grades?

A: Designating literacy coaches to the specific grade spans of primary, intermediary, and secondary would be the most effective approach for successful implementation. The various differences among these three age groups require a literacy coach with specific knowledge and experience of their unique needs. However, articulation meetings among the literacy coaches should occur regularly so as to maintain continuity in the program.

Q: Are there any other comments you would like to make about literacy coaching?

A: All aspects of a child's education are dependent upon his/her level of literacy. However, not all students arrive at the school's front door with the same level of literacy preparation/support from their homes. Therefore, to assume that additional literacy support is not needed in public education today only serves to further divide Americans into the *haves* and *have-nots*.

Source: Dr. Ken Koczur, Superintendent, Pine Hill School District, NJ.

SUMMARY

This chapter focused on the synergy that needs to exist among those in leadership positions that influence the advancement of literacy within schools. Several administrative roles were discussed. An interview with a district superintendent was included to offer an administrator's perspective. The collaborative role of the literacy coach in working with administrative leaders and teacher leaders was emphasized.

TOPIC EXTENSIONS FOR CLASS SESSIONS OR STUDY GROUPS

1. Prepare a presentation to a local school board concerning a budget for new reading curriculum in your district. What would you want to know about the members of the school board as you prepare for the presentation?

2. Discuss how, as a literacy coach, you would attempt to keep the superintendent of schools informed about the accomplishments of the work you and teachers are doing in your school. Discuss what you would do to keep the principal informed as well.

RESOURCE J: CHECKLIST FOR LITERACY COACH'S SCHEDULED MEETING WITH SUPERVISOR (BLANK)

Literacy Coach: _____

Date of Meeting: _____

Part A: Coaching of Classroom Teachers: Areas of Coaching Focus

Coaching Focus (Check the areas that apply and indicate the associated grade levels):

___ specific comprehension strategy(ies)
___ questioning techniques
___ word identification strategy(ies)
___ vocabulary instruction
___ guided reading group(s)
___ spelling instruction
___ content area strategy(ies)
___ study skills
___ physical room arrangement
___ instructional transitions

___ specific writing strategy (ies)
___ phonics instruction
___ fluency instruction
___ spelling instruction
___ guided writing group(s)
___ use of reading materials/ programs
___ classroom management
___ pacing of instruction
___ other:

Date	Grade/Department	Focused Outcomes

Part B: Collaboration With Reading Specialists

Collaboration	Dates	Focused Outcomes
___ review of assessment data		
___ reading program and/or materials issues		
___ planning presentations or workshops		
___ use of paraprofessionals		
___ other:		

Part C: Collaboration With Principal

Collaboration	Dates	Focused Outcomes
___ review of assessment data		
___ reading program and/or materials issues		
___ inservice needs		
___ grade level/department issues		
___ other:		

Part D: Professional Development Within the School

Professional Development	Dates	Description
1. Made additions to library collection of professional journals, books, CDs, etc.		
2. Provided links to Web sites.		
3. Placed journal articles in teachers' mail boxes.		
4. Made teachers aware of local, regional, and state conferences via brochures or links to online information.		
5. Facilitated/participated in study group: topic _____		
6. Facilitated/participated in book club: book _____		
7. Presentations, inservice: topic _____		
8. Arranged for teachers to observe each other (within school or in another school).		
9. Arranged for videotaping of teachers for self-reflection.		
10. Other:		

Part E: Log of Meetings*

	Dates	*Focus*
Principal		
Reading Specialist(s)		
Grade-Level/Department		
Classroom Teachers		
Parents		
Other:		

*A brief description rather than a detailed list or outline should be noted here for sharing at the meeting.

RESOURCE K: CHECKLIST FOR LITERACY COACH'S SCHEDULED MEETING WITH SUPERVISOR (COMPLETED)

Literacy Coach: <u>Charlene Martin</u>

Date of Meeting: <u>January 1</u>

Part A: Coaching of Classroom Teachers: Areas of Coaching Focus

Coaching Focus (Check the areas that apply and indicate the associated grade levels):

___ specific comprehension strategy(ies)

___ questioning techniques

___ word identification strategy(ies)

√ vocabulary instruction **(4 & 5)**

√ guided reading group(s) **(3, 4, 5)**

___ spelling instruction

___ content area strategy(ies)

___ study skills

___ physical room arrangement

___ instructional transitions

√ specific writing strategy(ies) **(K)**

___ phonics instruction

___ fluency instruction

___ spelling instruction

√ guided writing group(s) **(3)**

___ use of reading materials/ programs

___ classroom management

√ pacing of instruction **(K)**

___ other:

Date	Grade/Department	Focused Outcomes
11/1, 11/3, 11/8, 11/10	Gr. 3, all teachers	Guided reading groups alternately taught by classroom teachers and reading specialists.
Often: Oct. through Dec.	Kindergarten	Teacher using word wall more effectively to encourage students' writing. Teacher allowing more time for students' actual writing.
12/2–12/15	Grade 5	Demonstrated and later observed vocabulary lessons based on recent inservice suggestions.
11/15–11/24	Gr. 3, 1 teacher	Observed classroom teacher providing guided reading instruction and gave feedback.

Part B: Collaboration With Reading Specialists

Collaboration	Dates	Focused Outcomes
√ review of assessment data	12/12	Regrouping of students for small-group instruction
___ reading program and/or materials issues		
√ planning presentations or workshops	11/6	Planned parent workshop for 11/17
___ use of paraprofessionals		
___ other		

Part C: Collaboration With Principal

Collaboration	Dates	Focused Outcomes
√ review of assessment data	12/11 and 12/12	Follow-up with reading specialists
___ reading program and/or materials issues		
√ inservice needs	Regular weekly meetings	(1) guided reading; (2) vocabulary instruction
___ grade-level/ department issues		
___ other		

Part D: Professional Development Within the School

Professional Development	Dates	Description
1. Made additions to library collection of professional journals, books, CDs, etc.		
2. Provided links to Web sites.		
3. Placed journal articles in teachers' mailboxes.	Oct, Nov, Dec, Jan	One article per month (see portfolio)
4. Made teachers aware of local, regional, and state conferences via brochures or links to online information.	Oct. 1	State Reading Conference Oct. 21–24

Professional Development	Dates	Description
5. Facilitated/participated in study group: topic <u>Guided Reading Instruction</u>	Oct. 8, 15, and 22 Nov. 5, 12, and 19	4th- & 5th-grade teachers participated weekly in afterschool meetings.
6. Facilitated/participated in book club: book _____		
7. Presentations, inservice: topic <u>3 different topics</u>	Oct. 17 Oct. 23 Nov. 8	Parent Workshop Presentation at State Conf. Vocabulary (Gr. 4 & 5)
8. Arranged for teachers to observe each other (within school or in another school).		
9. Arranged for videotaping of teachers for self-reflection.		
10. Other:		

Part E: Log of Meetings*

	Dates	Focus
Principal	Every Tuesday afternoon in Oct., Nov., Dec., Jan.	Student assessment; coaching updates
Reading Specialist(s)	Bimonthly (Wednesday afternoons)	Small-group instruction (pullout and in-class)
Grade-Level/ Department	Grade 3 11/1, 11/3, 11/8, 11/10	Guided reading
Classroom Teachers	Various	Individual coaching plans (see portfolio)
Parents	N/A	
Other:	N/A	

*A brief description rather than a detailed list or outline should be noted here for sharing at the meeting.

Collaboration With **7**
Classroom Teachers

INTRODUCTION

Teaching is a dynamic process, and there is no fail-safe method of preparation or training to ensure continuous smooth sailing throughout one's teaching career. It seems likely that all teachers, novices as well as veterans, will struggle with some aspect of life in the classroom during their careers as various difficulties arise.

Literacy coaches are expected to be knowledgeable about the reading and writing processes and the content of the curriculum. The coaching experience involves assisting teachers who struggle with process or content to gain strength and stability in instructional techniques.

Another reality of coaching arises when the literacy coach encounters a teacher who is noncompliant with the coaching process. However, the literacy coach needs to have a positive approach when working with both the struggling teacher and the noncompliant teacher. A positive approach will effect positive change in the individual teacher's instructional techniques and professional demeanor.

This chapter describes the importance of the role of the coach as collaborator when interacting with teachers who struggle and teachers who may be noncompliant.

SCENARIO

Nancy Brennan has been the literacy coach at Thomas Jefferson High School for four years, working with each of the departments throughout the school. Her peers, the principal, students, and parents respect her. Nancy is always professional and personable and is generally perceived as helpful and trusting.

Recently, two situations surfaced that were challenging experiences for Nancy. In the first situation, Nancy became aware that Ms. Shallis, a tenth-grade English teacher, was struggling not only with lesson planning and implementation but also with management of her classes. Nancy had observed and coached in Ms. Shallis's classroom last year when Miss Shallis was a second-year teacher at Thomas Jefferson and taught ninth-grade English. The coach and the teacher worked well together all last year. With the start of the current school year, Nancy again noticed the difficulty this teacher was experiencing. Nancy spoke with Ms. Shallis, and they established times to meet and times for Nancy to observe.

In another situation, Nancy was surprised to observe Mr. Maenner, a member of the social studies department, intently reading the newspaper during an inservice she was conducting for his department. As a follow-up to the training, Nancy scheduled both observations and demonstration lessons for each of the seven social studies teachers. When Nancy arrived in Mr. Maenner's class for the observation, the students were independently reviewing study guides for their next test as the teacher worked at his computer. The teacher-student interaction that Nancy expected to see because of the planned observation did not occur. When Nancy arrived in Mr. Maenner's class the following week to conduct a scheduled demonstration lesson, she found a substitute teacher in the classroom that day.

Nancy felt hopeful about the first situation, frustrated about the second. How could Nancy work effectively with both of these situations?

COACHING THE STRUGGLING TEACHER

All teachers receive training in teacher education courses in college and, especially, in field experiences and student teaching. Although training can help prepare teachers for the complex, multifaceted life of the classroom, it seems likely that at one time or another, all teachers struggle with some aspect of their work. Some of the areas in which teachers have difficulties include management, curriculum, and pedagogy (Glickman, Calhoun, & Roberts, 1993; Snyder, 1993). The literacy coach may become aware of a struggling teacher's dilemma, whether minimal or huge, when the coach observes the teacher at work in the classroom or when the coach observes and interacts with the teacher as part of a professional development session. Part of the collaborative role of the literacy coach involves helping the struggling teacher overcome the area of challenge.

Struggling With Classroom Management

When a teacher has difficulty orchestrating literacy activities in the classroom, the teacher is struggling with classroom management. The untrained eye may scan a classroom in which the teacher is working directly with a small group of children as the majority of children purposefully engage in literacy centers or independent reading and consider it an organized situation because things are going smoothly. The untrained eye may think that the activities were easy to plan and implement. However, the trained eye may scan the same classroom with professional appreciation, realizing that the carefully planned and well-managed implementation of the various worthy activities occurred simultaneously in the teacher's classroom.

Whole-Class Versus Small-Group Instruction

During whole-class instruction, the teacher facilitates learning while interacting with the entire class engaged in the same literacy activity. The teacher observes the class for attention and participation and monitors students for understanding. However, whole-class instruction will not always be the preferred mode of instruction. Small-group instruction is appropriate when some students need explicit instruction and more careful monitoring by the teacher. During small-group instruction, the teacher facilitates learning by interacting with a small portion of the class while the majority of the class is engaged in literacy practice activity. According to Fountas and Pinnell (1996), conducting focused yet interrupted small-group instruction may present management challenges to teachers.

Small-group literacy instruction may include guided reading, guided writing, or reading or writing workshops. Workshops consist of a significant block of time for independent whole-class and small-group literacy activities. During workshops, students work independently and in groups at their instructional levels (Morrow, 2003). The teacher works with several groups and individuals during workshop time.

Small-group instruction may be conducted for 20 to 30 minutes per group. The groups may be as small as pairs or triads and generally do not consist of more than six students. The group size is purposeful so that the teacher can focus on the students' skill and strategy use (or misuse), make notes about the students' responses and miscues, and provide useful feedback to the students. If time allows, the teacher might convene a second small group during a class period. The first small group would become part of the majority of students, involved with practice activities, and the second group would become the focus group for the teacher.

The key to good management during guided lessons and workshops is ensuring that all students know their task and behavior responsibilities. These responsibilities need to be clearly taught and explicitly modeled for children so that when the teacher and small group separate from the whole group, on-task independent or interdependent work can be started and completed without interruption to the small group. If the children are to complete tasks in a specific order, the teacher should post a list of the tasks on the board or overhead. This reminder should help those who are off-task or who complete one or two tasks and then forget what to do next, without disturbing the teacher for further directions. Although the reminder is useful throughout the grades, elementary teachers will find this technique of reminding students especially helpful.

When teachers struggle with classroom management during small-group instructional sessions, the observant, collaborative coach should recommend management tips to teachers. The recommendations can be offered when the coach and teacher have an opportunity to meet after the coach's observation in the classroom. Figure 7.1 provides several suggestions that the coach can offer the teacher to improve classroom management when students are engaged in various literacy activities.

The suggestions in Figure 7.1 are not meant to be a complete "fix-it" list for the teacher struggling with classroom management. The literacy coach who observes a struggling teacher needs to pinpoint the exact reason management issues arise for this teacher. Additional causes of why teachers struggle with classroom management are discussed below.

Room Arrangement

Sometimes room arrangement could be causing classroom management problems for the teacher (Morrow, 2003). For example, suppose the teacher assigns the class the task of finding and summarizing two magazine articles related to a current topic of study. After she asks the small group of students to join her at the table, 18 students rise from their seats to go to a basket of magazines on the windowsill. The space is too small for the number of students, and most of them cannot reach the magazines. Voices can be heard across the room, and some furniture is displaced so students can get near the materials. Students complain to each other and to the teacher about the situation. There are at least three solutions to this problem: (1) rearrange the room so that there is more space for children to move in the required area, (2) put the basket in a more accessible place, or (3) remove the magazines from the basket and place them in two or more areas in the room.

Pacing

Pacing may also cause disharmony in a classroom involved with differentiated groups. Sometimes, the teacher allows too little time for

Figure 7.1   Suggestions for Helping the Teacher Who Struggles With Classroom Management

	Small Group (With Teacher)	*Large Group (Without Teacher)*
Materials	Have students' specific reading or writing materials, teacher's materials (visual aids, note-making form) at table where small group will work. Have materials that students need at various times during small-group work in nearby containers for easy access (pencils, markers, sticky notes, bookmarks, whiteboards, index cards, paper, tape recorder, etc.). Have an easel, whiteboard, or chalkboard in easy view of the children and within easy reach of the teacher. The teacher could use these materials to jot down phonic clues or vocabulary words or create semantic webs, list predictions, etc.	Have consumable materials that students need at various times during independent or group work in labeled containers for easy access (pencils, markers, sticky notes, bookmarks, whiteboards, index cards, paper).
Directions	Directions for small-group work should be specific. The teacher should give clear, concise directions so that the majority of time is spent with student engagement on-task, not teacher direction and redirection. General directions should be reviewed daily. It is helpful to have a list of general directions posted at the small-group work area for quick review.	Review general directions before each session. Keep a posting of general directions displayed in clear view for reference. Appoint one student to whom others may turn for clarification of directions about specific tasks. The appointee may be the Captain, Ambassador or Helper of the Day. Keeping a flag or sign at the student's desk will help others to recognize the designated student.
Students	Ensure that students handle materials within their own space at the table. This will help to avoid conflict among students.	Ensure that students know how many students are permitted to work with shared materials (computers, reference materials, etc.) at one time.
Resources	Professional books, journals, and Web sites that provide further information for the teacher to peruse independently or in collaboration with the coach could be suggested.	Professional books, journals, and Web sites that provide further information for the teacher to peruse independently or in collaboration with the coach could be suggested.

students to complete the work they are expected to do without direct supervision from the teacher (Evertson, Emmer, & Worsham, 2003). In other instances, the teacher allows too much time; the students may finish their work and then be unsure about the next steps. Both pacing situations can be problematic for the teacher working with a small group and trying to manage the rest of the class. The goal is to have children involved with quality literacy activities for the full time allotted. Wasted time disallows viable practice for students and causes management concerns for teachers. The coach needs to be cognizant of the time and task alignment for students as she observes in the classroom. If pacing is the issue, the coach can and should address that with the teacher.

Tasks

Task issues may also become evident classroom management challenges. Independent and interdependent tasks should be planned as practice activities for students. Familiar tasks (reading at independent levels, writing at independent levels, using software to review skills, or reviewing spelling or vocabulary with a peer) should afford the students time to practice skills. If assigned tasks are problematic because they are either unclear to students or too easy or too hard for students, the coach must surely discuss task issues with the struggling teacher to help him align time-task responsibilities for his students. The teacher who struggles with setting appropriate tasks may depend on the literacy coach to help select and assign tasks that are clear and valuable for the students. This situation provides an opportunity for the coach to revisit the classroom to demonstrate how to provide clear directions for worthy tasks.

Struggling With Curriculum

Some teachers struggle with curriculum because they are learning it themselves. Teachers first learn the curriculum when hired for an initial teaching position or when they change grade-level assignments or schools. Becoming familiar with required curriculum demands knowing more than the content of the curriculum or what is to be taught. It also involves knowing the standards to which the curriculum is aligned and what major evaluations and minor assessments are included in curriculum requirements. In this chapter's scenario, Ms. Shallis struggled with the high school English curriculum when she moved from ninth to tenth grade. Since she had no difficulty with curriculum while teaching ninth grade, we may assume that she had taught the grade for more than one year, received training or mentoring from experts within her district, and maintained good classroom management as a ninth-grade teacher. The new grade assignment requires that she know the content of the tenth-grade curriculum, especially the texts the students will be required to read. In addition, Ms. Shallis will have to create assignments related to the students' readings or incorporate assignments that are mandated by the district.

Considering Standards

Some teachers may struggle with curriculum when they neglect to consider standards that are specific to the curriculum areas in which they teach. Aligning standards with curriculum helps teachers focus instruction on the major goals of what is to be taught and learned (Biancarosa & Snow, 2004).

For example, in a certain state, one common language arts standard is designed to promote independent reading as part of the regular curriculum. A sixth-grade teacher may be accomplished at providing instruction that involves students' silent reading during the instructional time frame. The teacher may form the misconception that silent instructional reading is equivalent to independent reading. Consequently, instructional reading may be the only structure used for reading in that teacher's classroom.

Instructional reading is not the same as independent reading. Instructional reading takes place when the teacher guides and monitors the students' proficiency with text. Instructional reading levels are generally above independent reading levels. In contrast, independent reading is self-selected reading done at an independent comfort level, usually an easier level than the instructional level. When students do independent reading in school, they are accountable for logging what is read and for periodically conferring with the teacher about their reading. If the teacher does not realize this difference, independent reading may be neglected, and the standard for independent reading will not be met.

When the literacy coach is aware of an absence of alignment with standards in a particular classroom, a coaching intervention should take place. Collaboration with the teacher may involve discussing standards and explaining how curriculum and assessment are aligned to the standards. It may also involve demonstration teaching over time. After each demonstration, the teacher and coach can process why certain instructional methods were used and how the methods link curriculum and standards together.

The literacy coach can be of assistance to the teacher who struggles with the curriculum in several ways. First, the coach can make an appointment to review the district's curriculum manual with the teacher.

This document should at least outline the focus areas of teaching and assessment for each grade level. For example, if the tenth-grade writing curriculum emphasizes persuasive writing, it is very important that the teacher new to the grade level knows about the focus on this particular mode of writing. Of course, it will be more helpful to both the teacher and the students if the teacher is aware of curriculum focus at the beginning of the school year.

Second, the coach can help secure a mentor for the teacher if none has been provided or mandated by the school. For example, a veteran with six years teaching experience of tenth-grade English could certainly be an excellent resource person for Ms. Shallis, the teacher in the scenario at the beginning of this chapter.

Third, the coach and the struggling teacher could meet regularly to review curriculum mandates and options. They might also review curriculum standards. These meetings should help the teacher feel less isolated in decision making.

In each of these areas of assistance, the literacy coach is both a collaborator and a facilitator. The coach collaborates as a colleague who provides assistance and encouragement to the struggling teacher. The coach facilitates as a leader who helps the teacher recognize curriculum responsibilities. Curricula are often state-mandated and board-adopted. As a coach, one must ensure that teachers adhere to established curriculum guidelines. There are also two significant venues of assistance that cannot be overlooked when a teacher struggles with curriculum: participating in district-conducted professional development sessions and networking with other teachers in the same school or at the same grade level.

Knowing what to teach does not necessarily ensure knowing how to teach. The problem of struggling with the curriculum may or may not be accompanied by management and pedagogy issues as well. If management issues are evident as the teacher struggles with curriculum, the coach may refer to the suggestions in the preceding section. Demonstration teaching by the coach may help to alleviate the combination of difficulties the teacher is experiencing.

Bird Walking

Although well-intentioned, some teachers may stray from the curriculum by introducing several tangential areas of consideration to the students. This reversion from the curriculum becomes problematic when the topics take on a life of their own rather than making clear, focused connections to the curriculum being studied. Unfortunately, more classroom time becomes devoted to the overt topic rather than to the designated curriculum.

"Bird walking" is distinguishable from curricular connections when the tangential topic becomes dominant and the curricular topic becomes minor. For example, when reading a piece of literature related to Chinese culture, the teacher may ask either an expert or a person who is a recent visitor to China address the class. The teacher might also arrange a visit to a museum to provide a firsthand experience with artifacts related to the culture the students are studying. The teacher facilitates discussion with the class about these experiences and perhaps assigns response activities to them. These experiences are valuable in terms of both content and time because they will help students make text-to-world connections (Keene & Zimmerman, 2007). The experiences are directly related to the theme of the text the students have read.

On the other hand, a bird-walking situation would occur if the teacher spent an inordinate amount of time exploring Chinese culture to the detriment of other required areas of the curriculum. The literacy coach's intervention should help the teacher understand that guidelines and time lines are in place to help teachers meet curricular requirements.

Struggling With Pedagogy

Each teacher brings his own personality and teaching style to the classroom. The teacher's personality and pedagogy are major factors that contribute to the culture of the classroom. Ideally, a respectful culture that encourages risk taking and honors both process and product is the result of sound pedagogy. College methods courses help preservice teachers learn about pedagogy. Inservice teachers continue to learn about pedagogy throughout their careers.

The pedagogy that the teacher uses in the classroom should help the students understand what they are learning, why they are learning it, and how they learn most effectively. According to Marzano and Marzano (2003), effective classroom management is key to student achievement. In addition, teachers need to use strategies supported by research to influence teacher-student interactions positively and support student learning.

Pedagogy does not consist solely of questioning students. Good pedagogical techniques consist of modeling, demonstrating, or explaining learning tasks and strategies before guiding students to engage in the tasks. Guiding students connotes teacher assistance and intervention as needed. It can involve reteaching or re-explanation. The final step of using sound pedagogy is monitoring and assessing students' work. The final step is taken as students engage in the independent application of the task or strategy. The teacher's analysis of the information gained during the final step generates crucial information for subsequent instruction: what needs to be reviewed or retaught, what needs to be enriched, and what students should be placed in small groups for guided instruction.

Teachers may struggle with pedagogy due to one of the following reasons:

- Teacher modeling, demonstrating, or explaining is insufficient or omitted.
- Students' guided practice is insufficient.
- Students' guided practice is omitted, and independent application of literacy task or strategy is expected at a level of proficiency.
- The teacher neglects to assess student level of skill and moves forward with instruction even though student readiness is lacking.
- The teacher inaccurately assesses student level or skill and reviews or reteaches material excessively, delaying the students' opportunity to move forward with their learning.
- The teacher's pedagogy consists only of question-and-answer interaction. No dialogue about process or reasoning is evident in the interaction.

By observing in the classroom, the literacy coach gains awareness of teachers who struggle with pedagogy. The coach also gains awareness during professional development sessions by listening to teachers' oral comments or by reading journal entries or other written statements. This feedback provides data for the coach regarding the teachers' self-perceptions of difficulties during instruction. Of course, after gaining awareness of why teachers struggle, the coach needs to establish a plan to help them overcome weak pedagogical practices. Examples of gaining awareness from both oral and written modes follow.

Observing Teachers Struggling With Pedagogy

A coach assigned to the primary grades of an elementary school has been fortunate to observe quality teaching in most of the classrooms for which she has coaching responsibilities. However, the coach is concerned about one second-grade teacher's style of pedagogy. After several observations, the coach has consistently observed the same style: the teacher speaks to the whole class in an oral cloze manner. That is, he makes incomplete statements, leaving off the final word or phrase, and expects the class to complete the statement in unison. After the children give a response (or varied responses), the teacher repeats the "correct" expected response. This is the only pedagogical style the coach has observed after multiple visits to this second-grade classroom. The coach has several concerns about the pedagogy that this second-grade teacher uses: developmental inappropriateness, lack of change of pace, grouping, and response technique. The literacy coach recognizes an absence of actual instruction in this classroom.

Now that the coach has a clear picture of how this teacher is struggling with pedagogy, she needs to have a plan in mind as she prepares to meet with the teacher about steps to strengthen pedagogical practices. The steps include meeting with the teacher to set some goals for instructional improvement, providing some demonstration teaching in the class, and arranging for the teacher to observe in several other second-grade classrooms throughout the district. Enacting these steps allows the coach to assist the teacher. Multiple steps are needed since the teacher's pedagogy is characterized by several weaknesses. Continuing to work with this teacher over the course of the year (and even beyond that if warranted) is central to the coaching plan. In this role, the coach is both collaborating with the teacher and facilitating action steps.

Responding to Teachers' Feedback About Struggling With Pedagogy

After conducting a professional development session for seventh-grade teachers, the literacy coach asked the participating teachers to write comments on two sticky notes. She asked them to note a teaching method that they were using in the classroom with which they felt very comfortable on a yellow note. Teachers used a pink note to write about another technique about which they had questions. After reviewing the comments and sorting them by likeness, the coach noticed that several pink notes had similar comments. The four pink notes held the following comments:

1. I feel as though I model strategies for the students, but there is always some question about the strategy. How can I make sure I am doing a thorough job with the modeling?

2. Most of the explanations I give the students seem to be either incomplete or ambiguous. What can I do to choose words more carefully and be clear about what I'm attempting to explain?

3. Is modeling really necessary? After all, these kids are in seventh grade now.

4. I introduced using a time line on Monday, and by Wednesday several of the students were confused and frustrated with it. What can be done to help students remember steps and be successful?

The four statements are similar because they all deal with the introductory part of a lesson in which teachers model, explain, or use examples. Sorting the teachers' written responses helps the coach recognize concerns the teachers share about their instruction. These comments provide important data for the literacy coach. The coach can use the notes to plan topics for future professional development sessions and to reflect on the work that has been done so far with the teachers.

Whether observing or responding to teachers who struggle with pedagogy, the literacy coach should determine which of the following steps will lead to an effective action plan: (1) observing the teacher(s) several times during instruction, (2) having the teacher(s) observe the coach conducting demonstration lessons several times, (3) videotaping lessons and considering using full or partial segments of tapes to help teachers overcome their areas of challenge, (4) convening professional development sessions for teachers working in a particular grade level or department, or (5) involving others, such as reading specialists and consultants, in helping to improve identified areas of need.

COACHING THE NONCOMPLIANT TEACHER

Teachers, like other professionals, are constantly learning new techniques and acquiring information to help them refine their craft. Professional development is both an expectation and a requirement for those in professional settings. A good classroom teacher should embrace the time and effort needed to be an active participant in professional development. Then she should willingly implement the learned techniques and strategies in the classroom as important components of self-learning. The literacy coach's role in professional development involves a focus on continuous improvement in student achievement. According to Goleman (2000), the coach helps other professionals develop and invests in their capacity building. Capacity building within a staff is necessary for long-term improvements (Taylor & Gunter, 2006).

Ideally, all teachers will be accepting, active participants in professional development. According to Danielson (1996), professional responsibilities associated with being an educator include roles both within and outside the classroom. Danielson identifies some of the components of professional responsibility as reflecting on teaching, growing and developing professionally, and showing professionalism. Active participation in professional development typically involves all three of these components. Teachers who are active learners will certainly reflect on their own practice as well as on their students' responses to learning.

With the coach's encouragement, teachers realize that they will develop pedagogical skills over time. They will perform their duties professionally and exhibit professionalism in all school-related venues in and out of the classroom.

Since the literacy coach is responsible for either conducting professional development sessions or securing consultants and specialists to provide the sessions, the coach should hold firmly the expectation for all teachers to meet their professional responsibilities. The coach must be familiar with what needs to be conveyed to the teachers during professional development sessions and what teachers should be expected to do with the new information once they are back in their classrooms. According to Taylor and Gunter (2006), evidence of positive professional learning includes teachers' discussing ways of improving individual and group performance at their professional development meetings. In most cases, the coach will recognize which teachers meet their professional responsibilities regarding professional development.

Realistically, a few teachers may show nonaccepting reactions and inactive participation during professional development. Teachers' negative reactions to professional development are usually caused by either a level of discomfort with what is being taught or by an intransigent attitude toward any changes the training may require of them. This noncompliant teacher behavior may be observed during a professional development session. For example, the literacy coach may observe a teacher grading papers, reading a novel, or chatting on the cell phone. Fortunately, such exhibitions rarely occur, but the examples given here are from actual experiences.

Some noncompliance will not be obvious but may be covert and difficult to detect. In a few cases, noncompliance cannot be observed during professional training but will become evident during subsequent observations in the classroom or in discussions with teachers after professional development. Perhaps the literacy coach observes a teacher actively participating in a training session but later finds out that the teacher did not institute the training in the classroom.

It is important for the literacy coach to remain positive when addressing issues of teachers' noncompliance with professional development. Teachers may pose questions related to philosophy or rationale of a topic that is new or different as the topic is being presented to them. When a change is presented or mandated, "emotions frequently run high" (Fullan, 2001, p. 74). Teachers' questions should be accepted, and answers should be clearly and professionally explained. According to Fullan, respectful treatment of those with a resistive or noncompliant stance is essential to appreciate situations of diversity or complexity with which they are faced. When teachers fully understand why training is being conducted, what purposes and results are expected from the training, and how to implement what they have learned in their own classrooms, they are more likely to accept the new training and to feel professionally valued themselves.

Noncompliance Due to Discomfort

Noncompliance may be either passive or aggressive. Sometimes, professionals are noncompliant with an initiative or a mandate because they feel discomfort with the new task placed before them. There is a common saying among teachers that responsibilities are often added on to what teachers have to do but little or nothing is taken away. Classroom teachers may feel discomfort with changes in curriculum, assessment, or record keeping. When accustomed practices in these areas are disrupted, teachers can feel stressed. Additionally, the implementation of a time line to institute the change may cause more discomfort.

When the teacher is required to institute a change, she is sometimes assigned to work with a peer. This may cause an uncomfortable situation for the teacher. For example, after one session of training on using the computer to create a personal Web page, a veteran teacher may be paired with a younger teacher. The younger teacher is used to working on the computer and is familiar with creating Web pages. On the other hand, the veteran teacher has no computer at home and uses her classroom computer only to create newsletters and worksheets for her class. The veteran teacher would prefer to work alone, reviewing her carefully written notes at her own convenience. She feels uncomfortable with the peer learning situation, since the younger teacher has more background knowledge about the topic and talks and works quickly when they are together.

Conversely, many people may feel a sense of comfort when being assigned to work with a peer. Another veteran teacher may consider working with a younger peer to be very helpful. This veteran teacher is glad that the other teacher can assist him in a nonthreatening manner.

Whatever the area of discomfort, the literacy coach's supportive stance may be the first step in helping the teacher transition from discomfort to comfort and, eventually, from noncompliance to compliance. The literacy coach should reflect on the following questions for assisting the noncompliant teacher who expresses or demonstrates discomfort as the source of noncompliance:

- Can my one-to-one assistance with this teacher be effective for overcoming the particular area of discomfort?
- Might someone else be able to provide support to this teacher as she adjusts to the new task/mandate? If so, should I solicit another's

help for the teacher or ask the teacher whom he would like to have help him?

- Do I detect the teacher's willingness to accept help and to accept the new task/mandate?
- Is this the first time the teacher has been noncompliant? If so, why is this particular issue so upsetting to the teacher?
- Has this teacher been noncompliant in the past? If so, what seems to help this teacher move forward positively when new tasks are given?
- If the teacher remains noncompliant, what steps will I need to take to ensure that she meets the required professional responsibilities?

The collaborative literacy coach can do much to help the teacher who experiences discomfort from a change or an added job requirement. If a teacher feels overwhelmed, the coach can facilitate the teacher's implementation of the change/task by providing scaffolding support. Eventually, both the coach and teacher should realize that the teacher can continue the work without being codependent upon the coach. When the teacher is ready to transition from codependence to independence, the coach may use the checklist in Figure 7.2 to evaluate the three components of professional responsibility (Danielson, 1996).

Noncompliance Due to an Intransigent Attitude

Not all resistance is negative. Resistance can motivate us to think about our beliefs and actions. According to Fullan (2001), it is essential for all organizations to respect resistance. If resistance is completely ignored, it is only a matter of time before it takes its toll. Unfortunately, even when things appear to be working, the supposed success may be a function of merely superficial compliance.

If teachers' questions or comments during professional development cause contradictions for the coach, the coach should reflect on the beliefs that guide the school's literacy practices. The goal of overall instructional improvement needs to be examined as any new training becomes part of the school's literacy program. Positive change cannot occur without examining the constructs that drive decisions about methods and materials (Lester & Onore, 1990).

However, when resistance to professional development is characterized by defiance, it becomes refusal. Fullan (2001) states that a few hardcore resisters make a career out of being against everything. They act without moral purpose or commitment. Some teachers may feel that when a professional development initiative is presented, they can wait for it to pass so they can do what they were hired to do (Schlechty, 2001). The teachers may be arrogant enough to ignore the professional development and refuse to implement the initiative in their classrooms.

Figure 7.2   Checklist of Professional Responsibility Following Professional Development

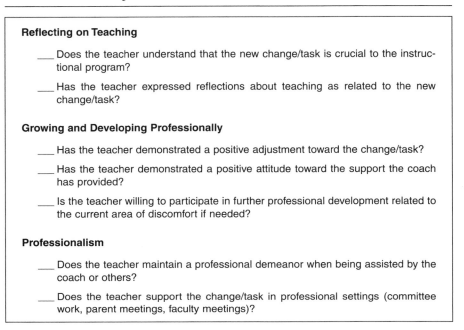

Reflecting on Teaching

___ Does the teacher understand that the new change/task is crucial to the instructional program?

___ Has the teacher expressed reflections about teaching as related to the new change/task?

Growing and Developing Professionally

___ Has the teacher demonstrated a positive adjustment toward the change/task?

___ Has the teacher demonstrated a positive attitude toward the support the coach has provided?

___ Is the teacher willing to participate in further professional development related to the current area of discomfort if needed?

Professionalism

___ Does the teacher maintain a professional demeanor when being assisted by the coach or others?

___ Does the teacher support the change/task in professional settings (committee work, parent meetings, faculty meetings)?

When the coach encounters teachers who maintain an attitude of refusal toward implementing a change or new task, this rare occurrence can be upsetting. The literacy coach has implemented the best collaborative and persuasive techniques in professional development but is met with blatant opposition. However, the noncompliance may be due to any of the following attitudes on the part of teachers: thinking that they are too busy, thinking that nothing is really new, or thinking that they are completely independent in the classroom (see Figure 7.3).

If the consistent positive stance of the coach is met with a constant negative stance of a teacher, the coach may have to proceed with two specific steps. The first step is to create an action plan to alleviate the teacher's refusal. The literacy coach who experiences such refusal may wish to use the scale in Figure 7.4 to determine the intensity of the teacher's refusal. The descriptors on the scale may also be used by the coach in preparing an action plan for working with the teacher.

The second step the coach may have to take is to hold a discussion with an administrator concerning the matter. This step should be taken

Figure 7.3 Examples of Noncompliance and Refusal Concerning Professional Development

Attitude	Misconception	Example of Refusal
Attitude #1: Busy teacher, busy students	Assigning equals teaching.	This teacher assigns tasks but does not model, explain, or demonstrate tasks. The teacher feels the modeling, explaining, or demonstration steps are unnecessary. There may or may not be any verbal refusal from the teacher during staff development; the refusal is demonstrated in the lack of implementation in the classroom. This teacher may tell others, including the coach and the principal, that all is going well when referring to the professional development requirements. However, in the classroom, he is not meeting his instructional obligations.
Attitude #2: Nothing is really new	You can't teach me anything new.	This teacher defiantly challenges the coach or other professional development facilitators about the change or initiative during the training session. The teacher's comments are negative and convey her intention of refusal. The comments may be made directly to the coach or only to those within close proximity to the negative teacher.
Attitude #3: Independent contractor	I can do what I want regardless of professional development.	This teacher may appear participatory during training but maintains an attitude of refusal in the classroom. The teacher sees himself as an independent contractor with no allegiance to the school's mission or commitment to the professional development training. He maintains a sense of independence rather than a sense of being a team member.

Figure 7.4 Scale for Determining Intensity of Refusal to Comply With Professional Development (Blank)

The literacy coach should read each descriptor related to professional development to rate the teacher's reaction. A scale of 1 (lowest resistance) to 4 (refusal) is provided. The scores can be tallied to determine intensity of refusal.

A. During Professional Development

	Low Resistance	Mild	Strong	Refusal
1. The teacher did not participate in cooperative small group work.	1	2	3	4
2. The teacher made challenging comments about the professional development topic.	1	2	3	4
3. The teacher distracted others with comments and/or behavior.	1	2	3	4
4. The teacher was late or absent during most of the professional development session.	1	2	3	4
5. The teacher did not bring the requested materials to the professional development session.	1	2	3	4
6. The teacher was not attentive and performed tasks unrelated to the professional development (reading a newspaper or magazine).	1	2	3	4

B. After Professional Development

	Low Resistance	Mild	Strong	Refusal
1. The teacher neglected to provide a written comment/evaluation of the professional development at the end of the session.	1	2	3	4
2. The teacher's lesson plans did not reflect implementation of the newly learned strategies.	1	2	3	4

	Low Resistance	Mild	Strong	Refusal
3. The teacher was not available to meet with the coach regarding implementation of the professional development topic.	1	2	3	4
4. The teacher directly states to the coach that the professional development initiative was unnecessary or unrealistic.	1	2	3	4
5. The teacher did not use the materials provided from the professional development training.	1	2	3	4
6. The teacher did not follow through with requested activities related to the professional development (providing reports, sharing at faculty meeting, etc.).	1	2	3	4
7. The teacher wrote and distributed a statement that is contrary to the professional development initiative to other stakeholders in the school community (parents, school board, principal, other staff members).	1	2	3	4
Column Scores				
TOTAL Score =				

Scoring:

1–13   Low resistance

12–26   Mild resistance

27–40   Strong resistance

41–52   Refusal

only if the first step is unsuccessful. If it becomes necessary for the coach and administrator to meet, the first thing the coach should report is what remedial steps have already been taken. The Intensity of Refusal Scale (Figure 7.4) would be one piece of documentation that the coach could use to substantiate her report to the administrator. An example of a completed scale can be seen in Figure 7.5. The coach could also show classroom observation notes and documentation of any other interactions with the teacher that demonstrate refusal to comply. The administrator will then determine if the teacher's actions of refusal constitute insubordination.

A teacher's refusal to comply with professional development led by a coach is very trying for the coach. Fortunately, most teachers do reflect on their teaching, grow and develop professionally, and consistently exhibit professionalism. It is important for the literacy coach to focus on the successes he has with assisting teachers and not the unusual situations of refusal to comply. Keeping the big picture in mind, schoolwide instructional improvement, should help the coach recognize the positive efforts being made by the majority of professionals in the school.

AN EXPERT'S THOUGHTS:
LAUREN RICHLIN, LITERACY COACH

Experienced literacy coaches who share their experiences and expertise do a great service to others embarking on coaching responsibilities. We posed questions about the skills needed to collaborate effectively with both struggling teachers and noncompliant teachers to Laura Richlin, a well-respected literacy coach from Pennsylvania. Laura's sound advice offers a cogent perspective on providing professional development for teachers while maintaining a positive stance toward the work the coach is doing will all of the teachers in a building.

Q: What skills do you think the literacy coach needs to collaborate effectively with classroom teachers?

A: The skills needed by an effective literacy coach are many. The first and foremost is patience. I found that my extensive background as a counselor and a mediator served me well. It helps to have compassion; sensitivity to the teachers' needs, feelings, and concerns; and solid, well-practiced listening skills. In addition, conflict resolution skills and creative problem-solving skills are a must. And did I mention patience?

Figure 7.5 Sample Scale for Determining Intensity of Refusal to Comply With Professional Development (Completed)

The literacy coach should read each descriptor related to professional development to rate the teacher's reaction. A scale of 1 (lowest resistance) to 4 (refusal) is provided. The scores can be tallied to determine intensity of refusal.

A. During Professional Development

	Low Resistance	Mild	Strong	Refusal
1. The teacher did not participate in cooperative small-group work.	1	2	3 X	4
2. The teacher made challenging comments about the professional development topic.	1	2	3 X	4
3. The teacher distracted others with comments and/or behavior.	1	2 X	3	4
4. The teacher was late or absent during most of the professional development session.	1	2 X	3	4
5. The teacher did not bring the requested materials to the professional development session.	1	2	3	4 X
6. The teacher was not attentive and performed tasks unrelated to the professional development (reading newspaper or magazine).	1	2	3	4 X

B. After Professional Development

	Low Resistance	Mild	Strong	Refusal
1. The teacher neglected to provide a written comment/evaluation of the professional development at the end of the session.	1	2	3	4 X
2. The teacher's lesson plans did not reflect implementation of the newly learned strategies.	1	2	3 X	4

(Continued)

Figure 7.5 (Continued)

	Low Resistance	Mild	Strong	Refusal
3. The teacher was not available to meet with the coach regarding implementation of the professional development topic.	1	2	3 X	4
4. The teacher directly states to the coach that the professional development initiative was unnecessary or unrealistic.	1 N/A	2	3	4
5. The teacher did not use the materials provided from the professional development training.	1	2	3 X	4
6. The teacher did not follow through with requested activities related to the professional development (providing reports, sharing at faculty meeting, etc.).	1	2	3	4 X
7. The teacher wrote and distributed a statement that is contrary to the professional development initiative to other stakeholders in the school community (parents, school board, principal, other staff members).	1 N/A	2	3	4
Column Scores	0	2	15	20
TOTAL Score = 37				

Scoring:

1–13   Low resistance

12–26   Mild resistance

27–40   Strong resistance

41–52   Refusal

Q: As a coach in a consultancy, you must have experienced both positive and negative aspects of coaching.

A: As a coaching consultant, I had the unique opportunity to visit and get a real feel for hundreds of classroom learning environments. I found myself awed by the creative genius in different classrooms. On most days, I went home inspired by something. And I loved having the opportunity to share that inspiration and new ideas with others. Personally, I appreciated having a flexible schedule that allowed me to attend to the needs of my own small children.

There are some interesting challenges about being a literacy consultant. The biggest one is the lack of a base or office. One has to drag materials from place to place and risk not having what is needed at any particular time. There can be a bit of worry. It's important to develop strategies for being prepared. I worked out of my car. I spent a great deal of time figuring out how to organize the trunk of my car to create a mobile coaching resource center. I had a mobile filing box, extra materials, easel, chart paper, art supplies, etc. This became problematic in that it informed the type of car I was required to have, and it limited the use of trunk space for my family needs.

Q: What thoughts or advice do you have about coaching the struggling teacher?

A: I think this topic could be a book in and of itself! I found that many teachers were initially threatened by the very fact that I was coming into their rooms. So the first thing I did was work on relationship building. I needed to create a modicum of trust with the teacher in order to proceed. I started slowly and carefully, focusing on successes before addressing deeper challenges. I worked little by little, doing everything I could to hold out the positive to the teacher. It is not a speedy process. I was more successful when I was assigned more coaching hours with an individual rather than less. Patience and extensive listening skills are essential. I think every coach should get certifications in conflict resolution and mediation. These skills are necessary for success. In many ways, knowledge and understanding about curriculum or pedagogy are secondary to the ability to work with people and take them from one place and move to another.

Q: What advice can you offer about dealing with noncompliant teachers during and after professional development sessions?

A: I have numerous stories about noncompliant teachers. One of my favorites is the kindergarten teacher who loved the three-day literacy development training where I was her instructor. She raved about the materials, the food, and the conference center. But when I arrived at her classroom door a couple of weeks later, she made it very clear that there was nothing I could help her with. She asked for my age (38) and then told me that she had been teaching for 35 years. "And do you know what that means?" she inquired. I responded, "That you could have been my kindergarten teacher?" "Exactly!" That was it! No amount of modeling, demonstrating, coaching, or anything moved her an inch. I almost never meet with a principal to talk about a coaching relationship. But this time I had to; I was so disappointed in my inability to make progress in this situation. The principal told me that he was amazed that I had managed to do as much as I had in that room. Apparently, this teacher had never even allowed anyone else to model a lesson, never mind rearrange her library center. So I learned to get less frustrated and keep on plugging along. I sometimes have to chant in my head, "It's okay, let them vent, just stay focused on what you're here to do, and eventually something will click."

Another story that supports my inner chanting theory: A young teacher took the stance of arguing with me about every aspect of our coaching relationship. She questioned the theoretical ideas, the use of particular children's literature, every classroom practice, be it content-based or classroom management skills. She basically told me that none of this would work and refused to try. And when I modeled lessons, she conveniently had a crisis with one or more students that she had to handle. After much wringing of hands, I decided that all I could really do here was listen, hear her out, focus on the positive, affirm any little thing I could affirm in her practice, and then let it be. I did all that I could. Three years later, a colleague literacy coach contacted me to tell me that she was now coaching this same teacher, who had been singing my praises. I was dying to hear about this teacher but didn't want to bias her new coach. Fortunately, my colleague, the new coach, was anxious to share about wonderful things that were happening in this teacher's room: rotating author studies, multilevel center activities, animated read-alouds with word cards and props, and lots of rich writing opportunities. I was thrilled and shocked! I guess, eventually, it clicked!

Source: Laura Richlin, Literacy Coach, Philadelphia, PA.

SUMMARY

The role of the coach as collaborator was stressed throughout this chapter. Two specific types of coaching situations, coaching the struggling teacher and coaching the noncompliant teacher, provided the structure for examining collaborative interaction between the literacy coach and the classroom teacher. Examples, sample forms, and suggestions related to both situations were provided throughout the chapter. In addition, a literacy coach's advice on working with struggling and noncompliant teachers was included.

TOPIC EXTENSIONS FOR CLASS SESSIONS OR STUDY GROUPS

1. Referring to the scenario in this chapter, step into Nancy Brennan's shoes and consider how you would deal with both the struggling teacher and the noncompliant teacher in her school. Discuss the action plans you would use in both situations.

2. What can the literacy coach do to introduce and maintain professional development that will elicit positive reactions from all teachers and eradicate noncompliance?

3. A literacy coach completed the scale in Figure 7.4 to determine whether he should confer with the administrator about the teacher's level of compliance or noncompliance. The coach scored the "during professional development" section with 3s and 4s with the exception of item #4. Item #4 was scored as a 2, since the teacher arrived just a few minutes late but was present for the rest of the session. The total score for the "during" section was 20.

   In the "after professional development" part of the scale, the coach gave no score to items #4 and #7, as she felt they were not pertinent to this teacher's situation. All other descriptors in the section were scored with 3s and 4s. The total for this section was 17.

   The overall score for the scale was 37. Using the scores provided, what decision would you make about conferring with an administrator about the teacher?

Collaboration With **8** Other Professionals and School Personnel

INTRODUCTION

Although classroom teachers are the primary group of professionals with whom literacy coaches interact, other professionals in the building and school district interact with the coach through the reading program as well. Throughout this book, we have treated the role of the literacy coach as a distinct one. In some districts, the reading specialist may also function as the reading coach, but in other districts, coaching is a distinct role. In Reading First school districts, the literacy coach may work with the primary-grade teachers, and the reading specialist may work with upper-grade teachers.

The literacy coach can also work outside her own building as a member of districtwide committees. This collaborative effort provides opportunities to interact with professionals throughout the school system. One hopes that the professionals would share the same goals in committee work that involves curriculum development, assessment, and professional development. This chapter explores instances in which the literacy coach collaborates with other professionals from within the school as well as outside the school.

SCENARIO

John Bruno has worked as a reading specialist in the Rocky Run School for 25 years. Recently, he was appointed as Rocky Run's literacy coach. Joyce

Ling, a teacher from another school in the district, was appointed to take John's place as the reading specialist in the building. As the new school year approaches, John wants to make certain that Joyce has access to all of the information that she needs to be able to function properly in her position as a reading specialist.

Joyce recently received a master's degree in reading from the state university. She has a reputation as an excellent classroom teacher and is looking forward to her new position as a reading specialist.

Another new position, a paraprofessional, has been assigned to assist Joyce with the instruction of the students. Joyce has never worked with a paraprofessional before and has many questions to ask John concerning the role of the paraprofessional in the reading specialist's classroom. Why has a paraprofessional been assigned at this time? What training, if any, has been given to the paraprofessional about reading instruction? On what type of continued training should Joyce focus with the paraprofessional? How many students are typically pulled out of the regular classroom at one time to receive reading intervention? What is the best way for Joyce and the paraprofessional to divide space in the classroom to facilitate two groups of students at the same time? For what types of tasks will the paraprofessional be responsible while Joyce coteaches in a regular classroom? What if parents disapprove of their children receiving instruction from a paraprofessional? What questions should Joyce expect from classroom teachers about the use of the paraprofessional in their classrooms?

COLLABORATING WITHIN THE SCHOOL

When literacy coaches are assigned to schools, it is important for them to have a collegial and collaborative relationship with the principal, the teachers, the librarian, the administrative assistants, the paraprofessionals, the parents, and other stakeholders in the school. Individual teachers recognize the direct impact of the coach's responsibilities in classrooms because the coach has conducted observations, demonstrations, and conferences. Others in the school, such as the reading specialist, the librarian or media specialist, and the paraprofessional, also have a direct impact on the reading curriculum. But the coach's indirect impact has the capability to influence the entire instructional program.

The two colleagues with whom the literacy coach may work most closely are the reading specialist and the reading paraprofessional. The coach, the reading specialist, and the reading paraprofessional share the goal of improving reading instruction within the school. The librarian or media specialist also plays a supporting role.

Working With Reading Specialists

There are many parallels between the role of the reading specialist and the reading coach. As stated in Chapter 1, the major difference between the roles is that the reading specialist works primarily with children and the reading coach works primarily with teachers. According to the International Reading Association's (2004) position statement concerning the role of the reading coach, the rapid proliferation of coaches is one response to increased attention to reading achievement and the reading achievement gap within the United States.

The common essential function of both the reading specialist and the literacy coach is to improve reading instruction. A common attribute is being an effective teacher. Stronge (2002) describes the effective teacher as one who recognizes complexity, communicates clearly, and serves conscientiously. These characteristics are certainly desirable in both the reading specialist and the literacy coach. To examine fully the role of coach as collaborator, a historical perspective of the role of the reading specialist and specific areas of collaboration between the reading specialist and coach are discussed in the next section.

Historical Perspective

The position of the reading specialist has been valued in American schools since the mid-1960s, when federal legislation provided funding for Title I programs (Bean, Swan, & Knaub, 2003). In this program, the reading specialist was responsible for supplementary instruction for students who experienced difficulty with reading (Dole, 2004). During that period, instruction took the form of a pullout program, and the materials that were used to instruct the children were different than those used in the classroom (Bean, Swan, & Knaub). Often, interaction did not occur between the classroom teacher and the reading specialist concerning the instruction that was happening in the classroom. Because of the lack of interaction, classroom teachers sometimes felt that they did not have the time to speak with the reading specialist about their students who were also being serviced by the reading specialist. Classroom teachers may have felt that the reading specialist was the expert and would take care of all of the students' problems.

As Title I programs were evaluated over time, a move away from total pullout reading classes took place. In the 1980s and 1990s, reading specialists serving Title I children were encouraged to provide instruction in the regular classroom in collaboration with the teacher (Vogt & Shearer, 2004). As the reading specialist and the teacher began to collaborate, the role of the reading specialist expanded to include much more than instruction. Reading specialists also took on responsibility for schoolwide assessment of students and for reporting results to teachers, administrators, and other stakeholders in the school community. The expansion of the role of the reading specialist was recognized by the IRA in position statements issued by the organization (IRA, 2000).

The Role of the Reading Specialist Today

In addition to the traditional role of remedial instruction, the reading specialist today has multiple roles and functions (Bean et. al., 2002; Vogt & Shearer, 2004). See Chapter 1 for a discussion of these roles and functions. The IRA position statement *Teaching All Children to Read: The Roles of the Reading Specialist* (IRA, 2000) states that the reading specialist has three major roles or functions: instruction, assessment, and leadership. The instruction function involves such tasks as planning and collaborating with teachers, supporting classroom instruction, and providing expert assistance (Wepner, Strickland, & Feely, 2002). The assessment function includes the administration and interpretation of diagnostic tools used by the reading specialist and assisting classroom teachers in the administration and interpretation of various assessments. The leadership function involves such activities as providing literacy program development and coordination and serving as a resource for teachers, administrators, and parents.

The research literature also reports that reading specialists do much more than teach (Bean, McDonald, & Fotta, 1990; Jaeger, 1996; Quatroche, Bean, & Hamilton, 2001). These findings also support the functions noted in the IRA position statement about reading specialists (IRA, 2000). The literature describes the expanded role of the specialist as one that includes the following functions:

- Providing resources to teachers
- Assessing reading difficulties
- Developing and implementing professional development and assuming leadership in the school's reading program

These components of the reading specialist's responsibilities are major sources of collaboration with school professionals, including the literacy coach.

Collaboration Between the Literacy Coach and the Reading Specialist

In Chapter 1, the essential differences between the literacy coach and the reading specialist were clearly explained. However, essential differences do not negate collaboration. The research findings stated in the previous section are accurate descriptors of the types of collaboration that occur between the literacy coach and the reading specialist. If either the reading specialist or the coach has a part-time assignment in a building, the other professional could be responsible for overseeing issues related to resources, assessment, or professional development. Many of the reading professionals that we interviewed from throughout the country serve as both reading specialist and coach. For example, some of them spend the morning in the coaching mode and the afternoon as reading specialists who provide small-group instruction to children. They work in one building. Others work in more than one building and fulfill the role of the coach for three days a week in School A and the role of the reading specialist for two days a week in School B.

Reading specialists and literacy coaches often depend on each other's support to carry out the multiple tasks necessary to implement a quality reading program. Both professionals share the goal of improved school-wide literacy instruction. The following sections share information about how the reading specialist and coach collaborate in providing resources, assessing reading, and implementing professional development.

Providing Resources. Providing resources to teachers is a task that can be expertly supplied by both the literacy coach and the reading specialist. The two professionals could collaborate in several ways regarding this task. First, the coach may observe in a particular teacher's classroom over a period of time. The results of the observations lead the coach to realize that the teacher needs some type of resources. These resources could be additional reading materials, ongoing mentoring, or the assistance of a team teacher in the classroom. The coach can solicit the reading specialist's aid in any of these situations by asking the reading specialist to meet with the teacher to offer the necessary support.

Second, the reading specialist may be a regular assistant in a teacher's classroom and become aware of a pedagogical or management need. It is not within the realm of the reading specialist's responsibility to address these issues with the teacher. Instead, the reading specialist should initiate a professional, confidential dialogue with the literacy coach about the situation. The literacy coach will then be able to observe the teacher for the area of weakness and ensure that the teacher receives adequate coaching to correct the issue.

Third, the coach and the reading specialist could meet together with the teacher to discuss an action plan and determine what role the coach will play in helping the teacher. They will also determine what role the reading specialist will play.

Assessing Reading Difficulties. The reading specialist often has direct responsibility for assessing reading difficulties of individual children who are referred for testing by the classroom teacher or by the child study team. The reading specialist may also have responsibility for testing certain grade levels within the school or for administering schoolwide assessments. The specialist's responsibilities could also include scoring the tests. When the reading specialist administers group tests, the testing information must be conveyed to the classroom teachers, principal, and parents. The reading specialist should find it beneficial to collaborate with the literacy coach on interpreting and reporting assessment results. When the two professionals collaborate, they may discover shortcomings of the test or shortcomings in their reading program.

If the test is either invalid or unreliable, the reading professionals should provide evidence of the deficiency and make a recommendation to find another test that better suits the needs of the school and more accurately assesses the students. This recommendation is likely to lead to committee work for both the reading specialist and the literacy coach as they collaborate with teachers and administrators to find a better assessment instrument.

If the test reveals gaps in the reading program, the reading professionals should work collaboratively to analyze the test results and pinpoint specific instructional areas that warrant attention. The literacy coach's role is to assist teachers in recognizing the problems and adjusting their instruction. The reading specialist's role is to help students through guided reading and direct teaching of strategies. For example, suppose that after carefully analyzing assessment information, the coach and reading specialist conclude that weak scores on the fifth-grade test for "determining fact and opinion" were not attributable to construction of the test items. Instead, they determine that the cause for the weak scores was insufficient instruction. The conclusion propels the coach to work proactively with fifth-grade teachers so that instructional techniques will improve. Grade-level professional development meetings may be convened to discuss appropriate places to embed "fact and opinion" teaching in the curriculum. Demonstration lessons can be planned and implemented to help individual teachers recognize the steps of modeling and guiding instruction for this strategy. Other resources, such as professional articles and videotapes or DVDs of exemplary lessons, should also be a part of the coach's plan to help ensure a better quality of teaching in this area. In addition, the reading specialist can work directly with students to ensure their mastery of the strategy. The reading specialist may also serve as a resource to the fifth-grade classroom teachers and to parents as they monitor their children's practice of the strategy with homework assignments.

Determining how to report the assessment information and any subsequent plans for maintaining or improving test scores is an awesome responsibility for anyone's shoulders. If the coach and reading specialist share this responsibility and present the information as a collaborative team, they send the message of collegiality both implicitly and explicitly to the other staff members.

Developing and Implementing Professional Development. Literacy coaches engage in professional development on a daily basis. Each observation and demonstration conducted in individual classrooms is an important part of professional development. Equally important are the group meetings and training sessions conducted within schools and throughout districts. The literacy coach's direct line to instructional improvement is through coach-teacher interaction. In addition to providing professional development for teachers, the literacy coach may be asked to provide principals and other administrators within the school district with awareness sessions, literacy program overviews, or explicit training. Examples of each of these administrative sessions may be found in Figure 6.1 in Chapter 6. The purposes for developing and implementing each type of session are noted here:

- *Awareness session.* The literacy coach provides information that may include coaching goals, data analysis, and implications or inservice plans. Awareness sessions are typically brief, ranging from an hour to a half day.
- *Literacy program overview.* The literacy coach previews materials and resources that are part of the reading program. Sometimes, the coach may co-present with a professional consultant or a reading specialist with whom she works. Program overviews typically range from at least two hours to a full day.
- *Explicit training.* The literacy coach demonstrates reading or writing techniques for the administrative staff. Since actual training is involved, these sessions typically last at least one day.

Reading specialists may engage in professional development on a daily basis or on an intermittent basis. Although reading specialists do not typically conduct formal observations of classroom teachers, they do have opportunities to observe informally when they teach small groups of children within the regular classroom. Reading specialists could be asked to coteach with a classroom teacher. Often, the invitation to coteach is extended by the classroom teacher because she has formed a trusting relationship with the reading specialist.

Sometimes coteaching is mandated by the building principal or by the reading supervisor. The administrator typically gives this directive because a classroom teacher has demonstrated weakness in teaching language arts or because a new teacher needs support from a seasoned teacher. While coteaching, a reading specialist may teach guided reading groups in the classroom. This is an opportunity for the reading specialist to model good pedagogy for colleagues. In addition, reading specialists are adept at providing sessions on specific topics (e.g., book conferences, writing workshop, responding to literature, literacy centers).

Obviously, both literacy coaches and reading specialists are capable of planning and implementing professional development. When a school (or a district) is fortunate enough to have both literacy coaches and reading specialists on the faculty, these professionals can work together to provide professional development for the teaching staff. Planning and implementing professional development is a challenging responsibility. Collaboration creates positive working relationships and conserves much of the energy one person might expend to go it alone. Literacy coaches and reading specialists have expertise to share with others. The wealth of experience and specialized training of the coach and reading specialist combine to make them extremely valuable resources in coplanning and implementing professional development. Figure 8.1 provides various examples of planning and implementing professional development and offers some insight into the collaboration that can take place between the coach and the reading specialist. A variety of examples represent districtwide, schoolwide, and individual classroom situations on which the coach and the reading specialist can collaborate.

The roles of the coach and the literacy specialist should be in syncopation, not in opposition. Both professionals can help to improve the quality of the overall instructional program. According to Johnson and Johnson (2003), the alignment of goals and daily practices across professional groups helps to create effective schools. When the literacy coach collaborates with the reading specialist, the two support each other on common ground. The examples provided here (see Figure 8.1) demonstrate how the collaboration between the coach and the reading specialist aids in the delivery of intersecting components of the language arts

Figure 8.1 Examples of Collaboratively Planning and Implementing Professional Development

Topic	Participants	Planning the Professional Development	Implementing the Professional Development
Schoolwide professional development (1 day): Using teacher read-aloud to extend students' responses to text	K–6 Elementary School Teachers (35): Coach (1), Reading Specialists (2)	• Coach and principal discuss need to revisit read-aloud to provide fresh ideas for the new school year. • Coach and reading specialists meet to plan day's events, choose appropriate books for demonstrations.	• Principal and coach share opening remarks to set the task for the day. • Coach and reading specialists conduct training sessions: grades K–2 (Reading Specialist #1); grades 3 & 4 (Coach); grades 5 & 6 (Reading Specialist #2).
Schoolwide professional development (ongoing): Integrating use of the Internet into research projects	Middle School Teachers (78): Coaches (2), Reading Specialists (4)	• Three summer planning meetings include coaches, reading specialists, principal, and technology coordinator; goals set and tasks divided. • Definite agenda set for sessions 1 and 2; tentative agenda for sessions 3–12. • Planning committee continues to meet throughout the year to assess progress and refine plans.	• Principal, coaches, and technology coordinator provide overview and goals at first session. • Coaches, technology coordinator, and reading specialists work with each department involved during sessions 2–12. • In-class assistance is provided to teachers by both coaches and reading specialists throughout the year.
Districtwide professional development (1 day): Introduction of new spelling program	Grades 1–8: All elementary and middle school teachers (234): Coaches (4), Reading specialists (14)	• Language arts supervisor convenes a committee consisting of coaches, reading specialists, and two representative teachers from each grade level; committee meets several times to review research, do a needs assessment, and evaluate published spelling programs. • Spelling program is selected; introduction of program to teachers is planned, and tasks are divided among coaches and reading specialists.	• Twenty-one committee members divide themselves so that at least two of them co-present the new program to specific grade levels. Procedures for pre- and posttests as well as practice activities are demonstrated. • Electronic surveys are sent to teachers three times throughout the year to gain feedback about use of the new spelling program.

(Continued)

Figure 8.1 (Continued)

Topic	Participants	Planning the Professional Development	Implementing the Professional Development
		• Committee continues to meet three times throughout the year to share feedback from teachers and parents regarding new spelling program.	
Districtwide professional development (ongoing): Use of electronic card catalog and other library media	K–12 teachers from the entire district (312): Coaches (4), Reading Specialists, (18)	• Librarians, coaches, and reading specialists meet with CDF company representatives to learn how to implement new technology (hardware and software). • Librarians, coaches, and reading specialists plan how to present new materials and support teachers in their use.	• A series of five half-day professional development sessions is scheduled for each of the buildings. Representative members of the committee co-present and assist teachers in becoming familiar with the materials. • Librarians follow through with individual issues and questions posed by teachers.
Grade-level professional development project (ongoing): Initiating guided reading in all third-grade classrooms in the school	Third-grade teachers from one elementary school (5): Coach (1), Reading specialists (3)	• Coach and reading specialists have initiated guided reading in grades 1 and 2 during the two previous years; they develop the third-grade initiative from past plans. • Monthly meetings allow updates on issues regarding this project.	• Coach and one reading specialist provide training and follow-up observations and feedback sessions for the five third-grade teachers. Other reading specialists will continue working with grades 1 and 2.
Schoolwide professional development project (ongoing): Linking reading, writing, and science	High school science department (8): Coaches (2), Reading specialists (3)	• After several observations of science staff, coaches determine that science teachers need more strategies for connecting science and the language arts. • Coaches and reading specialists meet to set goals, plan series of	• Session 1: Coaches provide overview, share literature and video. One coach conducts a "demonstration" lesson. • Sessions 2–8: Reading specialists provide demonstration lessons in individual science classrooms and then confer with teachers.

Topic	Participants	Planning the Professional Development	Implementing the Professional Development
		professional development sessions, set time line for follow-up observations with teachers.	• Sessions 9–15: Reading specialists confer with individual science teachers; provide feedback, resources.
Presentation for school board and/or administrators (one meeting): Information session about new primary grade assessments	School directors and district administrators (15): Coach (1), Reading specialists (2)	• Director of curriculum selects one literacy coach and the two reading specialists who work with that coach to present assessment information • Coach and reading specialists meet to plan presentation and select parts for presenting.	• Coach and reading specialists provide PowerPoint presentation accompanied by one page of succinct points about primary assessments. • Coach and reading specialists respond to questions from directors and public.
Individual classroom (one day): Use of word wall	Second-grade teacher: Coach (1), Reading specialist (0)	• Coach and teacher discuss word wall activities that integrate content area vocabulary. • Coach plans demonstration lessons for teacher.	• Coach conducts demonstration lesson. • Coach and teacher meet after demonstration to discuss techniques.
Individual classroom (ongoing): Strengthening modeling and guided practice during instruction	Sixth-grade language arts teacher: Coach (1), Reading specialist (1)	• Coach meets with reading specialist assigned to sixth grade to share concern about a teacher's lack of modeling and guided practice during instruction. • Coach and reading specialist meet with teacher to arrange schedule to include both demonstration teaching and observations of the teacher.	• Coach conducts week-long demonstration teaching with both teacher and reading specialist as observers; the three confer after the sessions. • Reading specialist provides demonstration teaching on ongoing basis for several weeks; confers with teacher frequently. • Reading specialist and teacher coplan several lessons and coteach them. • Reading specialists assist the teacher in planning lessons for independent teaching. • Coach observes teacher instructing; confers with teacher.

program. These professionals function as resources for each other as they engage in problem solving, planning sessions, and feedback sessions about the strengths and needs they observe in the literacy instruction within the school. Furthermore, the literacy coach serves as a liaison between the reading specialist and the regular classroom teacher. At the same time, reading specialists typically have more opportunities to be in contact with parents than the coach might have. Feedback regarding parent insights into instruction, initiatives, assessment, and motivational issues can be transmitted from the reading specialist to the literacy coach. When the literacy coach and the reading specialist collaborate, a win-win situation is evident for all stakeholders, especially the teachers and students who are directly involved in the instructional process.

Others' Perspectives on the Role of the Reading Specialists

Many schools recognize the key role that reading specialists play as leaders of successful reading programs (Bean, Swan, & Knaub, 2003). Literacy coaches and reading specialists who collaborate with each other as a habit of professional practice can provide exemplary professional development to teachers on both collective and individual bases. The demonstration teaching and coteaching performed in classrooms provide exemplary instruction and meet the needs of diverse students in classrooms. Literacy coaches and reading specialists should be mutually dependent and reliant on each other.

According to Bean (2004), the instructional role of the reading specialist is widely accepted by both administrators and teachers. The reading specialist plays an important role as an informal leader, especially when collaboration between the reading specialist and literacy coach is strong. How others view the role of the reading specialist is usually in response to how they perceive that professional's expertise, collegiality, and helpfulness. Perspectives of others who interact with the reading specialists are explored in the following sections.

Principals' Perspectives. According to Wepner and Quatroche (2002), when principals are knowledgeable about reading, they become even more supportive of the reading specialist. When the literacy coach informs the principal about instructional initiatives, professional development needs, and assessment data for the school, the principal can use the information to work closely with the reading specialist. Reading specialists spend a great deal of time in regular and special education classrooms. They instruct small groups of students in itinerant rooms as well as in regular classrooms. When the principal, literacy coach, and reading specialist collaborate, the principal has the advantage of relying on this reading team to keep the momentum of using the best instructional practices moving forward in the building. The principal understands that the reading specialist is a tremendous resource for the teaching staff and has direct links to students and parents. The principal may ask the reading specialist for agenda items regarding the school's literacy program to be included in monthly faculty meetings. The principal may also ask the reading specialist to make brief presentations at faculty meetings.

Some principals may not have a strong background in reading or in a certain area of reading such as early literacy or content area literacy. They may not seek the support of the reading specialists or render their support to them. If the principal feels unsure of himself when observing or conferring with classroom teachers about literacy instruction, he may not want to make his self-perceived deficiency evident to the other professionals on the staff. One way to help the principal improve observation and conferring skills is to arrange a classroom observation at which the principal, reading specialist, and the literacy coach observe together. After the observation, they could discuss the content and pedagogical techniques that were strong or weak areas of the instruction.

Both the literacy coach and the reading specialist could invite the principal to participate in professional development sessions that they conduct for teachers. In this way, the principal will receive firsthand knowledge of what is being disseminated to teachers about the literacy program. The principal will also gain an awareness of the expectations or changes that will result as an end product of the professional development.

As chief instructional leader of the school, the principal is responsible for the success or failure of the instructional program. Having the principal's support is both rewarding and challenging for the reading specialist. It is rewarding to have the ongoing support of one's supervisor. It is comforting to know that collegial interactions with the presentation of timely issues, honest feedback, and areas of concern will consistently be handled with professionalism and respect. It is challenging for the reading specialist to maintain a standard of excellence for herself and all those with whom she interacts. Meeting the standard will promote high levels of student achievement in the school's instructional program.

Teachers' Perspectives. Both new and veteran teachers welcome the help they receive from others who can assist them in the classroom. Reading specialists began their careers as classroom teachers and spend the rest of their careers in the classrooms of others. Because of their experiences, they relate well to the instructional demands and challenges that teachers face on a daily basis. Classroom teachers generally welcome the assistance of reading specialists because they recognize their expertise relative to children who have reading and writing difficulties. These children are more challenging to teach. The interventions supplied by the reading specialist, either through coteaching or pullout sessions, are critical to student improvement. When the interventions are shared and discussed with a colleague, the classroom teacher gains additional insight into how certain children in the class can best be taught.

Parents' Perspectives. Parents are appreciative of the efforts of others to help their children with academic achievement. Once parents understand the role of the reading specialist as a collaborator with classroom teachers, they will perceive the reading specialist as instrumental in helping their children. They also need to perceive the reading specialist as key in moving the instructional program forward. Sometimes the reading specialist and the teacher have joint conferences with the parent. The parent could also encounter the reading specialist during home and school meetings that the reading specialist conducts or in parent workshops on reading. Because the reading specialist does not have a classroom of his own, some parents are confused concerning his role. They may confuse the role of the reading specialist with other types of specialists in the school, such as special education teachers or therapists. Good communication between the reading specialist and parents is necessary to avoid confusion.

Similarly, parents' perspectives on the role of literacy coach could also change from confusion to appreciation once the coach's role is understood. The coach may be able to invite parents to participate in the following events to provide them with a clear view of how coaching impacts the improved performance of both teachers and students: (1) schoolwide committees or panels regarding text selection, assessment, technology, or progress reporting; (2) discussions following live or taped demonstration lessons by the coach; and (3) roundtable discussions about topics of the parents' choice. The discussion may also include the principal, classroom teachers, the reading specialist, librarian, school counselor, and any other professionals in the school's educational program.

Working With Paraprofessionals

Paraprofessionals instruct children in classrooms under the direction and supervision of certified teachers. The paraprofessional's function is to aid the teacher with instruction and classroom management. According to the U.S. Department of Labor (2003), over one million paraprofessionals are assisting classroom teachers in public and private schools throughout the country. Having paraprofessionals in the classroom enables teachers to spend more time with students who have specific needs that may be different from others in the class at a particular time. It also allows the teacher and paraprofessional to work with two small groups of students at the same time.

Many paraprofessionals do not hold college degrees. Paraprofessionals usually receive training conducted by the school district during induction meetings. The goal of the training is to ensure that paraprofessionals adequately provide services to the children and to the teacher. Induction meetings are normally held when the paraprofessionals are hired or during regularly scheduled professional development sessions. However, some districts provide no routine training for paraprofessionals. Instead, they rely on the teachers with whom the paraprofessionals work to train them.

Paraprofessionals can learn from observing the teachers whom they assist. Everyone hopes that they learn only sound techniques for both instruction and classroom management. However, it is possible that paraprofessionals will emulate weak techniques if those are all they observe.

Since paraprofessionals have direct contact with children, their modeling of language use for students needs to be conventional as well as humanistic. Idiomatic or unconventional language patterns are unacceptable, since the students with whom they interact will learn from the example of adults. Additionally, the paraprofessional's assistance in small-group or one-on-one instruction needs to be modeled after the classroom teacher's style of teaching. The delivery of all instruction, whether from a professional educator or from a paraprofessional, needs to be exemplary.

Paraprofessionals are often required or invited to participate in the same professional development sessions as the certified teachers. Literacy coaches can have a positive influence on the paraprofessionals in several ways: during the professional development sessions they conduct, in the model teaching lessons that they demonstrate in classrooms, and with the resources they share with teachers.

Working With Librarians/Media Specialists

The library/media specialist role has evolved from "keeper of the books" as changes have occurred in the curriculum. With the integration of technology and the use of computers in the curriculum, the librarian has also become a media specialist. In many reading and writing programs, the library/media specialist plays a major role (Radencich, 1995). Classroom teachers cannot be expected to know all of the resources that are available for use in enhancing the curriculum. It is difficult for classroom teachers to be familiar with the variety of books and materials that a library can house (Radencich, 1995). The library/media specialist can provide valuable assistance to teachers in learning about the volume of resources that may be available as well as how to use the materials. It may be helpful for the literacy coach to collaborate with the library/media specialist when the coach is preparing for professional development.

Teachers often team with the library/media specialist because the specialist is quite knowledgeable about children's literature. The literacy coach might also call upon the library/media specialist to provide literature resources for classroom teachers. The library/media specialist should be able to help the coach (a) find grade-appropriate books that could be used to teach a theme, (b) locate and download video clips that could be used as part of a demonstration or explanation, and (c) locate different types of text (narrative, informational, poetry) that teachers may be able to use to supplement reading from a basal or a mandated trade book.

The library/media specialist can assist the literacy coach with professional development when the specialist makes available current and past issues of professional reading journals in the teachers' lounge. The literacy coach may also ask the library/media specialist to locate specific articles from journals so the articles can be read by teachers and discussed in their professional meetings.

According to Dales (1990), the library/media specialist can aid classroom teachers in working with the curriculum to meet students' needs in the following ways:

- Provide flexible access to the library/media center so that teachers can take advantage of it for students.
- Use the following teaching modes to help students when they are in the library/media center: book talks, read-aloud stories, informational skill instruction, and use of electronic encyclopedias and indexes.
- Be available to answer reference questions or to help locate particular texts.
- Coplan with the classroom teacher about books used in literature circles.
- Help students discover all that has been published on a topic.
- Supply rotating book collections for the classroom.
- Furnish an attractive place in the library for student-authored books.
- Prepare book fairs. Be available during the fairs to talk about students' choices of books.
- Give teachers updates on current books.
- Use their knowledge of students to coach them on book selection.
- Make certain that students have library cards or electronic identification for using the school's library.

COLLABORATION OUTSIDE THE SCHOOL

The regular duties of the literacy coach take place within the school or, in some cases, across two schools. In addition to the routines established by the literacy coach, there may be other expectations, such as organizing and participating in committees that include members of the larger professional community. Engaging in committee work is part of the leadership role of the literacy coach. Bean (2004) states that leadership consists of any activities associated with working with others to accomplish a common goal. The common goal of a committee is the improvement of some aspect of the educational process: instruction, student achievement, professional development, assessment, curriculum, and standards. Those who convene and lead committees need to do so based on shared vision, program coherence, and problem resolution (Lambert, 2003). The literacy coach deals with these components of leadership when she works in individual classrooms. The coach also deals with these components as a chair, cochair, or participant on a districtwide committee.

Working With District Committees

Literacy coaches often serve on committees outside their own school. Because they are experts in literacy teaching and learning, have knowledge of curriculum and assessment, and have the ability to interact well with adult learners, literacy coaches are valued as contributors to districtwide committees. Districtwide committees are often formed to create or revisit program coherence. The coach may be asked to chair or cochair a major committee or a subcommittee. The coach could also be asked to contribute as a participating member, rather than as a leader, of the committee. Three common committees on which the literacy coach may be asked to serve are curriculum committees, assessment committees, and professional development committees.

Curriculum Committees

Someone once remarked that a committee was a group of people who designed a horse to look like a camel. Committee work can become cumbersome, but there are ways to lighten the load. Information can be disbursed ahead of time in the form of memorandums and written announcements. By disseminating written information ahead of time, the meeting can be spent sharing concerns and questions.

Curriculum committees are convened for the purpose of adopting new tests or new software or to renew the curriculum document and align it with standards and assessments. When the literacy coach facilitates the committee, he is in a more public leadership position than the role normally performed within the school (McAndrew, 2005). The more public leadership responsibilities of a committee facilitator include selecting committee members, choosing a site for the committee meetings, facilitating each meeting, and assessing the individual performance in as well as the collective sessions of the group.

Radencich (1995) indicates that how the committee is formed and operates is an important matter, and she provides the following pointers:

- Consider whether enough time and expertise are available to allow the committee to function effectively. A proposed time line for accomplishing the task is helpful.
- When forming a committee, consider the need for representation from all groups. If this is a district committee, every grade level should be represented, as well as each school. Skeptics as well as advocates should be included to maximize ownership of committee recommendations.
- Make certain that the group has sufficient time to examine materials, listen to presentations, and discuss issues among themselves. The member's active involvement gives that person a sense of contribution to and ownership in the committee.
- At the initial meeting, ensure that the goals of the curriculum committee are clearly stated in both written and oral modes.
- Ensure that the committee members appreciate the significance of the committee's work. Producing a few newsletters or memorandums throughout the course of the committee's work will keep the entire district staff informed of the committee's progress and goals. The committee membership could be listed in the newsletter or memorandums. Between meetings, committee members could be asked to collect surveys within their buildings or give brief committee updates during faculty meetings.
- Monitor whether committee members are completing their tasks and communicating regularly with their constituencies. If the committee is divided into subcommittees charged with performing tasks between committee meetings, the facilitator can visit each subcommittee during its working session to make suggestions or offer praise.
- Arrange for the appropriate closure. A final newsletter should be sent out to all teachers within the district, and the committee should be recognized with a celebration of its achievement with snack, a luncheon, or certificates of achievement.

Assessment Committees

At the present time in the United States, assessment and accountability are high priorities. Assessment committees are formed at both school and district levels. Literacy coaches are usually asked to serve on committees that are focused on reading and writing assessments. If asked to be a facilitator of such a committee, the coach should be prepared and organized. If the school has established assessment goals, the work of the committee should be aligned with those goals.

The literacy coach who conducts assessment committee meetings may be asked to share several standardized tests with the committee. She could also be asked to train committee members to give standardized reading assessments and show them how to interpret test results.

The assessment committee could also be involved in selecting the reading assessments that will be administered in the district. The guidance counselor or school psychologist may have access to catalogs that contain information on different types of assessments, and the literacy coach should seek their guidance. Another helpful tip when selecting assessments is to consult with another district with a similar student population that has used the tests being considered for adoption.

Sometimes, assessment committees are assigned the task of revising report cards after new assessments are selected or a new curriculum is written. Generally, the committee is given this task because its members are familiar with the assessments. They will need to provide clear descriptions of the literacy tasks assessed on the report cards. This is especially true at the elementary level.

Whether the coach serves on the assessment committee or a curriculum committee, the points mentioned in the above section on curriculum committees should be referenced. The following suggestions, adapted from Radencich (1995), can also help the literacy coach facilitate effective meetings:

- Provide sufficient notice. Send out notification at least a month ahead of time. Follow up with a brief note or e-mail a few days prior to the meeting.
- Start by defining the purpose of the committee meeting and clearly state the goals of the committee. Allow time for introductions, if appropriate.
- Start on time but remember that adults need breaks along the way.
- Self-imposed deadlines should be part of the structure of the meeting so that they do not run overtime. Interrupt if necessary to keep to the topic.

- Committee size is important. Smaller groups generally work more effectively.
- Serve refreshments
- Use humor to relax the group.
- Don't spend time on lengthy discussions that can be solved by a subcommittee.
- Watch for nonverbal cues indicating agreement or disagreement, a desire to speak, or impatience.
- Summarize and bring the meeting to a closure. Thank the teachers serving on the committee for their contribution.

Professional Development Committees

The literacy coach may join other coaches and administrators to determine professional development needs for the district. After the district needs are determined, the committee prioritizes the needs according to districtwide goals. The priorities could be consistent across the district or vary between elementary and secondary levels. Whatever the determination, the goal of professional development is to improve the teaching and learning occurring in the schools. Schoolwide or districtwide professional development is usually done for the purpose of training teachers in a specific technique or pedagogy. Training teachers is merely a first step (Hoffman & Pearson, 2000). Good professional development occurs over time. Vogt and Shearer (2004) indicate that "drive-in inservice" (a one-day session only) isn't very effective.

After professional development needs are established, the literacy coach serving on the professional development committee may be charged with several responsibilities. One responsibility would be to help create a projected time line for implementing the professional development. Several encounters with the topic, rather than only one, will help ensure a standard quality of implementation in classrooms.

A second responsibility of the committee is to determine which professionals will be the most effective presenters to the staff. Outside consultants who are considered experts in the field may be chosen. The literacy coaches themselves may be selected as presenters. For example, if one literacy coach is proficient in writing instruction, that coach could conduct several sessions related to writing techniques, conferring, and assessment. A second coach in the district who has an expertise in using children's literature could provide a series of workshops on how and why to use quality literature in the classroom. A third coach with a technology background may conduct sessions on working with media in the classroom to help with research projects.

A third committee responsibility is the assessment of how the meeting is flowing both during and after the professional development sessions. The literacy coach could be an observer or participant observer in the sessions. She can assess the effectiveness of the professional development through her own observation or through verbal or written feedback from the teachers involved.

COLLABORATING THROUGH PROFESSIONAL DEVELOPMENT

The literacy coach has a high level of expertise and should be comfortable working with adults as learners. Therefore, he is often asked to provide professional development. The coach can facilitate professional development both inside and outside the realm of his own school. Regardless of the venue in which the coach conducts professional development, he should exhibit expertise as collaborator, colleague, facilitator, and learner. The following sections will provide details about the types of professional development that the literacy coach may utilize, as well as some specific steps for planning and organizing sessions.

Facilitating Professional Development in the School District

The primary role of the literacy coach concerns coaching individual teachers in individual classrooms. However, another role of great importance is that of facilitator of groups of teachers participating in professional development. There are many keys to good facilitation:

- Be well planned and organized.
- Adjust pace and change of activities so that the audience keeps focused.
- Create a climate of "we're all in this together."
- Make certain that the teachers are participating.
- Maintain topic focus.
- Make a clear, concise presentation.
- Develop a checklist for the handling of details, logistics, etc.
- Summarize the presentation.
- Allow time for questions and airing of issues.
- Ensure that follow-up assistance and conferences will occur after the presentation.
- Provide resources.

- Collect data after the meeting (anecdotal information, surveys, students' work samples as a result of the professional development).
- Keep the principal informed of any initiatives, changes in coach's schedule, etc.

Facilitating Professional Development Outside the School District

As professional developers, literacy coaches become collaborators in a wider public arena. Networking of coaches and reading specialists within the district and across regional districts can lead to invitations to speak at other professional development venues. These meetings may be connected with schools or other educational organizations. For example, local or regional reading associations; literacy councils; public libraries; university-school partnerships; adult literacy organizations; and local, state, or national conferences are all venues that would appreciate the expertise of the literacy coach as a presenter.

According to Vacca and Vacca (1999), the following personal traits characterize effective presenters at professional development sessions:

- Demonstrates enthusiasm and interest in the topic.
- Relates to participants in an open, honest, and friendly manner.
- Answers questions patiently.
- Does not talk down to participants.
- Exhibits a sense of humor.

A coach may have developed expertise in one particular area and create several presentations that focus on that one area. One example might be concerning the use of guided questioning to enhance comprehension. The coach can model questioning techniques and discuss situations for which specific types of questions would be most helpful. The coach has developed scenarios that she and the participating teachers role-play to demonstrate explicitly the techniques being presented. At the close of the presentation, the coach can also provide resources for further reading or viewing.

Another coach has focused on the importance of note making when teaching guided reading and guided writing groups. The coach provides a rationale for why note making is important in small-group instructional settings. Information on how to record notes efficiently and effectively is shared about the strategies that students are, or should be, using. As part of the professional development training, the coach could conduct one or two mock situations that make the technique explicit for those participating in the session.

Sharing expertise with teachers outside the coach's own school is a professional growth experience for both the coach and those participating in the professional development meeting. Receiving good training on specific teaching strategies that help improve students' achievement is important for all teachers. Whether the person providing the training is an in-house expert or an outside expert, the benefit of good professional development sessions should carry over to the classroom.

AN EXPERT'S THOUGHTS: THERESA MANFRE, READING SPECIALIST

Theresa Manfre is a middle school reading specialist from Long Island, New York. In May 2006, Theresa was awarded the prestigious Nila Banton Smith Award from the International Reading Association for her influential work with content area literacy. The award is given yearly to a middle or secondary classroom teacher or reading specialist who has "shown leadership in translating theory and current research into practice for developing content area literacy" (IRA, 2007). We interviewed Theresa about the collaborative work she and other reading specialists do in schools.

Q: In what ways can the reading specialist and literacy coach collaborate?

A: The reading specialist and the literacy coach can collaborate on literacy initiatives that directly enhance the reading and writing skills in the content areas of English language arts and mathematics. Many educators agree that formal mathematics exams contain an exorbitant amount of reading. The learning standards and performance indicators can be reviewed and cross-referenced with two professionals working collaboratively.

The goal of any literacy initiative is positive change within a model of school reform. Specifically, the goal is to infuse and promote substantial reading research, standards-based methodologies, study skills, and test-taking learning strategies into the content areas of English language arts and mathematics, among others. This collaboration will increase student academic performance in general and certainly on the mandated NCLB state assessments. The educational strategies should be geared toward meeting the needs of a diverse student body and promoting equitable opportunities for student success.

The reading specialist and literacy coach can cultivate effective collaborative relationships with each other, as well as with the students, parents/guardians, caregivers, and other staff members, in order to meet the individual learning needs of each of the students and foster a positive model of school reform.

Q: What is the most rewarding part of your job as a reading specialist? What is the most frustrating part?

A: The most rewarding part of my job (truly my vocation) is teaching a lifelong skill that I judge to be the basis for all other learning. To witness a child really comprehending a story for the first time is what I live for. To have a student relate a passage to real life and attain the "wow factor" makes my heart skip a beat. I wish to ignite a torch of lifelong learning, encompassing the love of reading, for my students.

The most frustrating part of my job is the limited time allotted to help students reach the proficiency/grade level in reading. Sometimes, it appears administration is more concerned with data than with teaching to the total child (academically, socially, and emotionally). The state of a student's emotional intelligence has now been found to be a more accurate assessment of achievement potential than even academic records or national SAT scores. Emotional intelligence and the affective domain have positive implications for pedagogy, although they seem to be often overlooked in favor of district test scores.

Q: How do you assist the regular classroom teacher?

A: I facilitate both push-in and pullout models, although our data show better performance with the pullout model. A multitude of varied instructional strategies and materials are used during lessons and units of study. Some of these instructional strategies and materials include quality literature to motivate the students; educational technology; colorful, easy-to-see visual aids; graphic organizers to meet diverse learning styles; videos and artifacts; jigsaw techniques; skits; and role-plays. A goal is to engage students in open discussions.

Most of my materials are handmade, based on the individual needs and interests of the students, like educational games, contests, tangible awards, and incentives. Moreover, I offer ample provisions for the individual differences of students.

Q: What advice do you have for those who are currently seeking reading specialist certification/endorsement and are hoping to work as reading specialists?

A: I advise those seeking reading certification/endorsement to take appropriate graduate-level courses in special education and TESOL

(English language learners), since the best practices of those certification areas seem to overlap with reading. Additionally, I advise them to practice differentiated learning and to study the latest brain-based research along with the new buzzword *multiliteracies.*

Q: What recommendations do you have for reading specialists who encounter teachers who struggle with curriculum and/or pedagogy?

A: Reading specialists should always assist or mentor on the teacher's level, not in any formal administrative or evaluative manner. For teachers who struggle with curriculum and/or pedagogy, I communicate the importance of establishing "SMART" goals. This translates to the individual teacher's professional goals, which are (1) *s*mall and specific, (2) *m*eaningful and measurable, (3) *a*chievable and attainable, (4) *r*ealistic and reflective, and (5) *t*aught and timed. Then we proceed together.

Acceptance of change is easier as I offer warm and cool feedback, like that modeled in a peer review session. Being cognizant of a teacher's point of view, I offer empathy and read their body language. They will hear me use this statement: "We have no problems in life, just challenges we will overcome together." While I am aiding a struggling teacher, I often say, "Take what you need from me to help yourself succeed."

Q: Do you ever provide professional development for your teachers? If so, who asks/requires you to do this?

A: Yes, I occasionally provide professional development for teachers and other staff members. This includes comprehensive workshops, PowerPoint presentations, and team meetings on reading comprehension strategies and/or literacy concepts. I facilitate the Teacher Mentoring Program, so my professional development typically focuses on best practices, 4MAT (a school reform model from About Learning, Inc.), and the multiple intelligences relative to effective classroom organization and management with reader/writer workshops and literacy sessions.

Q: Is there anything else you would like to say about the role of the reading specialist and/or about the collaboration between the reading specialist and the literacy coach?

A: The role of the reading specialist is really that of a learning specialist for both students and other educators. The reading specialist can develop into the liaison between the English/language arts department and academic intervention services. My role provokes me to ask: "What specifically can I do to help you succeed with your goals?"

Source: Theresa M. Manfre, Reading Specialist, Long Island, NY.

SUMMARY

This chapter focused on the collaborative role of the literacy coach. Information was provided on specific collaborative situations: working with reading specialists, paraprofessionals, and librarians/media specialists. The common ground shared by literacy coaches and reading specialists was emphasized. Perspectives on the role of the reading specialist of principals, teachers, and parents were shared.

The coach's role in facilitating professional development and collaborating with reading specialists while planning and implementing professional development was explored. A nationally recognized reading specialist's thoughts about specific aspects of the varied tasks performed by reading specialists today, as well as the collaborative nature of their work, were shared.

TOPIC EXTENSIONS FOR CLASS
SESSIONS OR STUDY GROUPS

1. Taking on the role of John Bruno in the scenario described at the beginning of this chapter, what advice would you offer to Joyce Ling about the effective use of a paraprofessional in the reading specialist's classroom?

2. In addition to being effective teachers and working toward the improvement of reading instruction, what other significant parallels can you identify between the role of the reading specialist and the coach?

3. Discuss the positive and negative aspects of one person serving as part-time literacy coach and part-time reading specialist for a school.

4. This chapter provided information on the coach's role in providing professional development for teachers. What can the literacy coach do to ensure her own continued professional growth and development?

Assessment: Focus on Student Achievement 9

INTRODUCTION

Across the United States, local newspapers publish articles that contain achievement scores from schools or school districts. Radencich (1995) states that this creates a tunnel-visioned view because only one evaluation (which is not a perfect instrument) is used to measure school performance. Real estate agents have been known to use these reports to their advantage to sell homes in certain high-performing school districts. The news media creates public opinion, which has an influence on school boards and legislators who mandate state assessments. Thus, the pressure concerning assessment is a reality in today's schools, especially in view of NCLB (2001) legislation and Adequate Yearly Progress reports.

According to Winograd, Paris, and Bridge (1991), goals for assessment depend on goals for instruction. The alignment of the two, as sensible as it seems, is often not evident within the curriculum or among the practices of some teachers. Literacy coaches who play a role in administering assessments, collecting assessment data, or reporting on assessment information to stakeholders provide a lens for looking at the various views in the school or school district. The collection of data leads to a comprehensive overview of the curriculum and reading program. It informs the educators about the programmatic strengths and shortcomings of the curriculum. Analyzing the data can provide a clear understanding of the path that the school needs to take, which is the ultimate goal of assessment.

SCENARIO

At Belfield Middle School, literacy coaches Stefano Rodriguez and Peg Woods have met several times over the past few weeks. The principal provided them with copies of the state testing results and asked them to gather schoolwide benchmark data as well. He requested that they present results from both data sources to the staff at next month's faculty meeting. Additionally, the principal has asked them to translate the data and discern how it corresponds to strengths and needs of instructional strategies to affect student achievement positively within Belfield Middle School.

Stefano and Peg are willing to fulfill the principal's request, but they are struggling with issues related to the data. How do the data relate to the ongoing work they have been doing with classroom teachers over the past year? How do the data reveal the strengths of individual teachers and the weaknesses of others? Will the data support the school's focus on standards as well as the needs the coaches have prioritized for the school's literacy program? What other sources of information should be conveyed to the staff in terms of aligning assessment and instruction? As the coaches discuss issues and pose the questions, they begin to realize that a presentation at one faculty meeting will not be sufficient to convey both the general and specific information teachers will need to know.

Collecting and analyzing data in preparation for sharing it with the teachers is a typical expectation of literacy coaches. The opportunity to share information allows them not only to monitor progress but also to collaborate with teachers to affirm what is working well in their school and to determine what needs improvement.

COLLECTING AND ANALYZING DATA

Literacy coaches collect and analyze many types of data throughout the course of their work. On a daily basis, they collect data on instructional strategies. On a yearly basis, they collect and compile data about the schoolwide instructional program via benchmark and statewide assessments. Depending on the school situation, the coach may find herself the sole collector of data on the literacy program and the sole person responsible for analyzing and reporting it. In other situations, the coach may work in a team with the school's reading specialist to collect and analyze the data, and they can share the responsibility of dissemination illustrated by the above scenario. Both situations will be discussed in the sections that follow.

The Coach Alone

The literacy coach plays a major role in assessing a school's instructional program by observing in classrooms. The cumulative snapshots collected by the coach are a rich source of data. Continuing with the snapshot metaphor, the individual pictures of each classroom help to form an "album" for reviewing the broader systemic components of the literacy program. A wide-angle lens helps the coach appreciate the full spectrum of instructional considerations. Snapshots and albums are both important to collect and review routinely. The coach must look at the wider context of the school and the more narrow context of the classroom. Vogt and Shearer (2004) indicate that the school's vision, educational plan, standards, and provisions for looking at student's literacy needs should be examined. This is the wider context—the one viewed with the wide-angle lens.

The narrower context is the regular classroom situation. One of the major responsibilities of the coach is to collect data on the individual teachers in the classroom. Think of a zoom lens when considering observation and data collection in the classroom setting. Vogt and Shearer (2004) state that coaches need to observe possible mismatches between instructional approaches and students, curriculum and materials misalignments, and problems in grouping arrangements. Information about the classrooms in the building can be gathered through using teacher interviews, questionnaires, surveys, self-assessments, classroom observations (see coach's observation forms, Chapter 3, Resources E, F, G, and H), materials checklists, and conversations about literacy instruction.

The Coach With Reading Specialists

The triangulation of collaborator, colleague, and learner should be obvious to participants and observers as the literacy coach interacts with the reading specialist. These two professionals are mutually dependent upon and mutually supportive of each other. When grade-level or schoolwide tests are administered, reading specialists often play an active role. They may individually administer tests to children or assist in classrooms as group tests are given.

Some schools are fortunate enough to have both reading specialists and literacy coaches. In those schools, both professionals can assist in the administration, scoring, and review of grade-level or schoolwide tests. It is important for both reading specialists and literacy coaches to have a clear understanding of the scores themselves and of the implications of the scores for the school's literacy program.

The ultimate goal of the coach and reading specialist's mutually supporting each other is increased literacy achievement. Diligent review of test scores can help the coach assist teachers in improving their instruction. Improvement areas may pertain to identified areas of weakness in the test data (e.g., particular comprehension strategies or writing domains). Although the coach works with teachers, his efforts, combined with those of the teachers, should eventually affect student achievement at the classroom level.

The reading specialist's perspective on test scores should be focused at the individual student level. The reading specialist should be able to offer teachers suggestions based on assessment results (IRA, 2000). Because reading specialists may provide instruction in a variety of structures (individual or small-group pullout sessions, individual or small-group instruction within the regular classroom, coteaching with the classroom teacher), their own teaching should be refined to improve individual student achievement after an assiduous review of test scores. Modifications in instruction based on test results are necessary especially for students in need of reading interventions. "When the teachers and reading specialists work together and use assessments to inform and guide classroom instruction, students can experience literacy growth and teachers can feel a sense of ownership over classroom instruction and student learning" (Guth & Pettengill, 2005, p. 61).

SCHOOLWIDE DATA

A school literacy team that comprises the coach, the teachers, and the principals should determine what assessment instruments will be used, by whom, for what students, at what grade levels, and at what intervals during the school year (Vogt & Shearer, 2004). The types of assessments that are commonly used to collect data in the school and in the classroom are running records, fluency records, informal reading inventories, and, of course, standardized achievement tests.

Walpole and McKenna (2004) caution that "[c]onducting schoolwide assessments without training to ensure that all testers can administer the tests reliably is a waste of teaching and learning time" (p. 25). Walpole and McKenna state that data from testing should be used to drive instruction and, therefore, classroom teachers should administer the tests. The coach can play a significant role in training teachers how to administer tests correctly.

A testing model where the coach takes much of the responsibility for testing at first and then gradually releases the responsibility to the teachers is suggested by Walpole and McKenna (2004). They outline the following steps:

- The literacy coach first works with a small schoolwide assessment team to test all children.
- The assessment team simulates and practices testing with adults.

- The team then administers a group test to individual children.
- The team finally proceeds to testing throughout the whole school.
- Teachers are asked to watch some of the testing in the different steps to familiarize themselves with the procedures.
- Training is then provided to all of the classroom teachers by the assessment team.
- Next, the teachers function as members of the team in their own classrooms by administering their own tests to their own students.
- Other members of the team are still involved, because they assist teachers in collecting the data when a child is absent or needs some specialized assistance, such as having the test read to him.
- The data that have been collected are used by the whole faculty to drive instructional practices.
- To accomplish the goal of training teachers to collect assessment data, the coach must develop a calendar that gives an overview of the testing dates.
- After the testing dates have been scheduled on the calendar, the coach needs to plan backwards from the testing dates to schedule the teacher training needed to administer the tests.

If the literacy coach needs to garner testing information from the teachers in the building, he may have to devise a form for submission of this information. The reporting forms that are used by the teachers should be streamlined, made teacher-friendly for use in both inputting information and for reviewing the form. The literacy coach and teachers who have computers available can submit and review forms electronically with a click of the mouse. The forms can be stored on a server for review by the teachers, coach, principal, and any other interested school personnel.

Collecting the data is the first step, but for the picture to be complete, it must be followed by an analysis of the data. In our experience, we often find that classroom teachers do not know how to interpret data from assessments properly. We are concerned because in most schools, the data are used to make decisions concerning students based on just one overall score. Guth and Pettengill (2005) suggest that an assessment should not be used in isolation because it is merely a snapshot. In this instance, the literacy coach can assist the whole faculty in viewing data in a different light by providing summaries of schoolwide data. Walpole and McKenna (2004) state that the coach could use a spreadsheet to calculate the total number of students, the percentage, the mean or average, and the standard deviation easily.

CLASSROOM DATA

Pikulski (1994) believes that assessment should inform and support teacher decision making. Classroom assessments should also be used to develop a class picture. The class picture helps the teacher determine what instructional practices will produce optimal student learning in the classroom. Reading and writing assessments given in classrooms should be thoroughly reviewed by the teacher. If the teacher has difficulty analyzing the information or has some questions about it, the reading specialist or the literacy coach could support the teacher in understanding what information the assessment data reveal about the class as a whole as literacy learners.

Classroom data collection can be both formal and informal. Formal collection involves completing summary forms that are submitted to the principal or her designee. Classroom data are often collected at the district level as well. Informal data collection occurs in classrooms when teachers gather performance samples, such as writing drafts and fluency checks for reading. Checklists and teacher-made tests can be included as informal assessment pieces. When informal assessments are gathered by the teacher, they should be used to inform further teaching and determine any necessary interventions for individual students. The assessments are also valuable sources of information to share with parents during teacher-parent conferences.

When literacy coaches and teachers confer about what is happening instructionally in classrooms, teachers may want to bring some of the informal assessments they have collected to the conference. These artifacts can serve as a source for rich dialogue about instructional practices. They can also inform the literacy coach about what is important to the teacher and the areas of instructional focus in the individual classroom.

Thoughtful, informed, and collaborative review of student work and other assessment documentation can help provide direction regarding language arts instruction to both the classroom teacher and the literacy coach.

OBSERVATION DATA

Student Data: A Portrait of the Individual

Student assessment is a critical piece of the reading program development (Bean, 2004). Assessment results are used to guide instruction and improve student achievement.

Certainly, after going to the trouble of assessing each student, the teacher and the school should make the best use of the collected data.

Occasionally, the standardized test data collected and the performance of the individual student in class every day do not match. Radencich (1995) postulates that this type of discrepancy may be due to any of the following factors: illness on the day of the test, lack of student motivation, altered test scores, test administration errors, test anxiety, or a mismatch of test and curriculum.

The important point here is that the teacher should know how to determine which test scores are valid and which scores are not and how to use them wisely. The literacy coach and/or reading specialist should develop a plan to assist teachers with this task. They coach may also give suggestions to the teacher on how to manage and disseminate both the formal and informal test data that have been collected.

Radencich (1995) states that a wealth of teacher-collected assessment data needs to be managed, such as teacher observation notes of students, student self-evaluations, and student work samples. Therefore, professional development sessions on how to manage student portfolios are essential. It is important for the literacy coach to impart the message that assessing a child's literacy development is a recurring and continuous process. Observing and assessing each individual's literacy development should occur in several contexts and at different times. The reading specialist's observations concerning individual students' strengths and weaknesses should certainly be one context for examination.

Assessment portfolios should grow and be constantly reshaped because they are living documents. Since they are not private entities like grade books, they may include pieces of work chosen by the individual student and shared with the child's parents. Radencich (1995) suggests that parents be asked to make contributions to their child's portfolio so that they will learn more about the child's literacy development.

As a result of NCLB (2001) legislation, student data from formal standardized tests are also used to measure a school's Annual Yearly Progress. Across the country, student test data have been used to determine district funding levels and to determine which school districts need to be managed by the state. When school districts are placed in the hands of the states to manage because they have produced poor student scores, private corporations are sometimes hired to oversee the district. This action has often resulted in the firing of reading specialists and literacy coaches, because the budgets of the private corporations that manage the schools that need "corrective action" are very tight. Therefore, the standardized testing initiatives and the collection and analysis of data from these tests have had a major impact on schooling at this time in our country's history.

Classroom Data: A Group Snapshot

As stated in Chapter 3, the coach's observations in classrooms can be a great source of data about the school's instructional program. It is up to the coach to determine how to use the data to promote instructional improvement. When the coach's observational data are combined with formal assessment data for a particular classroom, a clear picture comes into view about the strengths and needs of instruction. As the literacy coach examines both types of information, she should be able to decide whether to discontinue, change, or intensify the current level of work she is doing with a specific classroom teacher.

In the wide-lens approach, the coach can conduct a similar examination of data for a grade level or department review. Focusing on several classrooms collectively allows the coach to determine how to proceed with a small group of teachers working in a similar context whom she is responsible for coaching.

The form shown in Figure 9.1 can be used to help literacy coaches collect data on several classrooms in a streamlined format.

REPORT WRITING

In this age of accountability, report writing is a fact of life. Written reports may be required by the principal on a regular basis. The process of report writing is expedited when proper documentation is in order. The literacy coach's log, e-mail, letters, and memorandums, when properly filed, are resources when writing reports.

Here are some tips for report writing:

- Keep the audience in mind. Are you writing reports for parents, teachers, school administrators, or school board members?
- Make certain that your report contains successes (even if they are small) as well as weaknesses.
- Don't forget to list examples or illustrations in your report.
- Double-check your spelling and grammar.
- Provide references from research where applicable. This will show that you have done your homework.
- Use clear, concise language. If you use educational terminology that your readership may not understand, be certain to explain it.
- If you have documentation to support your report, include it in an appendix.
- Your facts and figures must be correct. Have another knowledgeable colleague review them to make certain that they are accurate.

Figure 9.1 Data Review of Several Classrooms

Grade or Department	Teacher	Room #	# of Students	Dates of Observations by Literacy Coach	Dates of Conferences w/ Literacy Coach	Test Reviewed	Test-Indicated Strengths	Test-Indicated Weakness	Teacher's Concerns or Comments

Summary Statement:

Literacy Coach _____ Date _____

- Don't include extraneous information. In this information age, people are consumed with phone calls, e-mail, and other media. Keep your message to the point.
- If you do not have any idea of how to begin your report, ask for an example or model.
- Date the report. You many need to compare the current report with reports from prior (or future) years at the same time of year.

Sometimes, the coach may be asked both to submit and present written reports. Visual aides, such as PowerPoint slides or posters or charts, in addition to a report often accompany oral presentations.

At other times, the literacy coach takes the initiative to write a report that is not required by a school administrator. In this case, the coach should submit the report to her principal (or other supervisor) and ask for feedback and/or a meeting with the principal to review the report. The coach should not distribute the report to any other individuals or groups unless the administrator in charge has approved its distribution.

AN EXPERT'S THOUGHTS: DR. RICHARD ALLINGTON

Richard Allington, a distinguished educator who served as president of both the International Reading Association and the National Reading Conference, was named to the IRA Hall of Fame in 1995 for the significant contributions he has made to the field of education. He has written over 100 books about literacy teaching, learning, and assessment and serves on the editorial review boards for several journals. Dr. Allington shared his views of assessment information that is essential for literacy coaches.

Q: What data should the literacy coach collect and analyze as a result of individual classroom observations and demonstration teaching?

A: I'd say that gathering data on text-reader matches would be the first sort of data to collect. Do kids have books they can actually read with accuracy, fluency, and comprehension? This is especially important for struggling readers because often they have a desk full of books that are simply unmanageable for them. So check on how well the books in each struggling reader's desk "fit" that reader's current level of reading proficiency.

Q: Many times the literacy coach works closely with reading specialists in the school/district. What types of assessments should be familiar to and reviewed by both the coach and the reading specialist?

A: Both should know how to gather and interpret measures of oral reading accuracy and fluency. The most common assessment approaches here are running records and words-correct-per-minute data. Both focus on curriculum-based data gathering, and both provide good information on text-reader matches. In addition, both should know how to gather information on reading comprehension using free retell, prompted retell, and summary writing.

Q: After reviewing schoolwide standardized tests results, what should the literacy coach be prepared to do to work toward schoolwide improvement of literacy teaching and learning?

A: I'm not a big fan of trying to interpret schoolwide standardized test data. The group standardized tests have large standard error of measurement, assess only the lowest-level skills, and typically provide no information on the reading process (Why did the child respond that way?). The group standardized tests may provide users with a general sense of the levels of reading proficiency at each grade level, and so I'd look to see whether the numbers of lower-achieving readers are declining every year (and include pupils with disabilities in this count). In other words, when a school's reading program is effective, fewer students perform poorly each year, and more perform at adequate levels. In schools where the reading program (including remedial and special education programs) is not effective, the numbers of struggling readers get larger every year. So use standardized test data to map the size of the group of struggling readers in each grade. The goal is to reduce the number of poor readers with each passing year. If that is not happening, then you have to ask hard questions about the effectiveness of both classroom and intervention reading programs.

Q: What advice do you have for literacy coaches who are new to the role?

A: Don't spread yourself too thinly. Pick a grade level or two to focus on. Get to know six to eight classroom teachers really well. Focus your energies on helping those teachers improve their lessons. Then the next year, select another six to eight teachers to work closely with. And so on.

Q: In *A Guide to Literacy Coaching*, we are emphasizing the roles of collaborator, facilitator, colleague, and learner as significant to the working relationship the literacy coach has with teachers. Do you think that one or more of these roles are especially helpful when assisting teachers with administering assessments and then reviewing them?

A: I'd pick colleague and learner as the critical roles. Reading coaches just simply must have substantial expertise about reading development, reading assessment, and reading instruction and must be continually developing this expertise. Classroom teachers only need to know about reading development at the level they teach, but coaches need to know about development across the spectrum. As for collegiality, develop large amounts of shared knowledge about the teachers' lessons you are working with and share your expertise to foster further development of their expertise about teaching kids to read.

Q: All educators, from classroom teachers to the superintendent, feel the pressures of meeting Adequate Yearly Progress (AYP) in schools. Those in literacy leadership positions, such as literacy coaches, reading specialists, and supervisors, are often responsible for instituting programs to achieve AYP. What suggestions and cautions would you offer to those charged with putting programs into place?

A: First, be sure you know what the research actually says about effective reading instruction. There has been much distortion of the research by those with entrepreneurial interests, as documented in the report on the Reading First program by the Inspector General of the U.S. Department of Education. Second, realize that intervention for struggling readers has to be an all-day-long design. You cannot simply insert 30 minutes daily of good reading intervention instruction into a 330-minute school day and expect to solve the problems of struggling readers. Struggling readers need 90 minutes of high-quality classroom reading lessons, then 30 minutes more of small-group expert reading instruction to have any chance of catching up. Third, remember that commercial intervention programs are largely irrelevant in the design of good interventions. There is no "one-size-fits-all" approach that actually addresses the varying needs of any group of struggling readers. It is expert and intensive reading lessons that solve kids' problems, not programs.

Q: Any other thoughts related to the literacy coach and assessment?

A: The essence of good teaching is knowing what the reader knows and what they don't know and then designing lessons that build on what they know to develop the proficiencies they need. So good coaches help teachers learn how to observe and gather data from kids during their reading lessons. For instance, by fourth grade, you might expect to find some struggling readers who can read accurately but exhibit difficulties with comprehension; some of these kids may need lessons focused on effective comprehension strategy use, while others use appropriate strategies but have substantial vocabulary deficits that impair comprehension. Another group of struggling readers may have problems at the word level. But some of these kids lack basic decoding skills, and others have those skills but have not learned more advanced decoding skills (e.g., big word decoding), and another group may be able decode in isolation but fail to integrate this skill into their text reading. I could go on, but the point is that each of these potential groups of struggling readers needs very different interventions. The coach has to work to ensure that any assessments used help everyone focus lessons on what each student needs.

Source: Dr. Richard Allington, University of Tennessee.

SUMMARY

The assessment information in this chapter relates the role of the literacy coach in assisting classroom teachers, reading specialists, and the principal with the tasks of administering tests, collecting data, and reporting results to significant constituents. The collaborative role of the coach was emphasized.

The coach's responsibilities for collecting schoolwide test data and correlating that data with the coaching that has taken place within the school is discussed. Another potential responsibility, report writing, was also described, and suggestions for report writing were given.

A form for condensing and reviewing data from several classrooms was recommended. Such a form is a good tool for the coach and reading specialist to review together. Collaboratively, they can analyze student achievement at the classroom level. After a review at the classroom level, the coach and/or the reading specialist should meet with classroom teachers to discuss individual student achievement.

The expert's comments on assessment information collected and used by the literacy coach include both practical and philosophical aspects for consideration.

TOPIC EXTENSIONS FOR CLASS
SESSIONS OR STUDY GROUPS

1. Stefano and Peg, the literacy coaches in the scenario in this chapter, need help creating an action plan and a timetable for adequately conveying to the staff the information relevant to the data they have collected. Discuss the issues from the scenario with a colleague.

Together, create an action plan and timetable. Then, determine an appropriate method of presenting these documents to the principal and suggesting that more time and deeper discussion is needed to work with the faculty.

2. The daily work of the coach includes collecting data on instructional strategies. Discuss this topic with at least two other coaches or with teachers who work directly with literacy coaches. How do the coaches collect information about instructional strategies? What do they do with the information once they have it? Are the approaches of the two coaches alike or different? What are some overarching benefits of having this information?

3. Reading and writing assessments should be thoroughly reviewed by classroom teachers. What should a thorough review consist of? How could a literacy coach help a teacher to become more thorough in his approach to reviewing such data?

4. Report writing is a necessary component of the job for both formal and informal school leaders. Choose one of the following topics and, as a literacy coach, construct a mock report:
   a. A monthly report to the principal about the observations, demonstrations, curriculum review, etc., that you have done
   b. A project plan to be submitted to the language arts supervisor detailing the long-term professional development you designed for your school for the upcoming year. Be sure to include a rationale for your plan.
   c. A summary report to the principal and other administrators that provides information on recent standardized test data and its alignment (or lack of alignment) to state standards and district curriculum requirements

5. Create a list of additional questions you would ask Dr. Allington related to your work as a literacy coach. Be able to discuss why the questions you posed are of particular concern to you.

6. Choose one or two of the interview responses by Dr. Allington and discuss what stands out for you in terms of being critical to the work of the literacy coach and what might seem of lesser importance. You should be able to discuss why you have characterized the issues you have chosen.

Major Reports   **10**
That Impact
Literacy Coaching

INTRODUCTION

Literacy coaches should have a keen awareness of the content and implications of major literacy research reports, including those published by national commissions. Major reports generally have an impact on what schools, publishers, parents, and communities expect teachers to know and be able to do when they instruct and assess students. National reports also impact the content of textbooks and other materials used in published reading programs. This chapter provides an overview of the content and implications of five major reports: *The Report of the National Reading Panel, Reading First, Reading Next,* the *RAND Report,* and *Reading at Risk.* Much of the information offered is technical. In-depth information is given for documents that have a wider reputation than others.

Like Jeff Smith, the coach mentioned in the scenario below, all literacy coaches need to keep current with significant public reports so they can share their informed decisions about the documents' findings with stakeholders. The chapter emphasizes what the literacy coach should know about each of these documents. Knowing the documents and being able to decide judiciously which recommendations offer sound practices and which do not is crucial for the literacy coach's support of the professional development of individual and collective teachers.

SCENARIO

Jeff Smith is a literacy coach in the Midcity School District. He has been asked by the assistant superintendent for instruction to provide one of the full-day summer workshops for veteran teachers in the district. The assistant superintendent is especially concerned that the veteran teachers receive training and information on new national mandates and current trends in literacy, because a team from the Department of Education in their state is coming to examine whether national mandates and current trends are reflected in the teaching practices of the district.

Jeff Smith has decided to ask a panel of experts to lead a discussion of several national mandates and trends. As you read this chapter, consider the following questions:

- What issues do you think that Jeff should select for the panel discussion?
- Whom do you think that he might ask to be discussants on the panel?

WHAT THE LITERACY COACH SHOULD KNOW ABOUT THE *NATIONAL READING PANEL REPORT*

In 1997, the National Reading Panel (NRP), a group of 14 experts in the educational field, was charged by Congress to examine and report on a review of the research related to the "effectiveness of various approaches to teaching children to read" (National Institute of Child Health and Human Development [NICHD], 2000, 1-1). The result was a report titled *Teaching Children to Read: An Evidence-Based Assessment of Scientific Research Literature on Reading and Its Implications for Reading Instruction.*

Because the volume of reading research exceeded 100,000 studies, the NRP selected and prioritized areas to be included in its report. The criteria used to evaluate research were those generally accepted by scientists in medical and behavioral fields: experimental or quasi-experimental studies. The NRP determined that maintaining scientifically based research promoted rigorous analysis and common reporting procedures. In a nutshell, studies that were not considered scientifically based by the NRP were discounted from review and analysis.

Although experimental studies are often a part of educational research, other studies, such as correlational analysis, comparative analysis, case studies, and descriptive qualitative research, are common to the body of educational literature. The reason other types of studies are warranted in the educational field is that there is variability and uniqueness in student populations, school demographics, teachers, teaching techniques, reading programs, reading materials, and formal and informal assessments.

Qualitative research is important in education because it provides in-depth descriptions of populations and techniques (Garan, 2001; Yatvin,

2002). It also renders specific details concerning the strategies and skills that were successful or difficult for students in each particular study.

Despite the NRP's focus on scientifically based research, the literacy coach must know the report's content while recognizing what is not included. It is equally imperative that the literacy coach prudently discourage instructional practices that overemphasize singular skills and/or are developmentally inappropriate for certain age groups or types of learners. Literacy coaches should encourage the use of reading and writing strategies that will enable these communication processes to be taught and learned in a developmentally appropriate, strategic manner.

The results of the NRP's selection process included five major topics: (1) alphabetics (phonemic awareness instruction and phonics instruction), (2) fluency, (3) comprehension (vocabulary instruction, text comprehension instruction, and teacher preparation and comprehension strategies instruction), (4) teacher education and reading instruction, and (5) computer technology and reading instruction. Panel members joined one of five subgroups and focused their efforts on one topic. A discussion of each of the five topics follows.

Alphabetics: Phonemic Awareness Instruction and Phonics Instruction

Alphabetics (Harris & Hodges, 1995) is the study of the graphic symbols representing speech sounds used in writing a language. Phonemic awareness and phonics instruction are considered to be key elements in any beginning reading program. These two topics will be discussed further as they relate to the *National Reading Panel Report*.

Phonemic Awareness

The NRP stated that evidence suggests the "potential instructional importance" of phonemic awareness. Phonemic awareness is the ability to recognize and isolate unit sounds (phonemes) in words. There are 41 phonemes in the English lexicon, and several tasks are often used to determine a child's level of proficiency or deficiency of phonemic awareness (see Figure 10.1). According to the NRP, phonemic awareness is considered a contributing factor in helping children learn to read because the alphabetic structure of the English writing system is so complex. Therefore, the ability to "distinguish the separate phonemes in pronunciations of words so that they can be matched to graphemes" (NICHD, 2000, p. 2-2) is instructionally worthy. The report concludes that phonemic awareness can be effectively taught and learned in "a variety of teaching conditions with a variety of learners" (NICHD, 2-5), especially if teachers are trained to properly teach these skills. According to the NRP, phonemic awareness instruction has a stronger impact on children's learning to decode words than it does on their comprehending text, and it is beneficial to kindergarten and first-grade students in applying spelling. This seems to be a logical conclusion since phonemic awareness is a word-level skill for those whose reading and writing literacies are just emerging.

Although generally supportive of phonemic awareness instruction in schools, the NRP provides the following caveats about its implementation:

- Phonemic awareness instruction should not be considered a stand-alone early reading program.
- Phonemic awareness is a means to help children understand alphabetic principles applied to their reading and writing.

Figure 10.1 Samples of NRP's Descriptions of Instruction for Phonemic Awareness

Phonemic Awareness Task	Description	Sample Prompt
Phonemic Isolation	The recognition of individual sounds in words	What is the first sound in *mouse?* (/m/)
Phonemic Identity	The recognition of the common sound contained within several words	What sound is the same in these words: ten, top, tape? (/t/)
Phoneme Categorization	The recognition of the word with the odd sound in a series of three or four words	Which word does *not* belong here: mice, mask, and rabbit? (rabbit)
Phoneme Blending	Listening to a sequence of separately spoken sounds and combining them to form a recognizable word	What word is /p/ /ar/ /k/ ? (park)
Phoneme Segmentation	Breaking a word into its individual sounds by tapping/counting the individual sounds or by pronouncing and positioning a marker for each sound	How many sounds are there in *pig?* (three: /p/ /i/ /g/)
Phoneme Deletion	The recognition of what word remains when a specified phoneme is removed	What is *brake* without the *b?* (rake)

- Some children will need more phonemic awareness instruction than others.
- Early phonemic awareness instruction does not guarantee later literacy success.

Phonics

Phonics instruction differs from phonemic awareness instruction in that it is more broadly based to include sound-symbol relationships and spelling patterns, or rime patterns of words, to identify words in context. According to the National Reading Panel, "the goal in all phonics programs is to enable learners to acquire sufficient knowledge and use of the alphabetic code so that they can make normal progress in learning to read and comprehend written language" (NICHD, 2000, p. 2-89). Thirty-eight studies were analyzed to determine the effect of systematic phonics instruction on young children. The analysis provided information that some phonics instruction in the early grades (kindergarten and first grade) is better than none, both small and large instructional groups benefited from effective phonics instruction, and phonics instruction improved the spelling of kindergarten and first-grade students but "did not improve spelling in students above 1st grade" (NICHD, p. 2-95). The NRP states that phonics instruction should be integrated with other reading instruction to provide a comprehensive reading program for young readers and writers. The NRP cautions that phonics instruction is not meant to be the "dominant component" (p. 2-97) of any reading program.

Balancing Alphabetics With Other Forms of Instruction

The literacy coach should be cognizant of the information on alphabetics provided by the NRP so that practices involving overreliance on phonemic awareness or phonics by either classroom teachers or reading specialists is diminished. A balanced instructional program that moves students beyond word-level reading to the reading of connected text should be available for all young students. Sometimes, teachers tend to spend longer than necessary on word-level activities because programs that promote phonics are scripted and often follow routines. For example, a program may provide details for having children chant sounds, imitate sounds, visually recognize some phonic components, and engage in a word recognition game or phonic activity. If this series of activities is the only instruction provided to students, it deprives them of applying their alphabet skills to reading. Skills in isolation are futile; application of skills builds proficiency.

In remarks based on the NRP report, Botel (2000) states that

> publishers of phonemic analysis, phonics and other skills pro-
> grams are loaded with fat. That means that teachers are likely to
> spend so much time on this area that it will crowd out the other
> basic areas of a balanced literacy curriculum. (p. 1)

Tipping the scales with phonemic awareness and phonics instruction is a disservice to children because it deprives them of other vital nutrients of literacy. Reading, writing, talking, and viewing in response to literature and shared events should be included in every instructional program for the sake of the individual learners and for the sake of meeting standards as an educational institution. The literacy coach's ensuring that alphabetics does not crowd out opportunities for the teaching and learning of reading and writing at the application level needs to be evident in the feedback and professional development provided to teachers and administrators.

Fluency

Fluency entails the ability to read at an appropriate rate, with accurate word recognition, and with expressive prosody. Because fluency is a prominent concern among reading professionals (Dowhower, 1994; Opitz & Rasinski, 1998; Snow, Burns, & Griffin, 1998; Stanovich, 1986), the National Reading Panel chose it as one of the five subgroups for study. Procedures that emphasized repeated oral reading, such as paired reading and shared reading, were found to have an impact on dysfluent readers. The following statements summarize the major conclusions drawn by the NRP about fluency instruction:

- Classroom practices that encourage repeated oral reading with feedback and guidance lead to meaningful improvements in reading expertise for both good and struggling readers.
- Fluency represents a level of expertise beyond word recognition accuracy, and reading comprehension may be aided by fluency. Therefore, word recognition accuracy should not be considered the end point of reading instruction.
- Children who do not develop reading fluency will continue to read in a slow, laborious manner.
- Instructional practices that encourage repeated oral reading result in increased reading proficiency.

The information on fluency rendered by the NRP report stresses the need for guided practice in reading and re-reading of text to ensure fluency and aid comprehension. When literacy coaches are able to recommend fluency techniques to be included in teachers' instructional repertoires, they are enabling children to read better and to read more. At the same time, they are providing teachers with opportunities to assess students' strengths and needs related to reading rate, reading accuracy, and prosody. These recommendations seem to be especially important for the teacher who may provide just one reading of a text under her instructional guidance and question why the students read in a choppy manner. Coaching the teacher to provide more than one reading opportunity of full or partial text to improve students' fluency and understanding is a practical, uncomplicated technique to implement with students who may need fluency training.

Comprehension

Comprehension is the ultimate goal of reading. The NRP recognized the crucial nature of comprehension and the importance of quality teaching to enable all students to develop proficient comprehension. The NRP's review of comprehension research includes the topics of vocabulary instruction, text comprehension and instruction, and teacher preparation and comprehension strategy instruction. As a result, three themes have evolved and are used as the organizing criteria for reporting on comprehension. The three major themes linked to comprehension in the NRP report (NICHD, 2000, p. 4-1) follow:

1. Reading comprehension is a cognitive process that integrates complex skills and cannot be understood without examining the critical role of vocabulary learning and instruction and its development.

2. Active interactive strategic processes are critically necessary to the development of reading comprehension.

3. The preparation of teachers to equip them to facilitate these complex processes optimally is critical and intimately tied to the development of reading comprehension.

Each theme is extensive and complex, yet each must be thoroughly understood by those responsible for teaching students, as well as those responsible for coaching best practices in classrooms. Just as the NRP report delineated each of the three themes, the following sections will also address each theme as a strand of the overriding topic of comprehension.

Vocabulary Instruction

The first NRP theme of comprehension emphasizes the critical role of vocabulary instruction. The NRP examined studies on vocabulary instruction that "contained at least some experimental work on instructional methods" (NICHD, 2000, p. 4-16). A variety of instructional methods related to vocabulary were used across the studies, and the NRP recommended multiple methods of vocabulary instruction as more effective than any one method. Explanations of each method reviewed by NRP follow:

- *Explicit vocabulary instruction:* Preteaching vocabulary before instructional or independent reading (contextual settings and/or definitions of words are provided to students); analysis of roots or affixes also may be explicitly taught. This method not only facilitates the learning of new vocabulary but also promotes comprehension, because text becomes easier to negotiate when readers have an understanding of vocabulary used in context when it has been pretaught. It helps them to conceptualize accurately what they are reading.
- *Indirect instruction of vocabulary:* Students encounter new words as they read and infer meanings from the new words.
- *Multimedia methods of vocabulary instruction:* Teaching vocabulary from sources other than connected text such as graphic organizers, semantic maps, or hypertext is used to help students acquire new oral and written vocabulary. The computer may be considered "an adjunct to direct vocabulary instruction" (NICHD, p. 4-26) because of the many searching possibilities available to students as well as the capability to access definitions and synonyms for newly encountered terms.
- *Capacity methods:* Students concentrate on learning the meaning of words. This method may be used in isolation, separate from the reading process.
- *Association methods:* Students are encouraged to make associations between and among semantic and contextual uses of words. They are also encouraged to make associations based on images connected to words.

The NRP concluded that vocabulary instruction is a critical component of comprehension teaching and learning and offered the following guidance for instruction:

- *Vocabulary should be taught both directly and indirectly within rich contexts and may be acquired incidentally.* This tenet has strong implications for both the literacy coach and the classroom teacher. It imparts the notion of planned teaching of vocabulary, especially before students interact with text, as well as the unplanned, spontaneous teaching of vocabulary—taking advantage of the teachable moment when a word, figure of speech, or concept evolves within the instructional situation and lends itself to exploration. As the coach observes planned vocabulary teaching, he should reflect on whether or not the selected words will help to enhance the students' understanding of what they will read and whether or not the students were able to use the selected words appropriately in their oral and written responses to what was read. Just as important is the literacy coach's observation of the word, figure of speech, or concept that evolves and is not addressed by the teacher or questioned by the students. Neglecting language that may help to promote literate understanding is an omission of the teaching act and needs to be recognized so it can be corrected.

- *Repetition and multiple exposures to newly learned vocabulary is important.* Vocabulary tasks should be restructured when necessary; that is, group learning activities should be used and learning materials should be revised to provide students with varied approaches and several opportunities to explore new vocabulary. Students should be active participants in vocabulary learning tasks, whether oral or written, independent or interdependent, print or technological. How vocabulary is assessed and evaluated can have differential effects on instruction; the NRP report recommended that teachers and schools use "more than a single measure" (NICHD, 2000, p. 4-26) of vocabulary learning to ensure accurate assessment.

Text Comprehension Instruction

Another critical area of the NRP report was text comprehension, which overlaps the two previously mentioned themes concerning comprehension and interactive strategic processes. Before the 1970s, the explicit teaching of text comprehension was done primarily with content area text and not in the context of reading instruction. Durkin's work in the 1970s made it clear that teachers were not teaching reading comprehension strategies, nor were students using them. The NRP report (NICHD, 2000) clearly relays the historical background for this important research base:

An important development in theories about reading comprehension occurred in the 1970s. Reading comprehension was seen not as a passive, receptive process but as an active one that engaged the reader. Reading came to be seen as intentional thinking during which meaning is constructed through interactions between text and reader (Durkin, 1993). According to this view, meaning resides in the intentional, problem-solving thinking processes of the reader that occur during an interchange with a text. The content of meaning is influenced by the text and by the reader's prior knowledge that is brought to bear on it (Anderson & Pearson, 1984). Reading comprehension was seen as the construction of the meaning of a written text through a reciprocal interchange of ideas between the reader and the message in a particular text. (p. 4-39)

This research provided a new lens for looking at the teaching of reading. Comprehension instruction became an accepted practice; prior to Durkin's work, not much credence was given to the teaching of comprehension strategies. Rather, teacher question and student answer exchanges, with an emphasis on stating the "right answer," were considered an appropriate form of instruction. As a result of Durkin's seminal work, didactic methods of teaching reading were no longer the accepted norm. Strategic teaching and learning were recognized as important, and constructivist definitions of reading comprehension emerged.

Reading as Strategic Process

Reading is the process of constructing meaning (Kintsch, 1998; Rosenblatt, 1981). Proficient readers self-monitor their text reading by implementing strategies. The NRP report (NICHD, 2000) addressed the importance of strategy teaching and learning:

Explicit or formal instruction on these strategies is believed to lead to improvement in text understanding and information use. Instruction in comprehension strategies is carried out by a classroom teacher who demonstrates, models, or guides the reader on their acquisition and use. When these procedures have been acquired, the reader becomes independent of the teacher. Using them, the reader can effectively interact with the text without assistance. Readers who are not explicitly taught these procedures are unlikely to learn, develop, or use them spontaneously. (p. 4-40)

Instructional reading has transformed students from passive recipients of information to active processors and monitors of reading. Comprehension research from the 1970s through current times has rendered a large quantity of data supporting the use of strategy instruction for improving students' comprehension. According to the National Reading Panel, seven key strategies were found to be the most effective for classroom instruction: comprehension monitoring, cooperative learning, graphic and semantic organizers, story grammar, question answering, question generating, and summarizing. Figure 10.2 is an abridged and adapted version of the NRP's full listing of 16 categories for comprehension instruction, focusing on the seven key strategies mentioned above.

Figure 10.2   Abridged and Adapted Version of NRP's Categories for Comprehension

Strategy	Why Instruct?	How Effective?
1. Comprehension monitoring	Readers do not show comprehension strategy awareness.	Readers learn to monitor how well they comprehend. They gain metacognitive awareness and control over their thinking about reading.
2. Cooperative learning	Readers need to learn to work in groups, listen and understand their peers as they read, and help one another use strategies that promote effective reading comprehension.	Readers learn to focus and discuss reading materials. Readers learn reading comprehension strategies and do better on comprehension tests. Teachers provide cognitive structure.
3. Graphic organizers	Readers do not use external organization aids that can benefit their understanding.	Readers improve memory and comprehension of text; readers use graphic organizers for oral and written responses to what they read.
4. Story structure	Poor readers cannot identify structure of narrative texts.	Readers improve memory and identification of story structure.
5. Question answering	Readers do not know how to answer questions, nor do they know how to make inferences.	Readers improve answering questions; responses are directly linked to questions posed to readers.
6. Question generation	Readers do not know how to generate questions or inferences.	Readers learn to generate questions at the inferential level.
7. Summarization	Readers do not know how to summarize text.	Readers improve memory and identification of main ideas. They learn to sort major and minor details.

The literacy coach, as an expert of pedagogy and instructional strategies, should ensure that teachers and students have ample opportunities to employ these strategies in their language arts as well as content area teaching and learning. When working with teachers, the literacy coach needs to be keenly aware of the teacher's demonstration and explanation of strategies and how much (or how little) opportunity is provided for the teacher to guide the students' practice of these strategies. Because strategies are procedural, demonstration and practice are critical. Independent strategy application is not natural; it must be taught.

For students to become strategic readers, their teachers need to be strategic teachers. According to Duffy (1993), teachers need to engage in professional development experiences that allow them to discuss the complexities of strategic teaching and learning and practice explaining and demonstrating strategy instruction. This notion sends a strong message to literacy coaches. In their conferences with teachers, coaches need to highlight the active engagement of learners. Teachers' learning about and practicing their craft should be a part of teacher-coach sessions in both one-to-one situations as well as in group professional development settings.

Following is a discussion of the literacy coach's role in helping teachers instruct students on the key comprehension strategies.

Comprehension Monitoring. Teachers need to model comprehension monitoring for students. Comprehension monitoring involves the awareness of one's mental processes and strategies (Harris & Hodges, 1995). Often, students make word recognition errors when reading and have difficulty forming and supporting responses about what they've read. Teachers need to be observant of these shortcomings in their students and model self-correction strategies for them. They can also use guided questioning techniques to help students begin to self-monitor their use of strategies. The goal is for the student to gain control over his use of reading strategies.

During both classroom observations and conferences with teachers, the literacy coach can share ideas and techniques on comprehension monitoring. Follow-up observations and conferences can provide information about how well comprehension monitoring instruction has progressed. If progress is slow, the literacy coach may want to do a series of demonstration lessons for the teacher to model comprehension monitoring explicitly. Visual aids, such as charts for the classrooms, individual reminders on bookmarks, or sticky notes for specific students, may be helpful during the demonstration lessons. It is important for the literacy coach to process the demonstration lesson with the teacher (as an example of the metacognitive process itself).

Cooperative Learning. Cooperative learning techniques should be used when developmentally and instructionally appropriate. Under the direction of the teacher, students work together in small groups to achieve a learning goal. The goal is typically an outcome based on the shared reading and discussion of a narrative or an article. The small group is usually responsible to report to the entire class the result of its work and how it met its goal.

Literacy coaches can recommend situations when cooperative learning would be of advantage to learners. Cooperative learning with assigned roles for each participant and accountable time on-task is a technique that takes time for teachers to learn to implement and monitor. It also takes time for students to learn turn taking, role responsibilities, and the sharing and explaining of strategy use. When literacy coaches observe cooperative learning in classrooms, they need to be cognizant of the management aspects of this group technique as well as the active learning techniques of the students. The coach needs to remain mindful that cooperative learning is appropriate only when students have shared a common reading or listening activity to which they can respond in a variety of ways to share ideas and information; cooperative learning is not appropriate for every learning situation. Providing feedback to teachers about the appropriateness of cooperative learning or making suggestions for alternative strategies is an instructional responsibility of the literacy coach.

Graphic Organizers. Graphic organizers, such as T-charts, story frames, and Venn diagrams, are tools meant to help organize one's thinking. They can be added to as the student continues to read, participates in a cooperative learning group, or views a video. Guiding teachers to use graphic organizers that match the task at hand so that students are then able to use the organized representation in oral or written response may be another duty of the literacy coach. Unexplained or poorly selected graphic organizers are likely to hinder rather than promote students' comprehension.

Story Structure. Understanding characters, setting, and plot will help students to recall events, generate comparisons and inferences, and make personal connections to what they've read. These skills are evidence of students' knowledge of story structure. When teachers provide a clear framework for understanding story structure, students should be able to comprehend text and respond accurately to it. For some stories, a graphic organizer may represent story structure.

If the literacy coach becomes aware of a teacher's unclear presentation of story structure, the coach should probably review and explain the purpose of story structure to the teacher. In this situation, it may be necessary for the coach to model and explain story structure with the appropriate use of a graphic organizer. Subsequently, the coach should observe the teaching of another lesson with a focus on story structure. Finally, the coach should provide feedback to the teacher about the effectiveness of the second lesson.

Question Answering. Question answering with response specificity can be an intricate process. Teachers need to show children how to locate information directly from the text or from across the text to provide evidence for their responses. Holding readers responsible for telling why they provided an answer is important for both the teacher's and the students' assessment of the students' comprehension. Other strategies for helping the students enhance comprehension are restating, re-explaining, and citing and making additions to text evidence for their own and their peers' answers. It isn't just the product—the answer—that is important. The process—the how and why the answer was generated—is also important in understanding a student's thinking. Guiding questioning is an artful skill. Coaches may find it necessary to demonstrate or explain questioning techniques for teachers who show weakness in this area or who request help.

Question Generating. Question generating should be a strategy used by students as well as by teachers. Posing questions at the inferential level, questions that require reading between the lines or across passages to determine a response, requires knowledge of the text and the ability to explain inferences and implications. A by-product of question generating may be re-reading certain portions of the text to prove one's point or strengthen an explanation. Being metacognitively aware of one's own thinking process is inherent in generating high-level questions. When keeping the goal of improved instruction in mind, the literacy coach needs to encourage question generating and the processing of the questions and responses in all classrooms. When needed, modeling of question generating and processing by the literacy coach should occur.

Summarizing. Summarizing, providing a clear, concise rendition of a story or article, provides evidence of a student's understanding of the most important information contained or implied in text. It demonstrates the reader's ability to sort minor from major details, reconstruct the major details in a sequential fashion, and render the summary in a succinct, nonsuperfluous manner. Graphic organizers as well as verbal prompts can be used to teach students to summarize. Teacher modeling of this strategy is critical. Literacy coaches who provide feedback and assistance to teachers for modeling and guiding summaries will help promote comprehension strategy training in their schools.

Focusing on a Few Strategies. One of the major implications of the NRP report for literacy coaches is that choosing and focusing on a select number of comprehension strategies is wise. Promoting a thorough, well-orchestrated use of a few strategies, rather than a broad smattering of strategies, allows teachers to master the instruction of the selected strategies. Consistent focus on a few good strategies provides students with multiple opportunities to reuse and refine the strategies. Of course, the goal is for the students to apply the strategies independently without the teacher's guidance. Coaches who carefully assess strategy use in individual classrooms as well as among classrooms have the advantage of helping teachers select and implement core strategies to promote comprehension in their schools.

Teacher Preparation and Comprehension Strategies Instruction

Teacher preparation and comprehension strategies instruction, another area of comprehension explored by the NRP, is related to the third theme. The preparation of teachers to deliver comprehension strategy instruction should result in competent, self-regulated readers. This tall order begins with teacher training programs in universities for preservice teachers and continues with professional development programs provided by school districts and graduate programs for inservice teachers. The NRP report (NICHD, 2000) addresses the complexity of strategy instruction by stating that teachers

> must have a firm grasp not only of the strategies that they are teaching the children but also of *instructional* strategies that they can employ to achieve their goal. Many teachers find this type of teaching a challenge, most likely because they have not been prepared to do such teaching. Thus, although the literature on cognitive strategy instruction for reading comprehension has yielded valuable information, it has not provided a satisfactory model for effective instruction in the classroom. (pp. 4-119 to 4-120)

The NRP concluded that good teacher preparation could result in the delivery of instruction that improves students' reading comprehension. Two major approaches to comprehension strategy instruction were reviewed by the NRP: direct instruction (DI) and transactional strategy instruction (TSI).

Direct Instruction (DI). Duffy and colleagues have conducted most of the research on DI since 1986. The teacher's main role in DI is to provide an explicit explanation of the reasoning and mental processes involved in successful reading comprehension. In other words, the teacher helps the readers to think strategically about solving reading comprehension problems. In the initial study of the effectiveness of teacher training, explicit explanations by teachers were found to lead to greater general awareness of reading strategies among students (Duffy et al., 1986). A subsequent study concluded that "compared with students of untrained teachers, the students of trained teachers had higher levels of awareness of specific reading strategies as well as great awareness of the need to be strategic when reading" (Duffy et al., 1987, p. 4-122).

Transactional Strategy Instruction (TSI). In the TSI approach, teachers also use explicit explanations of reading strategies. However, another layer of processing is involved: students are required to collaborate so that an "interactive exchange," a transactional process, occurs among the readers. The collaborative discussion that takes place is a priority in the TSI approach. Anderson (1992) trained teachers in the TSI approach and found that the preparation given teachers had a significant effect (80 percent) on reading comprehension performance.

The NRP report found that approaches, not reading programs, were effective because "intensive instruction of teachers can prepare them to teach reading comprehension strategically" (p. 4-125). Based on the information from the NRP report, literacy coaches should not assume that all teachers enter the profession with the same level of training in strategy instruction. Because strategies are taught within the context of reading, the explanations and prompts used by teachers will vary. Ongoing refinement of strategy training should occur for all teachers.

The literacy coach should be well prepared to model and share a wide variety of strategies during professional development opportunities. The more strategies a teacher knows and can use, the better the teacher is able to individualize instruction for students. The goal of both the teacher and the literacy coach is instructional improvement.

Teacher Education and Reading Instruction

During its investigations, the National Reading Panel found that teacher education and professional development "emerged as one of the most frequently mentioned areas of concern" (NICHD, 2000, 5-1) when analyzing reading and reading instruction. The words of the National Reading Panel explain the need to continue studying effective teacher education (education received preservice or before initial certification is earned) and professional development (education received inservice or after initial certification is earned):

Teacher education and professional development represent two aspects of the ways in which teachers acquire knowledge. In teacher education programs, prospective teachers are taught in structured programs before being certified as teachers. The experiences these preservice teachers have include coursework in theory and methods as well as supervised teaching. Once teachers are in the field, having assumed teaching positions, the emphasis shifts from teacher education to professional development. This latter context is often referred to as inservice education. Because there are dramatic differences in the amount of time spent, the structure of the program, and the continuity of the education, the NRP has chosen to analyze the two contexts separately. (NICHD, 5-1)

Only experimental studies of teacher education or professional development were included in the NRP's analysis of these contexts. After an initial selection of 300 studies, only 32 were chosen because they met the criteria set by NRP, including 11 preservice studies and 21 inservice studies. Three major questions were formed to guide the analysis of these studies: (1) How are teachers taught to teach reading? (2) What do studies show about the effectiveness of teacher education? and (3) How can research be applied to improve teacher development?

More than half of the 11 preservice studies included in the NRP research revealed that either comprehension strategy instruction or general methods were taught in preservice courses. Ten of the 11 studies reported improvement in teacher knowledge. However, the NRP offers a word of caution here: "There is no way of knowing whether this increased knowledge actually translates into effective teaching because none of the studies reports data on the teachers after their participation in the experimental program" (p. 5-6).

The 21 inservice studies largely concerned elementary inservice, but there were a few studies at middle and high school levels. Inservice topics fell into four areas: comprehension and strategy instruction, general methods, classroom management, and improving teachers' attitudes. However, the amount of time spent in inservice, both in individual sessions and continued training over time, was very difficult to determine since, according to the NRP, many of the studies were nonspecific and/or inconsistent in providing information about duration.

The NRP summarized the analysis of teacher education and reading instruction by stating that "there are simply too many approaches in this small sample to allow conclusions about any one specific method" (NICHD, 2000, 5-13) regarding how teachers are taught to teach reading. There was evidence that interventions in teacher education improve instructional practice; however, no specific interventions were mentioned. Research can be applied to improve teacher education by determining which interventions are most effective, continuing research at the inservice level (and encouraging the provision of "extensive support" in terms of time and money) for extended time frames.

Literacy coaches need to make firm commitments to professional development that is consistent and ongoing for individual teachers as well as for the full faculty. Knowledge of interventions and techniques develops over time with practice. Coaches should also be encouraged to keep records of the time spent in these professional development sessions, keep data about the teachers' change and proficiency development with the interventions, and, if possible, record data about the positive effect on students' learning as a result of the interventions. Such reports need to be published to provide data for the field about the types of professional development and the change it effects on both teachers' and students' learning.

Computer Technology and Reading Instruction

The NRP suggests the need for further research in the area of computer technology and reading instruction for two reasons: first, the use of computers in reading instruction is relatively new (since the 1960s), and second, the capabilities of computers have changed over time. Currently, some computers are capable of implementing a complete program of instructional reading. New capabilities, such as multimedia presentations and speech recognition, and information resources, especially the Internet, are having a tremendous impact on how computers are used in schools today. The NRP analyzed 21 experimental studies on the topic of computer technology used for reading instruction. These studies involved vocabulary instruction, word recognition instruction, and comprehension instruction. Most of the studies involved speech-text connections. The NRP states that it is "extremely difficult" to make conclusions specific to computer technology and reading instruction based on the small research sample analyzed. However, the NRP did come to two broad conclusions: (1) it is possible to use computer technology for reading instruction and (2) the use of word processing has the potential to make reading instruction more effective.

The NRP offers the following implications for instructional practice using the computer as a tool for reading instruction and suggests further research related to them:

- Computers can be used for some reading instructional tasks.
- Word processing is a useful addition to reading instruction.

- Multimedia computer software can be used for reading instruction.
- Computers do have a motivational use in reading instruction.
- Hypertext has a great deal of potential in reading instruction.

The NRP also suggests further research as new uses for the computer are conceptualized and penetrate literacy instruction. It poses the following questions as a basis for the research:

- What is the proper role for integration of computers in reading instruction? In what contexts can they be used either to replace or supplement conventional instruction?
- What are the conditions under which multimedia presentation is useful or desirable in reading text?
- What are the requisite characteristics of software to teach reading?
- What is the appropriate mix of reading and writing instruction delivered by computer?
- How can professional development programs be structured to help teachers effectively integrate computer solutions with instruction?
- How are the effects of computer usage in pedagogy most effectively measured? Do conventional assessments measure all of the learning that takes place in computer environments?
- What is the utility of hypertext in instructional contexts?
- How can Internet resources be incorporated into reading instruction?

These questions are excellent for the literacy coach to use to begin assessing the importance of the computer in the school's reading program; teachers' willingness and abilities to incorporate technology into the literacy program; and the recommendations for continued or reduced use of certain types of technology, software, and Web sites. Depending upon the specific technology issues in the school, the literacy coach may generate additional questions. The assessment of technology integration may best be made when the literacy coach collaborates with the technology coordinator and a committee of teachers, including reading specialists, librarians, and a representative team of classroom teachers.

WHAT THE LITERACY COACH SHOULD KNOW ABOUT THE *READING FIRST* INITIATIVE

In 2002, the *Reading First* Initiative was established by the Bush administration to improve reading achievement in kindergarten through third grade. Nearly $5 billion was allocated and distributed over several years to states that applied for funding. Grants were awarded to state and local educational agencies to establish reading programs that were developed from scientifically based reading research. The programs were to be structured on these five key topics as outlined in the National Reading Panel's report: phonemic awareness, phonics, fluency, vocabulary development, and comprehension.

The main goal of the *Reading First* program is to increase the percentage of early readers who read proficiently. One of the purposes of the funding is to provide a comprehensive program so that students can read proficiently, as measured by the state reading assessments, and at grade level or above on the National Assessment of Educational Progress (NAEP) reading assessment.

Reading First grants are also issued to participating schools for the implementation of programs to assist at-risk students who are deficient in reading. Another goal of the program is to decrease the percentage of kindergarten through third-grade students participating in the *Reading First* program who are referred to special education programs based on their problems with learning to read.

Reading First funding is also allocated to school districts to select, implement, and provide professional development for teachers. The significance of this funding is that it has enabled school districts to employ literacy coaches to support classroom teachers, provide a budget for purchasing instructional materials, and administer assessments or diagnostic instruments. Thus, *Reading First* was a historical educational initiative because of its focus on one-to-one literacy coaching in America's classrooms. It placed the role of the literacy coach and the need for support for classroom teachers in the limelight.

WHAT THE LITERACY COACH SHOULD KNOW ABOUT *READING NEXT: A VISION FOR ACTION AND RESEARCH IN MIDDLE AND HIGH SCHOOL LITERACY*

The Alliance for Excellent Education is a national policy, research, and advocacy organization with the goal of helping to make every American child a high school graduate. Representatives from the philanthropic Carnegie Corporation and the Alliance for Excellent Education combined forces to produce a 2004 report called *Reading Next: A Vision for Action and Research in Middle and High School Literacy (Reading Next)*. The report was funded and written to provide a focus on the serious need to improve reading comprehension in our secondary schools. Educational research and reports at the end of the 20th century and the beginning of the 21st were laden with early-reading concerns and ideas for improved implementation of teaching practices. As discussed previously, *Reading First* focused on reading from kindergarten through third grade. However, reports for secondary education were neglected in comparison to those for primary reading issues. In response, the Alliance for Excellent Education, a panel of five nationally known educational researchers headed by Catherine Snow of Harvard, drafted a set of 15 recommendations (see Resource L) to "meet the needs of our eight million struggling readers while simultaneously envisioning a way to propel the field forward" (Biancarosa & Snow, 2004, p. 3).

In *Reading Next,* the panel provides an overview of statistics that clearly paints a picture of the urgent need for reform in addressing education, particularly reading, in our secondary schools. Figure 10.3 provides a synopsis of these statistics as reported in *Reading Next.* The experts determined that the problem for older students was not illiteracy but comprehension. Struggling middle and high school students cannot understand what they read. Therefore, *Reading Next* focused on interventions that will be helpful to these struggling readers. It created a "list of promising elements of effective adolescent literacy programs" (Biancarosa & Snow, 2004, p. 12), which it sorted into two categories: instructional improvements and infrastructure improvements. The infrastructure elements can help literacy coaches and other school leaders support the instructional elements for improvement. There is no hierarchy to the list, and the report clearly states that the "elements have a dynamic and powerful interrelationship" (Biancarosa & Snow, p. 12).

Instructional Improvement

Nine elements for instructional improvement are outlined in *Reading Next*: comprehension strategies, content connection to skill and strategy instruction, motivation and self-directed learning, text-based collaborative learning, strategic tutoring, diverse texts, intensive writing, technology component, and ongoing formative assessment. These elements are aligned to the key problem identified in the report: secondary school students who struggle with literacy do so because they do not comprehend what they read. In the report, direct, explicit comprehension instruction is recommended as an effective adolescent literacy intervention. Programs are not recommended. An ideal intervention should be based on the teacher's diagnosis of the students' needs. However, key components of approaches to comprehension instruction are explicitly stated. The following sections provide a summary of each of the nine instructional elements.

Figure 10.3   Synopsis of Statistics from *Reading Next* Regarding Literacy Concerns in American Secondary Schools

Concern	Statistic
Dropouts	Every day, 3,000 students drop out of high school, most because they lack the reading and writing skills to keep up with the demands of their high school classes.
Nonproficient readers	Of students entering ninth grade, 70 percent are nonproficient readers.
Struggling readers	More than 8 million students in grades 4–12 are struggling readers (NCESa, 2003).
African-American and Latino graduates	Only 70 percent of high school students graduate on time with a regular diploma, and fewer than 60 percent of African-American and Latino students graduate with a regular diploma (Greene, 2002).
Postsecondary remedial courses	Approximately 53 percent of high school graduates enroll in remedial courses in postsecondary education (NCES, 2001).
Need for differentiated instruction	Of American students in middle and high schools, 70 percent require differentiated instruction.

Comprehension Strategies

The first instructional element is that comprehension strategies should be taught and learned so that students use strategies both instructionally and independently when reading a variety of texts. Comprehension monitoring, being metacognitively aware of how they understand while they read, is also critical. In addition, teacher modeling, scaffolded instruction, and apprenticeship models are cited as excellent approaches to direct, explicit comprehension instruction. As mentioned earlier, no programs are singled out as being able to remedy the struggling readers' woes, but two examples of instructional approaches are succinctly explained in the comprehension portion of the report. These approaches are reciprocal teaching (Palincsar & Herrenkohl, 2002) and reading apprenticeship (Jordan, Jensen, & Greenleaf, 2001). *Reading Next* emphasizes that whatever approach is selected by teachers, it should be thoroughly explained. Students should be instructed in how to use the strategies and when the strategies should be used.

Content Connection to Skill and Strategy Instruction

The second instructional element is that effective instructional principles should be embedded in content. The importance of content connected skill and strategy instruction is inherent in this element. When addressing this element, *Reading Next* conveys that

> learning from reading in content-area texts requires skills that are different than the skills needed to comprehend literature. Language arts teachers need to expand their instruction to include approaches and texts that will facilitate not only comprehension but also learning from texts. (Biancarosa & Snow, 2004, p. 15)

Motivation and Self-Directed Learning

The third element, motivation and self-directed learning, reinforces the need for students' active engagement in what they read and write. It reminds teachers that adolescent readers should have opportunities to select both reading materials and topics for research. The goal of this intervention, self-regulation, emerges when middle and high school students have these opportunities for choice in a supportive classroom environment with ample instructional assistance to help them be successful with their choices.

Text-Based Collaborative Learning

Text-based collaborative learning, the fourth element, promotes small-group work for middle and high school students. The text may be assigned by a teacher or selected by the group of students. In either case, the goal is to interact with a focus on the content of the text. According to *Reading Next*, "learning is decentralized in these groups because the meaning drawn from a text or multiple texts is negotiated through a group process" (Biancarosa & Snow, 2004, p. 17). It is vital that teachers scaffold these group interactions and even provide concrete examples or sample problems as models for students before they participate in an actual collaboration. An example of text-based collaborative learning offered in *Reading Next* is "Questioning the Author" (McKeown, Beck, & Worthy, 1993).

Strategic Tutoring

In strategic tutoring, the fifth element, tutors work one-on-one or with a small group of struggling readers to teach them learning strategies as they help them complete their content assignments. These sessions don't necessarily have to take place during the regular school day. The emphasis is on teaching the students to be strategic readers so they eventually employ accurate strategies independently.

Diverse Texts

The sixth element, diverse texts, should include books that have both a range of levels and a range of topics. *Reading Next* endorses having a variety of multiple ability levels of text in every middle and high school classroom.

Intensive Writing

The seventh element of *Reading Next* is intensive writing. This intervention increases both the quantity of writing that students do as part of their assignments as well as the quality of instruction and assignments given to them. According to *Reading Next*, "writing instruction also improves reading comprehension. Many of the skills involved in writing . . . reinforce reading skills, and effective interventions will help middle and high school students read like writers and write like readers" (Biancarosa & Snow, 2004, p. 19).

Technology Component

The eighth element of *Reading Next* stresses the importance of technology. Including a technology component can also be an effective intervention in adolescent literacy programs. Technology can be used as both an instructional tool and an instructional topic to support struggling readers and writers. Because technology is quickly altering the reading and writing demands of our society, using technology interventions in secondary classrooms should equip students with literacy skills they'll use beyond their school years.

Ongoing Formative Assessment

The final element of *Reading Next* mentioned under the instructional improvement category is ongoing formative assessment of students. The report states, "The best instructional improvements are informed by ongoing assessment of student strengths and needs" (Biancarosa & Snow, 2004, p. 19). Student progress should be recorded on individual profiles and on class profiles. The purpose of such assessment is to inform instruction on a regular basis in order that "adjustments in instruction" truly help struggling adolescents succeed.

Infrastructure Improvements

The second category of interventions, infrastructure improvements, consists of six elements: extended time for literacy, professional development, ongoing summative assessment of students and programs, teacher teams, leadership, and a comprehensive and coordinated literacy program. The infrastructure category represents those things that can be put into place to allow instructional interventions to occur. Although both categories, instructional improvements and infrastructure improvements, are extremely important for the literacy coach at the middle and high school level to know about, infrastructure interventions seem to be the actions that can be owned, implemented, and overseen by the literacy coach. These are improvements that will permeate the entire culture of the literacy program within the school.

Extended Time for Literacy

The expert panel for *Reading Next* "argued the need for two to four hours of literacy-connected learning daily" (Biancarosa & Snow, 2004, p. 20) at the middle and high school levels, especially where literacy interventions are needed. The processes of reading and writing combined with text-centered skills and content take time to teach and to learn. Strugglers need increased interaction with texts as well as multiple exposures to strategies and trial applications. These events take time to process. In some secondary schools, a lunch period may be adjusted so that part of the time is spent in remedial or support literacy classes. In other schools, elective subjects are often given half the time of a required area of study. Remedial or support literacy classes are often assigned to struggling students in lieu of an elective subject. Short time periods such as those described in these examples are insufficient to promote the metacognitive teaching and learning that need to occur so that valuable reading and writing can be done independently, shared with teacher and peers, and processed for improvement.

Professional Development

Professional development is the linchpin that will secure the infrastructure interventions in adolescent literacy programs. The comments regarding professional development in *Reading Next* clearly describe the who, what, and why of this critical intervention:

> Professional development does not refer to the typical onetime workshop, or even a short-term series of workshops, but to ongoing, long-term professional development, which is more likely to promote lasting, positive changes in teacher knowledge and practice. The development effort should also be systemic, including not only classroom teachers but also literacy coaches, resource room personnel, librarians, and administrators. Effective professional

development will use data from research studies of adult learning and the conditions needed to effect sustained change. Professional development opportunities should be built into the regular school schedule, with consistent opportunities to learn about new research and practices as well as opportunities to implement and reflect upon new ideas. Effective professional development will help school personnel create and maintain indefinitely a team-oriented approach to improving the instruction and institutional structures that promote better adolescent literacy. (Biancarosa & Snow, 2004, p. 20)

Ongoing Summative Assessment

Ongoing summative assessments are different from the ongoing formative assessments of students mentioned in the first category. Summative assessments are generally evaluations and usually include districtwide standardized tests as well as statewide proficiency tests. The goal of summative assessment is to allow teachers and schools to track students' progress throughout their entire 13 years in school. Administrative teams who must report to stakeholders such as school boards, parents, and the wider community often do the progress-monitoring reviews. The information provided from such reviews should also be shared with teachers to help them plan for instruction.

Teacher Teams

Teacher teams can be an outstanding intervention when teachers meet regularly "to discuss students they have in common and to align instruction" (Biancarosa & Snow, 2004, p. 21). This is especially true in secondary schools since students are instructed by multiple teachers of separate subjects. Establishing coordinated instruction in secondary schools can become a reality when collegial teacher teams meet with a focused agenda: improved literacy teaching and learning.

Leadership

Regarding leadership, *Reading Next* sagely states, "without someone with an informed vision of what good literacy instruction entails leading the charge, instructional change is likely to be beset with problems" (Biancarosa & Snow, 2004, p. 21). Of course, the emphasis on leadership is replete with references to the school principal and her knowledge of reading and writing instruction at the secondary level. Although the principal should have an overarching vision for the educational program of the school, it is often impossible to do it all and do it well. An assistant principal and/or other administrators may have responsibility for the supervision of language arts. Those administrators and teachers responsible for implementing language arts instruction, including literacy coaches, may take a more prominent role in coordinating literacy programming and professional development than the building's principal. Informed decisions about literacy interventions need to be based on research, teachers' input, and assessment data.

Comprehensive and Coordinated Literacy Program

The final infrastructure intervention, a comprehensive and coordinated literacy program, is especially linked to leadership and the establishment of teacher teams. If secondary teachers are asked to coordinate their instruction so that strategies can be reinforced for students, they need to participate in development opportunities that foster their work as interdisciplinary teams of professionals who share instructional responsibilities for a common group of students. The comprehensive and coordinated literacy program described under this tenet involves the instructional elements in the first category mentioned in *Reading Next*.

The report touts the possibility of enhancing "adolescent literacy achievement now while at the same time refining and extending the knowledge base of the entire field" (Biancarosa & Snow, 2004, p. 31). It also extends the challenge for further research to both funding organizations and educators. Importantly, the report clearly represents the dilemma facing American secondary schools today in educating diverse populations with a broad range of literacy needs. Positive actions need to take place now; professional reflection and insight need to guide future actions.

WHAT THE LITERACY COACH SHOULD KNOW ABOUT THE *RAND REPORT*

While *Reading Next* focused on improving reading and comprehension in secondary school, the Carnegie Corporation of New York and other businesses became concerned that students entering the job market after graduation were not well prepared to face the reading skill challenges that they must confront in the business world. Consequently, the Carnegie Corporation of New York requested the services of the RAND Corporation (a nonprofit research organization) to conduct a study to research the status of adolescent literacy in the United States. The result was a 2005 report titled *Achieving State and National Literacy Goals, a Long Uphill Road.*

The RAND Corporation enlisted a small group of investigators to focus upon the state of academic achievement of adolescents (students in grades 4–12) (Snow, Burns, & Griffin, 1998). The investigators asked three questions:

1. As measured by state assessments, to what extent are adolescents achieving state literacy goals?

2. As measured by the National Assessment of Educational Progress (NAEP), to what extent are adolescents achieving national literacy goals?

3. How do the results from state assessments and the NAEP compare to one another?

Since each state must meet standards-based education requirements presented in NCLB, students were to be tested by 2005–2006 in reading and math. In this accountability system, grades 3, 4, 5, 6, 7, 8 and one grade in high school receive an annual test in these two subject areas. States were also to test students in grades 3–5, 6–9, and 10–12 in the content area of science by 2007–2008. According to the standards set in NCLB, all students must pass their state tests by the year 2014. Schools that do not make "adequate yearly progress" may face penalties over time such as reduced decision making, changes in school staffing, extending the school day/year, and being required to hire an outside expert to provide consultation to the school.

The RAND Corporation researchers gathered data from state assessments and the National Assessment of Educational Progress (NAEP) on adolescent achievement and progress. Their report suggests that the goal of 100 percent efficiency in reading for all students presented a major challenge for states because fewer than half of the students met the state proficiency standards. Furthermore, in no state did even half of the students meet the NAEP standard of proficiency in literacy.

The *RAND Report* states a wide disparity exists in the achievement of subgroups of students, causing some school districts a more challenging task of reaching the 100 percent proficiency goal.

A problem that occurs with the "proficiency" mandate is the difference in performance level on assessment tests the states designate as "proficient." The level of proficiency that each state expects depends on the type of assessment that is administered and what cutoff score each state considers to be proficient. Another issue of concern is that subgroups of students in each state may perform differently on state assessments than on the NAEP. State assessments may show small performance gaps, while the NAEP may show large performance gaps between the same subgroups of students. Therefore, the *RAND Report* states, it is important to give attention to multiple sources of information regarding literacy.

Finally, the *RAND Report* indicates that our nation may not be able to raise the literacy skill of adolescents simply by making mandates and requiring assessments. Resources and paying attention to the issue of ill-prepared adolescents who do not have the skills to face the marketplace is a problem that legislators, school districts, and teachers must continue to work together to solve.

Literacy coaches at the middle school and high school levels can give content area teachers the support they need in working with adolescents as they provide demonstration lessons and professional development sessions for teachers. Much of the focus of this support should be on test-taking skills, study skills, note making, and test interpretation.

WHAT THE LITERACY COACH SHOULD KNOW ABOUT *READING AT RISK: A SURVEY OF LITERACY READING IN AMERICA*

Sponsored by the National Endowment of the Arts (NEA), the 2004 report *Reading at Risk: A Survey of Literary Reading in America (Reading at Risk)* focuses on adult reading in America rather than instructional reading. However, we felt that including it in this chapter was important because of the clear message it sends about the decline of independent literacy activities engaged in by adults. Although a generally brief report, with five chapters and an executive summary, this document is based on a sample of over 17,000 American adults. It provides statistical measures by age, gender, education, income, region, race, and ethnicity (NEA, 2004).

The percentage of adult Americans reading literature has made a significant drop (10 percentage points) over the past 20 years. In other words, less than half of American adults currently read literature. The decline in literary reading parallels a similar decline in total book reading. The decline is consistent across ethnic groups, education levels, and all age groups. However, the strongest decline in literary reading is in the youngest age groups, between the ages of 18 and 34. As you might expect, the decline in book reading correlates with increased participation with electronic media.

The preface of *Reading at Risk* states the gist of the dire condition of this national trend:

> Advanced literacy is a specific intellectual skill and social habit that depends on a great many educational, cultural, and economic factors. As more Americans lose this capability, our nation becomes less informed, active, and independent-minded. These are not qualities that a free, innovative, or productive society can afford to lose. (NEA, 2004, p. vii)

The concern of the National Endowment of the Arts is that reading as a leisure activity will disappear from the American cultural scene over the next 50 years. Educators know that readers need to be motivated and inspired to read. They also know that those who read proficiently are more likely to choose to read than those who struggle. Whether reading for leisure or reading to be informed consumers and citizens, adults can transform themselves and their communities through wide reading. Educators need to be aware of the reading decline and take steps to reverse this trend. High school teachers and those who work with them need to be especially sensitive to the issue so that they can influence their students to choose to read throughout their lifetimes for the pleasure, stimulation, and information it will bring to them. We hope that the literary decline reported in *Reading at Risk* will not continue and that reading will increase because of the efforts made by teachers in our schools.

HOW DO LITERACY COACHES OBTAIN NEEDED KNOWLEDGE?

Jeff Smith, the literacy coach in the scenario at the beginning of this chapter, knows full well that an abundance of reading material comes across teachers' desks. He also knows that sometimes teachers get lost in the daily routine and lose the vision of the big picture. Laying a foundation for all of the teachers' work in the building and helping the teachers see the connection to the bigger picture of national, state, and local school district goals and visions is an important part of his role.

If at all possible, literacy coaches and others with school and district responsibilities for literacy achievement should carefully read primary source reports regarding literacy teaching and learning. Reports that are not accessible as full documents should be learned about from attending district and regional professional meetings in which experts share pertinent information and discuss the major tenets of reports as well as cautionary elements of each. Most reports are available online, at least in summary form. Coaches should reflect on the information they find by asking the following questions:

- What does each report say to me and the position I hold?
- What does each report say to the school's literacy practices?
- How will the information from these reports help me to provide useful feedback to the teachers with whom I work?

SUMMARY

In this chapter, the National Reading Panel's report, the *Reading First* Initiative, the *Reading Next* report, the *RAND Report*, and the *Reading at Risk* report were discussed at length to provide literacy coaches with the salient points of each. We feel this information is worthy of review by literacy coaches because of the national trends and mandates facing education at this time. America's literacy coaches need to be aware of these reports and how they impact the nation as a whole and their schools in particular.

TOPIC EXTENSIONS FOR CLASS SESSIONS OR STUDY GROUPS

1. Read the Executive Summary and Report on Phonemic Awareness Instruction in the *Report of the National Reading Panel: Teaching Children to Read* (pp. 2-1 to 2-45) and discuss the implications for reading instruction in both sections. How do the implications relate to your beliefs and/or your school's current practices concerning phonemic awareness instruction? What suggestions could you make to the coach who observes an overemphasis on phonemic awareness instruction in a school?

2. You are a literacy coach who has been charged with the task of helping teachers create a "planned variation" of their current literacy program, and you need to present the plan to the board of school directors and parents. Help the teachers select a minimum of three of the elements for intervention from the NRP report about which they will provide a comprehensive overview to the stakeholders, explaining how these elements will bring about a change in classroom practices, homework assignments, and overall student achievement.

3. As a literacy coach, what recommendations would you make to teachers regarding integrating vocabulary into comprehension instruction? Ensure that your recommendations guarantee that developmentally appropriate techniques and assessments occur in the classroom. Describe how you will provide evidence of students' vocabulary use during and after instruction.

4. If you were to discuss the *Reading First* Initiative and *Reading Next* with the teachers in your building, what would you suggest are their highlights, and what implications might they have for the programs in your current school setting?

RESOURCE L: FIFTEEN RECOMMENDATIONS FROM *READING NEXT: A VISION FOR ACTION AND RESEARCH IN MIDDLE AND HIGH SCHOOL LITERACY*

1. Direct, explicit comprehension instruction, which is instruction in the strategies and processes that proficient readers use to understand what they read, including summarizing, keeping track of one's own understanding, and a host of other practices

2. Effective instructional principles embedded in content, including language arts teachers using content-area texts and content-area teachers providing instruction and practice in reading and writing skills specific to their subject area

3. Motivation and self-directed learning, which includes building motivation to read and learn and providing students with the instruction and supports needed for independent learning tasks they will face after graduation

4. Text-based collaborative learning, which involves students interacting with one another around a variety of texts

5. Strategic tutoring, which provides students with intense individualized reading, writing, and content instruction as needed

6. Diverse texts, which are texts at a variety of difficulty levels on a variety of topics

7. Intensive writing, including instruction connected to the kinds of writing tasks students will have to perform well in high school and beyond

8. A technology component, which includes technology as a tool for and a topic of literacy instruction

9. Ongoing formative assessments of students, which is informal, often daily assessment of how students are progressing under current instructional practices

10. Extended time for literacy, which includes approximately two to four hours of literacy instruction and practice that takes place in language arts and content-area classes

11. Professional development that is both long term and ongoing

12. Ongoing summative assessment of students and programs, which is more formal and provides data that are reported for accountability and research purposes

13. Teacher teams, which are interdisciplinary teams that meet regularly to discuss students and align instruction

14. Leadership, which can come from principals and teachers who have a solid understanding of how to teach reading and writing to the full array of students present in schools

15. A comprehensive and coordinated literacy program, which is interdisciplinary and interdepartmental and may even coordinate with out-of-school organizations and the local community

Source: © 2004 Carnegie Corporation of New York. Reprinted with permission.

References

Ackland, R. (1991). A review of the peer coaching literature. *The Journal of Staff Development, 12*(1), 22–27.

Allington, Richard L. (2006). Reading specialists, reading teachers, reading coaches: A question of credentials. *Reading Today, 23*(4), 16–17.

Alvermann, D., Boyd, F., Brozo, W., Hinchman, K., Moore, D., & Sturdevant, E. (2002). *Principled practices for a literate America: A framework for literacy and learning in the upper grades.* Athens: University of Georgia.

Alvermann, D., Moore, D., & Conley, W. (Eds.). (1987). *Research within reach: Secondary school reading.* Newark, DE: International Reading Association.

Anderson, R. C., & Pearson, P. D. (1984). A schema-theoretic view of basic process in reading. In P. D. Pearson, R. Barr, M. Kamil, & P. Mosenthal (Eds.), *Handbook of reading research* (pp. 255–292). Mahwah, NJ: Lawrence Erlbaum Associates.

Anderson, V. (1992). A teacher development project in transactional strategy instruction for teachers of severely reading-disabled adolescents. *Teaching and Teacher Education, 8*(4), 391–403.

Aseltine, J., Faryniarz, J., & Rigazio-DiGilio, A. (2006). *Supervision for learning.* Alexandria, VA: Association for Curriculum Development.

Au, K. H., Carroll, J. H., & Scheu, J. A. (1997). *Balanced literacy instruction: A teacher's resource book.* Norwood, MA: Christopher-Gordon Publishers.

Bean, R. (2004). *The reading specialist.* New York: The Guilford Press.

Bean, R. (2005, May). *How is coaching defined?* Paper presented at the meeting of the International Reading Association, San Antonio, TX.

Bean, R., Cassidy, J., Grumet, J., Shelton, D., & Wallis, S. (2002). What do reading specialists do? Results from a national survey. *The Reading Teacher, 56,* 736–744.

Bean, R., McDonald, L., & Fotta, B. (1990). *Survey of Chapter 1 programs in Pennsylvania.* Technical Report. Harrisburg, PA: Pennsylvania Department of Education.

Bean, R., Swan, A., & Knaub, C. (2003). Reading specialists in schools with exemplary reading programs: Functional, versatile, and prepared. *The Reading Teacher, 56,* 446–455.

Becker, J. M. (1996). *Peer coaching for improvement of teaching and learning.* Retrieved December 30, 2007, from www.teachersnetwork.org/tnpi/research/growth/becker.htm

Benjamin, L., & Lord, J. (1996). *Family literacy.* Washington, DC: Office of Educational Research and Improvement.

Biancarosa, G., & Snow, C. E. (2004). *Reading next: A vision for action in middle and high school literacy; A report from Carnegie Corporation of New York.* Washington, DC: Alliance for Excellent Education.

Booth, D., & Roswell, J. (2002). *The literacy principal: Leading, supporting and assessing reading and writing initiatives.* Portland, ME: Pembroke Publishers.

Botel, M. (2000, December). *My sense of what to do about phonemic awareness/phonics based on the report of the National Reading Panel.* Philadelphia: Newsletter of the Penn Literacy Network.

Cady, B. (2005). Ohio creates new career path with literacy specialist endorsement. *Reading Today, 22*(6), 1.

Carmichael, M. (2001). Creating a "teachers as readers" group in your school. *Teacher Librarian, 28*(5), 22–24.

Come, B., & Fredericks, A. (1996). Family literacy in urban schools: Meeting the needs of at-risk children. *The Reading Teacher, 48,* 392–403.

Dales, B. (1990). Trusting relationships between teachers and librarians. *Language Arts, 67,* 732–734.

Daly, J. (1994). Teachers as readers: "Things got better and better." *Teaching PreK–8, 25*(3), 53.

Daniels, H. (2003). Our best idea: Teachers who read. *Voices From the Middle, 10*(4), 38–39.

Danielson, C. (1996). *Enhancing professional practice.* Alexandria, VA: Association for Supervision and Curriculum Development.

Danielson, K., & Rogers, S. (2000). You can't pass it on if you don't have it: Encouraging lifelong reading. *Reading Horizons, 4*(1), 35–45.

Dole, J. (2004). The changing role of the reading specialist in school reform. *The Reading Teacher, 57,* 462–471.

Dole, J. (2006). "What am I supposed to do all day?" Three big ideas for the reading coach. *The Reading Teacher, 59,* 486–488.

Dowhower, S. L. (1994). Repeated reading revisited: Research into practice. *Reading and Writing Quarterly: Overcoming Learning Difficulties, 10*(4), 343–358.

Duffy, G. (1993). Rethinking strategy instruction: Four teachers' development and their low achievers' understandings. *Elementary School Journal, 93*(3), 231–247.

Duffy, G. G., Roehler, L. R., Meloth, M. S., Vavrus, L. G., Book, C., Putnam, J., et al. (1986). The relationship between explicit verbal explanations during reading skill instruction and student awareness and achievement: A study of reading teacher effects. *Reading Research Quarterly, 21,* 237–252.

Duffy, G. G., Roehler, L. R., Sivan, E., Rackliffe, G., Book, C., Meloth, M. S., et al. (1987). Effects of explaining the reasoning associated with using reading strategies. *Reading Research Quarterly, 23,* 347–368.

Durkin, D. (1993). *Teaching them to read.* (6th ed.). Boston: Allyn & Bacon.

Education Commission of the States. (2007). *Homeschooling.* Retrieved December 30, 2007, from www.ecs.org/html/issue.asp?issueid=72

Enz, B., & Searfoss, L. (1996). Expanding our views of family literacy. *The Reading Teacher, 49,* 576–579.

Erickson, L. (1995). *Supervision of literacy programs: Teachers as grass-roots change agents.* Boston: Allyn & Bacon.

Evertson, C., Emmer, E., & Worsham, M. (2003). *Classroom management for elementary teachers* (6th ed.). Boston: Allyn & Bacon.

Fountas, I., & Pinnel, G. (1996). *Guided reading.* Portsmouth, NH: Heinemann.

Fuchs, D., & Fuchs, L. (2006). Introduction to response to intervention: What, why, and how valid is it? *Reading Research Quarterly, 41,* 93–99.

Fullan, M. (2001). *Leading in a culture of change.* San Francisco: Jossey Bass.

Garan, E. M. (2001). Beyond the smoke and mirrors: A critique of the National Reading Panel on Phonics. *Phi Delta Kappan, 82*(7), 500–506.

Garmston, R. (1987). How administrators support peer coaching. *Educational Leadership, 44*(5), 18–26.

Glickman, C. (2002). *Leadership for learning.* Alexandria, VA: Association of Supervision and Curriculum Development.

Glickman, C., Calhoun, E., & Roberts, J. (1993). Clinical supervision within the school as the center for inquiry. In R. Anderson & K. Snyder (Eds.), *Clinical supervision: Coaching for higher performance* (pp. 51–59). Lancaster, PA: Technomic Publishing Company.

Goldberg, S. M., & Pesko, E. (2000). The teacher book club. *Educational Leadership, 57*(8), 39–41.

Goleman, D. (2000, March/April). Leadership that gets results. *Harvard Business Review,* 78–90.

Greene, J. P. (2002). *High school graduation rates in the United States: Prepared for the Black Alliance for Education Options* (rev.). Retrieved January 10, 2008, from the Manhattan Institute for Policy Research, Center for Civic Innovation Web site: www.manhattan-institute.org/html/cr_baeo.htm

Guiney, E. (2001). Coaching isn't just for athletes: The role of teacher leaders. *Phi Delta Kappan, 82*(10), 740–743.

Guth, N., & Pettengill, S. (2005). *Leading a successful reading program.* Newark, DE: International Reading Association.

Harris, T., & Hodges, R. (Eds.). (1995). *The literacy dictionary.* Newark, DE: International Reading Association.

Hoffman, J. V., & Pearson, P. D. (2000). Reading teacher education in the next millennium: What your grandmother's teacher didn't know that your granddaughter's teacher should. *Reading Research Quarterly, 33,* 169–197.

Individuals With Disabilities Education Improvement Act (IDEA) of 2004. Pub. L. No. 103-266. Retrieved January 12, 2007, from http://idea.ed.gov

International Reading Association. (2000). *Teaching all children to read: The roles of the reading specialist: A position statement of the International Reading Association.* Newark, DE: Author.

International Reading Association. (2004). *The role and qualifications of the reading coach in the United States: A position statement of the International Reading Association.* Newark, DE: Author.

International Reading Association. (2006). *Standards for middle and high school literacy coaches.* Newark, DE: Author.

International Reading Association. (2007). *Nila Banton Smith Award.* Retrieved January 8, 2008, from www.reading.org/association/awards/teachers_smith_award.html

IRA/NCTE Literacy Coaches Clearinghouse. (2005). *Reading Today. (23)*3, 3.

IRA, others develop middle, high school coaching standards. (2005). *Reading Today, (23)*3, 1.

Jaeger, M. (1996). The reading specialist as collaborative consultant. *The Reading Teacher, 49,* 622–629.

James, F. (2004). *Response to intervention in the Individuals with Disabilities Education Act (IDEA), 2004.* Newark, DE: International Reading Association.

Jay, A. (2005, May). *Leading a winning literacy team: The complex roles of coaching, training and management.* Paper presented at meeting of the International Reading Association, San Antonio, TX.

Jay, A., & McGovern, J. (2006). Literacy leadership in the elementary school: The principal's role in professional development. *Pennsylvania Reads: Journal of the Keystone State Reading Association, 7*(2), 22–33.

Jay, A., & McGovern, J. (2007). Not just a manager anymore: Principal's role as literacy leader moves to the front. *Journal of Staff Development, 28*(4), 51–57.

Johnson, D. W., & Johnson, F. W. (2003). *Joining together: Group therapy and group skills* (8th ed.). Boston: Allyn & Bacon.

Jordan, M., Jensen, R., & Greenleaf, C. (2001). Amidst familiar gatherings: Reading apprenticeship in a middle school classroom. *Voices From the Middle, 8*(4), 15–24.

Joyce, B., & Showers, B. (1982). The coaching of teaching. *Educational Leadership, 40*(1), 4–10

Joyce, B., & Showers, B. (1996). Staff development as a comprehensive service organization. *Journal of Staff Development, 17*(1), 2–6.

Keene, E. O., & Zimmerman, S. (2007). *Mosaic of thought.* Portsmouth, NH: Heinemann.

Kintsch, W. (1998). *Comprehension: A paradigm for cognition.* New York: Cambridge University Press.

Kise, J. (2006). *Differentiated coaching: A framework for helping teachers change.* Thousand Oaks, CA: Corwin Press.

Klinger, J., & Edwards, P. (2006). Cultural considerations with response to intervention models. *Reading Research Quarterly, 41,* 108–117.

Lambert, L. (1998). *Building leadership capacity in schools.* Alexandria, VA: Association for Supervision and Curriculum Development.

Lambert, L. (2003). *Leadership capacity for lasting school improvement.* Alexandria, VA: Association for Supervision and Curriculum Development.

Lefever-Davis, S., & Heller, M. (2003). Teacher study groups: A strategic approach to promoting students' literacy development. *The Reading Teacher, 56,* 782–784.

Lester, N., & Onore, C. (1990). *Learning change.* Portsmouth, NH: Heinemann.

Lyons, C. (2001). Developing successful collaborative literacy teams. In V. Risko & K. Bromley (Eds.), *Collaboration for diverse learners* (pp. 168–187). Newark, DE: International Reading Association.

Lyons, C. (2002). Becoming an effective literacy coach. In E. Rogers and G. S. Pinnell (Eds.), *Learning from teaching in literacy education: New perspectives on professional development* (pp. 140–163). Plymouth, NH: Heinemann.

Marzano, R., & Marzano, J. (2003). The key to classroom management. *Educational Leadership, 61*(1), 6–13.

McAndrew, D. (2005). *Literacy leadership: Six strategies for peoplework.* Newark, DE: International Reading Association.

McBrien, J., & Brandt, R. (1997). *The language of learning: A guide to education terms.* Alexandria, VA: Association for Supervision and Curriculum Development.

McKeown, M., Beck, I., & Worthy, M. (1993). Grappling with text ideas: Questioning the author. *Reading Teacher, 46,* 560–566.

Micklos, J. (2006). Persistence pays. *Reading Today, 23*(4), 8.

Miletta, M. M. (1996). *A multiage classroom: Choice and possibility.* Portsmouth, NH: Heinemann.

Morrison, T., Jacobs, J., & Swinyard, W. (1999). Do teachers who read personally use recommended literacy practices in their classrooms? *Reading Research and Instruction, 38,* 81–100.

Morrow, L. (1997). *Literacy development in the early years: Helping children read and write*: Boston Allyn & Bacon.

Morrow, L. (2003). *Organizing and managing the language arts block: A professional development guide.* New York: Guilford Press.

Moxley, D., & Taylor, R. (2006). *Literacy coaching: A handbook for school leaders.* Thousand Oaks, CA: Corwin Press.

Murphy, C. (2002). Use time for faculty study. *Journal of Staff Development, 20*(2), 20–25.

National Association of Elementary School Principals. (2001). *Leading learning communities: Standards for what principals should know and be able to do; Executive summary.* Alexandria, VA. Retrieved December 30, 2007, from www.naesp.org/client_files/LLC-Exec-Sum.pdf

National Center for Education Statistics. (2001). *Internet access in public schools and classrooms: 1994–2000.* Washington, DC: U.S. Department of Education. Retrieved January 9, 2008, from http://nces.ed.gov/pubs2001/2001071 .pdf

National Center for Education Statistics. (2003a). *The nation's report card: Reading 2002.* Washington, DC: U.S. Government Printing Office. Retrieved January 9, 2008, from http://nces.ed.gov/pubsearch/pubsinfo.asp?pubid= 2003521

National Center for Education Statistics. (2003b). *Public school teacher questionnaire.* Washington, DC: U.S. Department of Education. Retrieved January 9, 2009, from http://nces.ed.gov

National Endowment of the Arts. (2004). *Reading at risk: A survey of literary reading in America* (Research Division Report #46). Washington, DC: Author.

National Institute of Child Health and Human Development. (2000). *Report of the National Reading Panel: Teaching children to read; An evidence-based assessment of scientific research literature on reading and its implications for reading instruction* (NIH Publication No. 00-4754). Washington, DC: U.S. Government Printing Office.

No Child Left Behind Act of 2001, Pub. L. No. 107-110, 115 Stat. 1425 (2002).

O'Donnell-Allen, C., & Hunt, B. (2001). Reading adolescents: Book clubs for YA readers. *English Journal, 90*(3), 82–89.

Office of Vocational and Adult Education. (2002). *High school reading: Key issue brief.* Washington, DC: U.S. Department of Education.

Opitz, M. F., & Rasinski, T. V. (1998). *Good-bye round robin.* Portsmouth, NH: Heinemann.

Palincsar, A., & Herrenkohl, L. (2002). Designing collaborative learning contexts. *Theory Into Practice, 41*(1), 26–32.

Pikulski. J. (1994). Preventing reading failure: A review of five effective programs. *The Reading Teacher, 48,* 30–39.

Poglinco, S. M., & Bach, A. J. (2004). The heart of the matter: Coaching as a vehicle for professional development. *Phi Delta Kappan, 85*(5), 398–400.

Portin, B. (2004). The roles that principals play. *Educational Leadership, 61*(7), 14–19.

Pressley, M. (2001). Barbara Wiesner (case study). In M. Pressley, R. Allington, R. Wharton-McDonald, C. Collins-Block, & L. Morrow (Eds.), *Learning to read* (pp. 95–114). New York: Guilford Press.

Pressley, M. (2002). *Reading instruction that works* (2nd ed.). New York: Guilford Press.

Quatroche, D. J., Bean, R. M., & Hamilton, R. L. (2001). The role of the reading specialist: A review of the research. *The Reading Teacher, 55,* 282–294.

Radencich, M. (1995). *Administration and supervision of the reading/writing program.* Boston: Allyn & Bacon.

Robbins, P., & Alvy, H. (1995). *The principal's companion.* Thousand Oaks, CA: Corwin Press.

Rosenblatt, L. M. (1981). *The reader, the text, the poem: The transactional theory of the literary work.* Carbondale, IL: Southern Illinois University Press.

Sanacore, J. (2003). Promoting the lifetime reading habit in middle school students. *The Clearing House, 73*(3), 157–161.

Schlechty, L. (2001). *Shaking up the school house: How to support and sustain educational innovation.* San Francisco: Jossey-Bass.

Shaw, M., Smith, W., Chesler, B., & Romeo, L. (2005). Moving forward: The reading specialist as literacy coach. *Reading Today, 22*(6), 6.

Smith, M. E. (1994). Teachers as readers: Quality time and impact. *Teaching PreK–8, 25,* 51–52.

Smith, W., & Andrews, R. (1987). Clinical supervision for principals. *Educational Leadership, 45*(1), 45–55.

Snow, C. E., Burns, M. S., & Griffin, P. (Eds.). (1998). *Preventing reading difficulties in young children.* Washington, DC: National Academy Press.

Snyder, K. (1993). Schooling transformation: The context for professional coaching and problem solving. In R. Anderson & K. Snyder (Eds.), *Clinical supervision: Coaching for higher performance* (pp. 77–96). Lancaster, PA: Technomic Publications.

Stanovich, K. (1986). Matthew effects in reading: Some consequences of individual differences in the acquisition of literacy. *Reading Research Quarterly, 22,* 360–406.

Strong, M., & Lander, M. (2005). Promoting a teachers as readers group in your local council. *Pennsylvania Reads: Journal of the Keystone State Reading Association, 6*(1), 40–47.

Strong, M., & Traynelis-Yurek, E. (2006, October). *The relationship between the reading specialist and the special education teacher.* Paper presented at the 50th annual conference of the College Reading Association, Pittsburgh, PA.

Stronge, J. H. (2002). *Qualities of effective teachers.* Alexandria, VA: Association for Supervision and Curriculum Development.

Sturtevant, E. G., Linek, W., Brozo, W., Hinchman, K., & Boyd, F. (2005). *Principled practices for adolescent literacy: A framework for instruction and policy.* Boston: Allyn & Bacon.

Symonds, K.W. (2003a). *The literacy coach: A key to improving teaching and learning in secondary schools.* Washington, DC: Alliance for Excellent Education.

Symonds, K. W. (2003b). *Literacy coaching: How school districts can support a long-term strategy in a short-term world.* San Francisco: Bay Area School Reform Collaborative. (ERIC Document Reproduction Service No. ED477297)

Taylor, B. M., Pearson, P. D., Clark, K., & Walpole, S. (2000). Effective schools and accomplished teachers: Lessons from primary-grade reading instruction in low-income schools. *Elementary School Journal, 101*(2), 121–165.

Taylor, R., & Gunter, G. (2006). *The K–12 literacy leadership fieldbook.* Thousand Oaks, CA: Corwin Press.

Teale, W., & Yokota, J. (2000). Beginning reading and writing perspectives on instruction. In D. Strickland & L. Morrow (Eds.), *Beginning reading and writing* (pp. 1–28). Newark, DE: International Reading Association; New York: Teachers College Press.

Toll, C. (2005). *The literacy coach's survival guide.* Newark, DE: International Reading Association.

U.S. Department of Labor. (2003). *Occupational outlook handbook.* Washington, DC: Bureau of Labor Statistics.

Vacca, R. T., & Vacca, J. L. (1999). *Content area reading: Literacy and learning across the curriculum* (6th ed.). New York: Longman.

Vogt, M., & Shearer, B. (2004). *Reading specialists in the real world: A sociocultural view.* Boston: Allyn & Bacon.

Walker, D. (1995). *The constructivist leader.* New York: Teachers College Press.

Walmsley, S., & Allington, R. (1995). Redefining and reforming instructional support programs for at-risk students. In R. Allington & S. Walmsley (Eds.), *No quick fix* (pp. 19–44). Newark, DE: International Reading Association; New York: Teachers College Press.

Walp, T., & Walmsley, S. (1995). Scoring well on tests or becoming genuinely literate: Rethinking remediation in a small rural school. In R. Allington & S. Walmsley (Eds.), *No quick fix* (pp. 177–196). Newark, DE: International Reading Association; New York: Teachers College Press.

Walpole, S., & McKenna, M. C. (2004). *The literacy coach's handbook*. New York: Guilford Press.

Wepner, S. (1989). Roles and responsibilities of reading personnel. In S. Wepner, J. Feely, & D. Strickland (Eds.), *The administration and supervision of reading program* (3rd ed., pp. 22–44). New York: Teachers College Press.

Wepner, S., & Quatroche, D. (2002). The evolving roles and responsibilities of reading personnel. In S. Wepner, D. Strickland, & J. Feeley (Eds.), *Administration and supervision of reading programs* (3rd ed., pp. 16–28). New York: Teachers College Press.

Wepner, S., Strickland, D., & Feeley, J. (2002). *Administration and supervision of reading programs.* New York: Teachers College Press.

Wepner, S., Valmont, W., & Thurlow, R. (Eds.). (2002). *Linking literacy and technology.* Newark, DE: International Reading Association.

White, D., & Fraser, J. (2001). Insights from authors: What readers can learn about self and society. *Journal of Children's Literature, 27*(2), 39–44.

Winograd, P., Paris, S., & Bridge, C. (1991). Improving assessment of literacy. *The Reading Teacher, 45*(2), 108–116.

Wong, K., & Nicotera, B. (2003). *Enhancing teacher quality: Peer coaching as a professional development strategy; A preliminary synthesis of the literature.* Washington, DC: Institute of Education Sciences. (ERIC Document Reproduction Service No. ED483035)

Yatvin, J. (2002). Babes in the woods: The wanderings of the National Reading Panel. *Phi Delta Kappan, 83*(5), 364–369.

Index

CORWIN PRESS